The Forest People without a Forest

The Forest People without a Forest

Development Paradoxes, Belonging and Participation of the Baka in East Cameroon

Glory M. Lueong

berghahn
NEW YORK · OXFORD
www.berghahnbooks.com

First published in 2017 by
Berghahn Books
www.berghahnbooks.com

Library of Congress Cataloging-in-Publication Data
A C.I.P. cataloging record is available from the Library of Congress

British Library Cataloguing in Publication Data
A catalogue record for this book is available from the British Library

Printed on acid-free paper

ISBN 978-1-78533-380-4 hardback
ISBN 978-1-80073-216-2 paperback
ISBN 978-1-78533-381-1 ebook

Contents

FIGURES AND TABLES

Figures

Tables

Acronyms

ACHPR	African Commission on Human and People's Rights
ASBAK	Association des Baka du Cameroun (sometimes referred to as 'Association Baka')
BBP	Beyond Being Pygmies
BRD	Baka Rights and Dignity
CADDAP	Centre d'Action pour le Développement Durable des Autochtones Pygmées
DO	divisional officer
DRC or DR Congo:	Democratic Republic of Congo
FGD	focus group discussion
FONDAF	Foyer Notre-Dame de la Forêt
GDP	gross domestic product
GTM	grounded theory methodology
GTZ	Gesellschaft für Technische Zusammenarbeit
ILO	International Labour Organization
INGO	international non-governmental organization
IPDP	Indigenous People Development Plan
IWGIA	International Work Group for Indigenous Affairs
MINADT	Ministry of Territorial Administration and Decentralization
MINAS	Ministry of Social Affairs
MINEP	Ministry for the Environment and Protection of Nature
MINFOF	Ministère des Forêts et de la faune/Ministry of Forests and Wildlife
NGO	non-governmental organization
NTFP	non-timber forest product
OKANI	Association OKANI ('okani' means 'rise up' in the Baka language)
PNDP	Programme National de Développement Participatif
PPDP/FESP	Pygmy People Development Plan of the Forest and Environment Sectorial Programme

PPEC	Programme Pygmées de l'Est Cameroun
RACOPY	Réseau Recherche-Actions Concertées Pygmées
REPALEAC	Réseau des Populations Autochtones et Locales pour la Gestion durable des Ecosystèmes forestiers d'Afrique Centrale
SAP	structural adjustment programme
SDO	sub-divisional officer
UNDP	United Nations Development Programme
UNDRIP	United Nations Declaration on the Rights of Indigenous Peoples
UNPFII	United Nations Permanent Forum on Indigenous Issues
USAID	United States Agency for International Development
WWF	World Wide Fund for Nature

PREFACE

Many people, including my interlocutors, have asked me how I became interested in the 'Pygmies'. To this end, I have chosen to start writing this book by narrating my inspiration for the topic.

When I was a child growing up in the northwest region of the country, which is about 1,000 kilometers away from the eastern region where the Baka live, I heard so many fascinating stories about the Pygmies. I heard that Pygmies were very short people whose only friends were wild animals, birds and trees; people who built their houses on treetops like the nests of birds, and wore no clothes. More so, when we misbehaved, our guardian tended to rebuke us by saying 'I will send you to go and live in the forest with those Pygmies since you do not want to behave like normal people'. Some villagers also told us that Pygmies climbed on trees like monkeys and depended on wild fruits and raw meat for food, and that they were never sick because they knew a lot of traditional medicines. Deep inside of me, I wondered who the Pygmies were and how they looked physically.

As I grew older and more academically advanced, issues of identity, belonging and participation became very sensitive to me. This was because of my own family background and ancestral 'roots'. My paternal grandparents originated from two different villages in the western region of the country, as did my maternal grandparents. My paternal grandparents, upon fleeing from the 'Maquisard' war that took place in the country during the 1950s and 1960s, settled in the village where my maternal grandfather originated, the same village in which we were born. Taking into consideration such a family history, I have always found it difficult to define myself and where I belong. My friends always joked by referring to me as '*une Camerounaise, sans village*' (a Cameroonian without a village).

Entangled in this difficulty of defining who I was and where I belonged, my childhood dreams about the Pygmies gradually changed. Instead of just being curious to go and see for myself who the Pygmies were, I became interested in learning how they asserted their belonging on the roadsides where they have come to live, considering that they have a forest ancestry.

Introduction

❧ • ☙

Indeed, one of the paradoxes of our times is the upsurge in our strong preoccupation with belonging … Appeals to the soil – as in the notion of autochthony ['sons of the soil'] – play a particular role in this respect as some sort of primordial form of belonging, with equally radical forms of exclusion as its flipside. The emotional charge these notions have recently acquired in different parts of Africa – Ivory Coast, Cameroon, Congo, to mention the most blatant examples – will be well known (Geschiere 2011a: 81).

This book draws from my PhD research in development sociology and is based on fourteen months of research conducted in different phases between October 2011 and January 2016 in the East Region of Cameroon. In total, there were twelve months of ethnographic fieldwork (split into six months, four months and two months) during which I collected ethnographic data from both Bantu and Baka communities. During the two months of desk research, I visited both the national and missionary archives to collect historical data. Secondary sources consulted spanned scholarly works, accounts of early travellers and missionaries in the region, government policy documents and legal texts, and reports from local, national and international nongovernmental organizations (INGOs) working in different capacities both with the Baka as well as with the Bantu.

The book explores the ways in which the Baka, who now live on roadsides in the East Region of Cameroon, assert their belonging in order to participate in development projects within the region. The book inscribes itself into the broader scope of development sociology, with a focus on the so-called 'forest peoples'. The title of the book, *The Forest People without a Forest: Development Paradoxes, Belonging and Participation of the Baka ('Pygmies') in East Cameroon*, highlights three key issues that have been explored in the book.

Firstly, the expression 'the forest people' is borrowed from Turnbull's classic anthropological publication, *The Forest People* (1961). In this book, Turnbull provided 'thick descriptions' of the Mbuti Pygmies of the Ituri forest, calling them forest people. He presented these Pygmies as being hunter-gatherers, who were intimately attached to the forest, and whose being and survival were inconceivable without the forest. These descriptions sold an imagined image of all African Pygmies as 'forest people'; thus, in contemporary times, it is common to read and hear about Pygmies being referred to as 'forest people'. Nonetheless, while this book borrows the phrase 'the forest people' from Turnbull, it does not consider the Pygmies as people whose being and survival is dependent on a forest. Rather, it calls to question the presumed forest-boundedness of the Baka as Pygmies considering that, in Cameroon, they have been ejected from the forest and made to resettle on the roadsides with no or very limited access to the forest. Hence the book's title, *The Forest People without a Forest*.

Secondly, the 'development paradoxes' in the book's subtitle have their roots in a cumulation of contrasting development policies and interventions that have been implemented among the Baka both by the government, as well as by non-governmental organizations. In effect, the above-mentioned eviction of the Pygmies from the forest and their resettlement on roadsides were motivated by developmental policies, most of which equated development to sedentary agriculture and assimilation for the Baka (Abega and Logo 2005). At post-independence, it was assumed at the national level that the 'savage' could evolve to become a citizen mainly by contributing to national development through agriculture (ibid.). In light of this, the Baka, then considered as 'savages', were made to resettle on the roadsides to be assimilated as sedentary agriculturalists like the majority of the Cameroonian population, and thus become integrated citizens (Pemunta 2013). This assimilatory approach to the integration of the Baka in Cameroon was in line with the then integrationist stipulations provided by the International Labour Organization's (ILO) Convention 107 of 1957 on 'indigenous and tribal people', which Cameroon, intriguingly, did not ratify.[1]

Paradoxically, although Cameroon has not ratified ILO Convention 169 of 1989, which emphasizes respect for diversity and the protection of indigenous cultures and livelihoods, it voted for UNDRIP. In this regard, while the Baka continue to reside on the roadsides – where integrationists' approaches to development made them resettle – the forest is being staged as their homeland, where they belong. Cameroon's vote in support of the adoption of UNDRIP did not initiate an end to the existing sedentary agricultural assimilative development approaches for the Baka. To this end, both approaches to development are being implemented among the Baka, who now live on roadsides with no or very limited access to the forest and its resources. These phenomena are captured in this book as 'development paradoxes'.

Following the above-mentioned vote for the adoption of UNDRIP which emphasizes respect for cultural and livelihood diversity of indigenous peoples – in this case the Baka, who now reside on roadsides, but who are also experiencing assimilative sedentary agricultural development interventions – two anthropologists, Rupp (2011) and Pyhälä (2012), independently conducted research on the sociocultural situation of the Baka in eastern Cameroon. Interestingly, these two anthropologists came out with contrasting findings that reflect the paradoxical development policies and interventions implemented among the Baka. In effect, Rupp, in her groundbreaking ethnography *Forests of Belonging* (2011) questions the making of the Baka ('Pygmies') as a 'distinct category' (indigenous forest peoples). She calls it simplistic, and goes further to argue that such dichotomous categorizations of 'Pygmies', 'hunter-gatherers' and 'indigenous peoples' versus 'villagers' (Bantu tribes) are very stereotypical, misleading and blind to ongoing interactions between the Baka and their neighbouring Bantu peoples. According to Rupp's findings, the Baka are integrated, assimilated citizens. Beguilingly, Pyhälä in her own ethnographic report titled 'What Future for the Baka?' (2012), defines the Baka as being 'an indigenous hunter-gatherer society inhabiting the western range of the Central African rainforests … whose culture and lifestyle differ significantly from those of the dominant Cameroonian society, not only in terms of language, customs and traditions, but also in that, their livelihoods and identity depend entirely on their rights and access to their traditional lands and natural resources' (2012: 18, 16). Based on Pyhälä's findings, the Baka are excluded and marginalized indigenous forest peoples.

Bearing in mind the above-mentioned development paradoxes, as well as the disparity in the conclusions arrived at by Rupp (2011) and Pyhälä (2012), the main question that guides the discussions in this book is: How do the Baka assert their belonging in order to participate in development interventions and in the community? Do they assert belonging on the roadsides where most of them have been residing for more than three decades, or do they assert belonging to the forest where many of them have never resided? Do they consider themselves to be assimilated citizens or indigenous forest peoples, and why? Is there any differentiation in the way that the Baka assert their belonging? How do the ways in which they assert their belonging influence their participation in development interventions? These questions are analysed taking into particular consideration the fact that, in the East Region of Cameroon, belonging is highly contested and gives access to differentiated livelihood resources (Geschiere 2009). In effect, this book focuses on the confrontation of two versions of belonging (autochthony and indigeneity). The book does not aim to analyse interethnic relations between the Baka and the Bantu, nor the state of protection of indigenous peoples' rights in Cameroon.

Key Words and Concepts

In this book, I have used some contextualized words and concepts that need to be discussed. The words include: Pygmies, Baka, Bantu, roadsides and camps. The concepts are: autochthony, indigeneity, development, participation, home and belonging.

Pygmy: In countries that make up the Central African subregion, including Cameroon, the term Pygmy is generally used to refer to a category of Africans who either currently live in the forest and survive mostly from hunting and gathering, or those whose ancestry is linked to forest dwelling, hunting and gathering. For the most part, Pygmies were and still are represented as short, 'primitive' and 'uncivilized' people (Barns 1922: 149; Ray and Varma 2008: 35; Dasen 2013: 179). Some of these representations have also been captured by Mendosa[2] and Shahin,[3] just to name a few. The etymology of the word 'Pygmy' has been traced from the Greek word '*pygmaioi*' (meaning 'fist', or the measurement equivalent to the length from the elbow to the knuckles). Homer, the ancient Greek poet, first used this word in the *Iliad* to describe a tribe of dwarfs[4] (Breverton 2011). Since the nineteenth century – especially following the German ethnologist and collector of African art Felix von Luschan – they are usually described with the ethnologically obsolete term 'Pygmies'. Some scholars consider the word 'Pygmy' to be derogatory and scientifically incorrect, charged with prejudices, stereotypes and imagined physical characteristics of a group of people (Cummings, Jordan and Zvelebil 2014: 935; Hewlett 2014: 1890). More so, some of these scholars argue that most of the people concerned 'do not use the term Pygmy to refer to themselves' (Giles-Vernick 2001: 131).

In some African countries like the Republic of Congo, the use of the word is said to have been banned.[5] In effect, Paragraph 2 of Article 1 of law no. 5-2011 on the promotion and protection of indigenous peoples' rights prohibits the use of the term Pygmy in the Republic of Congo because of its pejorative connotation, and it is punishable by the Congolese Penal

Code.[6] Nonetheless, in Cameroon, the word is still in use. It is often used synonymously with appellations like 'hunter-gatherers', 'forest peoples' and 'primitive people'. Some government officials even hold that Pygmies are 'a people who are culturally evolving and moving up' (Hewlett 2000: 380). In like manner, the word is inscribed in policy documents like the famous 'Pygmy People Development Plan of the Forest and Environment Sectorial Programme' (PPDP/FESP). In Cameroon, the word is used to refer to three 'groups' of people; the Baka in the East and South Regions, the Bakola in the South Region and the Bedzang in the Centre Region. In the context of this book, the Pygmy 'group' Baka are the subject of study. For the majority of the Baka, the word 'Pygmy' is considered to be insulting. Only a few of them use the term on rare occasions for 'cultural marketing'.[7]

Baka: In the East Region of Cameroon, the appellation Baka is the name by which the people categorized as Pygmies call themselves. This appellation is very much based on the definition of their ethnicity, and is widely accepted both by those concerned as well as by anthropologists (Rupp 2011). In this work, I have sided with using the term Baka, as opposed to Pygmies. However, when discussing development policies and approaches that were designed 'for Pygmies', I use the word 'Pygmies' because the policies were designed for the Baka, as well as the Bakola and the Bedzangs. Moreover, these development policies were, and often still are, officially titled as being 'Pygmy development policies and/or strategies'. This is, for example, the case with the above-mentioned PPDP/FESP. Linguisitically, 'Baka is a[n] Ubangi-Adamawa language (ALCAM no. 309) spoken by 50–60,000 Baka, also know[n] as Pygmies, in southeast Cameroon. The language shares similarities primarily with Ngbaka Ma'Bo' (Léonard 2011: 1), and it varies phonetically as one moves from one region to another (RASED, 2006). In Cameroon, the Baka are one of three ethnic groups historically referred to as 'Pygmies'. Nonetheless, the Baka are also found in other countries of the Central African subregion. In Cameroon, they are found inhabiting the southeastern region of the country, in the Republic of Congo, in DR Congo and Gabon, they are found in the northern regions, and in Central African Republic, they are found in the southwestern region. Although the exact numbers are difficult to determine, either because of their lack of inclusion in national census programmes, or due to their sometimes mobile nature, 'the Baka are currently estimated to have a total population of somewhere between 50,000–70,000, of which a large portion (approximately 40,000–60,000) are found in Cameroon' (Pyhälä 2012: 14).

Bantu: The word 'Bantu' as used in this book is meant to refer to a category of Cameroonians whose livelihood has for the most part been historically associated with sedentary agriculture. While it is largely agreed that not all Bantus are sedentary agriculturalists (Selin 2003), Feierman and Janzen have shown that 'the spread of food cultivation and sedentary society southward through and around the equatorial rainforests has come to be associated with the spread of the Bantu languages … of Bantu-speakers, in what is now the border area of Cameroon and Nigeria' (1992: 170). In the East Region of Cameroon, the word 'Bantu' combines a number of ethnic groups, including the Maka, the Pols, the Badjoué and the Bangando, just to name a few. In this region of the country, the word is used synonymously with the words 'villagers' and 'agriculturalists'. The word 'Bantu' is very much applied in linguistics, and is considered to refer to a family of languages spoken by the above-mentioned ethnic groups. In this regard, people whose mother tongue is Bantu are considered to be Bantus. This linguistic underpinning of the word has been criticized as being incorrect (Robillard 2010: 39). However, although the use of the word is criticized by some scholars, the Bantu, unlike the Pygmies, do not express discontent about this appellation. I use the term in this book, because in Cameroon it is accepted and used by policy makers and development actors, as well as by the Bantu themselves. To this end, my use of the term is not suggestive of my approval of its correctness.

Roadsides: In the East Region of Cameroon, roadsides refer to territorial land surfaces located in the vicinities of a constructed road, which may or may not be tarred. In most cases, these land surfaces constitute part of the agricultural areas defined in the country's 1994 forest law as the agro-forestry band ('*bande agro-forestière*'). Administratively, these roadsides are considered to be part of village lands where residents also practise agriculture and other livelihood activities. Nonetheless, due to the tensions surrounding the politics of belonging in the East Region of Cameroon, the Baka tend to contest this administrative positioning of roadsides in relation to villages (which are on the most parts, mainly Bantu villages). It is important to mention that there is a difference in meaning here from the regular English meaning of the term roadsides: roadsides are not only limited to the immediate sides or verges of the road with distances between zero and five metres. Rather, roadsides refer to land surfaces located at distances of up to five hundred metres from a constructed road. The designation is well known and understood, and in the francophone forest regions of the country is referred to as '*bordure de route*'. Figure 0.1 illustrates two different Baka roadside 'camps'.

Camp: In the East Region of Cameroon, the term camp is used to refer to different Baka settlements. For the Baka, the term invites a lot of controversy and is subject to contestations, as will be discussed later on in this work. For most Bantus however, the term is used to suggest a dimension of 'temporariness',

Figure 0.1 Examples of Baka roadside 'camps' in the East Region of Cameroon.
Source: photographs by the research assistant in Mendjou and Abakoum respectively (Nov. 2011).

'unrootedness in the soil', 'not belonging' and 'stranger' status of the Baka who reside on the roadsides. In effect, since the birth of multiparty politics in 1990 and subsequent decentralization in 2004, the country has witnessed the re-emergence of ethnoregional polictics,[8] such that the presumed 'unrootedness in the soil', as well as the 'stranger' status of the Baka have awaken discussions about the concept of 'autochthony', being a local, as well as the 'politics of belonging' which were actively suppressed by former president Ahidjo in his attempt to cultivate a single national identity that would dominate any ethnic or local identities. These discussions around autochthony, being a local, as well as the 'politics of belonging' have become dominant in everyday negotiations of access to power and resources among Cameroonians (Geschiere 2009), to the point that they have created a 'pervasive and disturbing issue of exclusion' (Sama 2007: 192), which has made people to express their identities in ways that are profoundly more entrenched in the local than the national (Geschiere 2009). The process of expressing this identity in a deeply rooted 'local' is called the politics of belonging (Geschiere and Nyamnjoh 2000). Its most prevalent form is 'autochthony', which means 'born from the soil' and confers an undeniable primordial right to belong, which is often employed in politically charged attempts to exclude 'others' (Geschiere 2009).

In like manner, the emergence of the global category of 'indigenous peoples'[9] as interpreted by the UN and ILO has further opened up another space for people in Cameroon to assert their belonging, since the category of 'indigenous peoples' also confers some sort of 'authenticity' and programmed development assistance. Thus, in Cameroon, autochthony and indigeneity are highly sensitive because they are directly linked to the question of governmentality and development. Even though autochthony and indigeneity offer different spaces for people to assert their belonging in a bid to access related resources, Pelican (2009: 52) has noted that these concepts, although different, are interrelated and often interpreted differently by the many different actors at the local, national and international levels. Sonné also alludes to the same twist of interpretation in the Cameroonian context when he writes that an autochthon originates from the country/territory in which s/he lives, while 'indigenes' are the first occupants of a given territory:

> An autochthon is an individual originating from the country or territory in which he lives. He shares the same soil as other members of his community. So it is with indigenous or aboriginal populations: they are the first inhabitants of a region or of a given territory (Sonnè, Wang. UNESCO-MOST); my own translation).

In this light, the understandings of the terms indigenous and autochthons as applied in Cameroon are not immediately clear.

'Indigenous Peoples': Multiple Understandings

To use Pyhälä's words, 'another extremely complex and sensitive subject in Cameroon is that of "indigenous peoples"' (2012: 15). Unlike most countries in Africa, where all Africans are considered indigenous (Lutz 2007) without any further special categorization, Cameroon is one of the few African countries that voted in favour of the UN Declaration on the Rights of Indigenous Peoples in 2007 and is currently in the process of recognizing the existence of 'indigenous peoples' as a distinct category in its territory. Nonetheless, in the country, on the ground (local) understandings of the concept differ significantly from its Euro-American/international conceptualizations (Pelican 2009). This arises from a long history behind the use of the word 'indigenous' in Cameroon. As Niezen puts it, 'the agendas of international institutions do not reveal or reflect cognizance of the history of the terms they use or the cultural innovations introduced by conceptual-diplomatic efforts' (2010: 105–106).

In the African continent, and Cameroon in particular, the use of the word 'indigenous' has drifted from its etymological meaning since colonial times. The word originates from the Latin '*indigena*', made up of '*indi*' meaning 'within' and '*gen*' or '*genere*' meaning 'root', thereby translated as 'born in' (Barume 2010: 20). During colonial times for example, the word was used in English Africa to refer to peoples found in colonized territories, regardless of whether or not they had been born there, or if they were newcomers. The term was used interchangeably with the word 'natives' (ibid.). This colonial understanding of the term continued until after the creation of the ILO,[10] the first organization to deal with the issue of the term 'indigenous'.

The ILO introduced the first formal definition of the term, which considered indigenous people as 'workers belonging to, or assimilated to indigenous populations of the dependent territories of members of the organisation, and workers belonging to, or assimilated to the dependent indigenous populations of the home territories of members of the organisation' (Barume 2010: 22) in Convention 50. This definition was highly criticized for its double meaning since, at the same time, it implied indigenous by origin and indigenous by assimilation. Countries like South Africa, which had assimilated whites and black Africans, were sharp examples used to criticize the definition, which only lasted until the mid-1950s. Following this criticism, the definition was amended in 1957 and called Convention 107 titled 'Convention Concerning the Protection and Integration of Indigenous and Other Tribal and Semi-tribal Populations'. This new convention redefined the term 'indigenous' as:

> members of tribal or semi-tribal populations in independent countries which are regarded as indigenous on account of their descent from the populations

which inhabited the country, or a geographical region to which the country belongs, at the time of conquest or colonisation and which, irrespective of their legal status, live more in conformity with the social, economic and cultural institutions of that time than with the institutions of the nation to which they belong. [In this definition,] the term semi-tribal includes groups and persons who, although they are in the process of losing their tribal characteristics, are not yet integrated into the national community (ILO Convention 107, Articles 1(1b) and 2).

In other words, the convention defined indigenous peoples as 'peoples who are indigenous because of some historical event such as conquest or colonisation and who are still living in the tribal or semi-tribal form' (ibid. 2010: 24). This redefinition added the point that governments shall have the primary responsibility for developing coordinated and systematic action for the protection of the populations concerned and their progressive integration into the life of their respective countries (ibid. 2010: 26). After some decades, this convention again came under severe criticism for its assimilationist and integrative dimensions, thereby leading to the adoption of the current Convention 169 of 1989 which applies to:

1. (a) tribal peoples in independent countries whose social, cultural, and economic condition distinguish them from other sections of the national community, and whose status is regulated wholly or partially by their own customs or traditions or by special laws or regulations;
(b) peoples in independent countries who are regarded as indigenous on account of their descent from the populations which inhabited the country, or a geographical region to which the country belongs at the time of conquest or colonisation or the establishment of present state boundaries and who, irrespective of their legal status, retain some or all of their own social, economic, cultural and political institutions [and];
2. [Emphasis on] Self-identification as indigenous or tribal ... as a fundamental criterion for determining the groups to which the provisions of this Convention apply (ILO Convention 169, Article 1).

This last convention, therefore, removed the assimilationist orientation of Convention 107, which encouraged integration (Hogdson 2002: 1038) and rather emphasized the recognition of, and respect for, ethnic and cultural diversity. The UN as an international development actor does not, for its part, have a legally binding definition for indigenous peoples (Hogdson 2002: 1039). Although these new interpretations to help identify indigenous peoples were indicative rather than legally binding, most African countries rejected their adoption, as well as their implementation in the continent, arguing that all Africans are indigenous and deserve equal access to natural resources (Barume 2010; Lutz 2007). In 2007 however, some African countries including Cameroon made an exception by voting in favour of the adoption of the United Nations Declaration on the Rights of Indigenous Peoples (UNDRIP). Since the adoption of this convention in 2007 by the UN General Assembly (Pelican 2009: 52), Cameroon in some of its policies in 2008 branded the Pygmies and Mbororos (non-agricultural populations of the country) as indigenous peoples on its territory. This is the case for example with the World Bank-funded Chad-Cameroon pipeline project whereby, 'under the World Bank's policy on indigenous peoples, the Baka, Bagyeli, Bakola and Bedzang – all Cameroonian indigenous hunter gatherers – are considered as 'indigenous peoples' and the government has recognised and taken ownership of the Pygmy/Indigenous People's Development Plans of the Chad Cameroon Pipeline'. Despite this, the official government terminology for indigenous peoples in Cameroon in other contexts not related to World Bank projects is 'marginalized people' (Ndobe 2013) and their affairs are managed by a department in the Ministry of Social Affairs. Intriguingly however, during the 2014 celebration of the UN International Day of the World's Indigenous Peoples in Cameroon, Cameroon's Minister of Social Affairs explicitly said that only Mbororos and 'Pygmies' are considered to be indigenous peoples (IWGIA 2014).

This process of recognition of indigenous people in Cameroon based on ILO Convention 169 has opened doors to local, national and international non-governmental organizations to implement targeted development programmes for the said indigenous peoples, thereby making the country's own rather assimilative and integrative approach to indigenous peoples an 'extremely complex and sensitive subject' (Pyhälä 2012: 15–16). Each of the three reinterpretations of indigeneity applied to the African continent demonstrates clearly that the term 'indigenous' embodies different categories of people.[11] Firstly, the colonial interpretation of the term made all Africans indigenous. Secondly, only people living in tribal and semi-tribal states were considered indigenous; and finally, the term referred to people who defined themselves as indigenous or who were identified as such by NGOs and INGOs.

Autochthony, the sister term to indigenous people, is another complex term that calls for clarification.

'Autochthony' Versus 'Allogeny' (Strangerness)

The word 'autochthony' is as 'old as the world or at least the state' (Bayart and Geschiere, 2001: 128). It has been traced back to France and Great Britain during the sixteenth-century state formations, and political conquests where divides between 'son of the soil' and strangers tended to emerge (ibid.).

Nevertheless, in French colonial Africa, the concept of autochthones was rarely used. Rather, the word *'indigène'* referred to natives, who at that time were people whom colonial masters met in the colonies. The term was used to mean that natives were sons and daughters of the soil (Pelican 2009). In recent years, the concept now coined in anthropological literature as 'autochthony' has become very prominent. It has become a special political watchword in the 'unexpected corollary of democratization and the new style of development policies ("by-passing the state" …) [to get to the local grass roots level]'[12] (Ceuppens and Geschiere 2005: 385). The prominence of this concept as engraved in development policies that seek to get to the locals has resulted in 'the exclusion of supposed "strangers" [*'allogènes'* – people not born of the soil] and the unmasking of "fake" autochthons, who are often citizens of the same nation-state' (ibid. 2005: 385). Sonnè, discussing autochthon-stranger relations between Cameroonians living in Cameroonian territory notes that within a given community in the country, an autochthon can have an *'allogène'*/stranger as a neighbour:

> An autochthon may have a stranger (*'allogène'*) as a neighbor. This is an indi-
> vidual 'born elsewhere'. He is settled on this land undoubtably for various
> political, economic or cultural reasons. He knows his origin and genealogy;
> irrespective of the efforts that he makes in his area of residence, he knows from
> the depth of his heart that his land is 'elsewhere'. … There are many strangers
> whom the autochthones have generously welcomed on their soil (Sonnè in
> UNESCO MOST) programme, not dated; my own translation).

From this it can be argued that, in Cameroon, the concept of autochthony builds on the argument of 'prior settlement' to establish and legitimize specific political rights for the benefit of those who see themselves as natives, and to exclude those whom *they* label as 'aliens or strangers'. Bayart and Geschiere (2001) have aptly summed up this process using the French description *'J'étais là avant'* ('I was there first'). In this regard, the characteristic of political, social, economic and cultural struggles between autochthones and *'allogènes'* (strangers) are of the order 'I was here first'.

This is the intriguing case observed between the Baka and their Bantu neighbours. The Bantu claim that they were first on the roadsides, and only brought the Baka out of the forest recently to settle with them on 'their roadside villages'. So the Bantu consider themselves the real autochthones (Leonhardt 2006), while the Baka are strangers. The Baka on their part, however, argue that they were first in the forest, but have been dispossessed of their ancestral lands. This constant struggle of 'we' rightfully belong and 'they' are strangers is the politics of belonging which Rupp has aptly summarized as having 'brought together two powerful political currents: autochthony as a vehicle to ensure that power and resources remain in the hands of the regional elite and their followers, and the international insistence that resources are channeled to communities that conform to Euroamerican, institutional definitions of "indigenous people"' (2011: 52).

Development

Development is a wide concept that cannot be defined independently without considering historical, social, economic and political factors that come into play in the process. In this light, development is qualified as being a complex concept to define, and for which there is no single agreed-upon definition. The commonest definition is one that approaches development from an economic perspective, thereby reducing it to economic growth and increased national gross domestic product (GDP). However, Sen has criticized this economic perspective as too narrow, arguing that development should be conceived of as the process of expanding the real freedoms that people enjoy (2000). In the same light, the United Nations Development Programme (UNDP) uses the term 'development' from a human development perspective to mean, 'to lead long and healthy lives, to be knowledgeable, to have access to the resources needed for a decent standard of living and to be able to participate in the life of the community' (UNDP: http://hdr.undp.org/en/humandev.)

For his part, Escobar critically questions the very rise of the concept of development. To him, the whole concept of development is a pervasive hegemonic discourse which created the so-called Third World (1996). Escobar argues that the whole project of development needs to be rethought with possibilities for counter-hegemonic alternative development. Escobar's stance on what development is questions development as reflected in the writings of Heilbroner. According to Heilbroner in Bodley, development means helping to 'transform "tradition-bound" societies into modern societies. Nothing short of a pervasive social transformation will suffice: a wholesale metamorphosis of habits, a wrenching reorientation of values concerning time, status, money, work, and an unweaving and reweaving of the fabric of daily existence itself' (1963: 53 in Bodley 1990: 96).

Even though the concept of development is contested, the focus of this book is neither to evaluate development projects initiated for and/or by the Baka, nor is it to analyse how the various understandings and interpretations of development are good or bad. Rather, this book focuses on understanding how 'development' interventions shape relations between different communities, as well as whether people within these communities instrumentalize the construction of their belonging in a bid to be included in 'development' interventions. To this end, this book does not adopt a given definition of development. Rather, development in the context of this work is taken to mean programmes and interventions thus named, and implemented in the East Region of Cameroon as such, irrespective of whether they are geared towards economic 'growth', 'increased' freedoms, 'improved' health and education or 'a wholesale metamorphosis of habits'. The reason for taking development as a given, defined by those implementing it, is to enable me to analyse how shifting framings of development affect the social dynamics of targeted communities.

Participation

The concept of participation cuts across disciplines, and its meaning changes as one switches between disciplines. As a concept, participation can be variously understood in terms of its content and forms. In social sciences and development theorizing most especially, participation has a long history (Hickey and Mohan 2004). Oakley (1991: 6) has aptly condensed these various interpretations into the following four categories:

- … A voluntary contribution by the people in one or another of the public programmes supposed to contribute to national development, but the people are not expected to take part in shaping the programme or criticising its contents.
- With regard to rural development … participation includes people's involvement in decision-making processes, in implementing programmes, their sharing in the benefits of development programmes, and their involvement in efforts to evaluate such programmes
- Participation is concerned with … the organised efforts to increase control over resources and regulative institutions in given social situations on the part of groups and movements of those hitherto excluded from such control.
- Community participation [is] an active process by which beneficiary or client groups influence the direction and execution of a development project with a view to enhancing their well-being in terms of income, personal growth, self-reliance or other values that they cherish.

The World Bank, for its part, understands participation as 'the process by which stakeholders influence and share control over priority setting, policy-making, resource allocation, and program implementation' (Klugman 2002: 237). In this way, the World Bank argues that participation can enable stakeholders to improve on their decision-making processes, strengthen project ownership and help poor people and disadvantaged groups (World Bank, Social Assessment Guidelines, 10 May 1994).

From these, it is clear that the concept of participation, just like that of development, is contested. The concept of participation is engraved into the bigger project of participatory development which was seen as a panacea for the failures of top-down development approaches. Particiation is projected to increase the involvement of socially and economically marginalized peoples in decision making (Cooke and Kothari 2001). Participatory development envisages the recognition of 'the importance of entrusting citizens with the responsibility to shape their own future' (Jennings 2000: 2). To this end, participatory approaches are believed to be capable of helping to extend the concept of participation to citizenship, so as to 'recast participation as a right, not simply an invitation offered to beneficiaries of development' (Gaventa 2004: 29). This dimension to participation is said to enhance local people's capabilities (Hickey and Mohan 2004: 62). Namara has, however, argued that the word 'participation' has been highly instrumentalized by NGOs to secure donor funding without any effective participation on the part of a project's beneficiaries (2009, 2010).

Nonetheless, considering that the objective of this book is not to evaluate the effectiveness of participatory development programmes in the East Region of Cameroon but rather to investigate how the Baka negotiate their belonging to participate in development interventions, this book focuses more on what the different development interventions consider participation to be. It is also worth noting here that, during the past decade in Cameroon, decentralized local development interventions have supplanted national development approaches such that, in general, people can participate in and benefit from local decentralized development interventions only if they belong as locals (autochthones) at local community levels. In other words, a local decentralized development project destined for indigenous peoples in the East Region of Cameroon is considered to be for the Baka (because they belong as indigenous peoples). This is what Robillard (2010) has called positive discrimination in the East Region of Cameroon.

Home and Belonging

The conceptual relationship between home and belonging has been widely explored in migration and refugee studies. In the past, scholars explored migrants' experiences of leaving their countries of origin which they called home, to settle in a new country, which they called 'strange lands' (Ahmed 1999; Ahmed et al. 2003). In contemporary times however, the focus of these studies has often been to understand how migrants reconstruct 'home' in these new countries. A couple of these studies have shown that the concept of home is much contested (Malkki 1995). In general, one reads a tension between the conceptualizations of home as either a physical place, a symbolic place, or both. Traditional conceptualizations of the concept define it to be a safe and territorially fixed place to leave and return to, a space under one's own control and of familiarity. In this conceptualization, a home could be a house, a village, a region or a nation, a space of right and/or entitlement (Rapport and Dawson 1998: 7). Olwig (1998) and Demuth (2000) have nonetheless shown that the concept of home entails both a concrete physical space and an emotional feeling of belonging such that feelings of home are intricately tied to where one belongs or wants to belong. In this way, one may conceive of home as being both a concrete geographical place of origin and/or where one feels one can belong and participate in the everyday life of the community.

Exploring the relationship between home and belonging, however, is not only peculiar to scholars of migration and refugee studies. Recent 'obsessions' about autochthony and decentralized local developments in most African countries has brought this relationship between home and belonging into question for internal migrants or displaced populations within a given country (Geschiere 2009). This is especially because in most of these countries, Cameroon included, displaced populations face challenges with issues of home and belonging. In the context of Cameroon for example, citizens construct home at two levels – the national and the local – such that feelings of belonging are often expressed in terms of 'national' and 'local' citizenships. In this regard, the home of displaced citizens is at first often taken to be a fixed locality from where they originated, while they are considered to be strangers in the community in which they have resettled. They are considered to be not at home and to not belong, even though they are citizens of the same country within which they have been displaced. These challenges significantly increase the value of claims to belonging and local participation for these displaced citizens. Lund illustrates this phenomenon when he says that, 'while people may share national citizenship, the idea of autochthony – first arrival – is often invoked as a mechanism of inclusion and exclusion ... [such that] not belonging [at the local level], i.e., not being a local citizen, may outright deny [a] person a legitimate opportunity to stake a claim' (2011: 74).

This is the situation that this book explores among the Baka, who are to a large extent considered Cameroonians at the national level, yet their claims to belonging and to home at the local level within the East Region of the country remain contested. This study takes into consideration the fact that at the local level in the East Region of Cameroon, local citizenship is developed in line with the modalities of land occupation and exploitation, which are closely linked with the metaphor of 'rootedness in the soil'. This conceptual relationship between home and belonging for the Baka in the context of development interventions and participation is of particular interest for this book. This is because in this era of decentralization and local development, local citizenship defines who can participate in and/or benefits from these local decentralized development interventions. In this light, the ways in which the Baka construct home and belonging at the local level (in roadside communities) need to be properly understood. It is worth mentioning here that, while the challenges surrounding the Baka's local level citizenship could well be conceived of as discrimination against them, this book will not explore discrimination, because such analysis risks demonizing the Bantu as discriminatory without throwing significant light on the local social dynamics of community life in the region.

Organization of the Book

This book is divided into five chapters. Chapter 1 briefly discusses local and national constructions of Pygmies in Cameroon. The chapter also highlights the ensuing challenges to the belonging and participation of the Baka in East Cameroon. Chapter 2 examines how the Baka assert their belonging, considering that they now reside on roadsides while their belonging continues to be ascribed in terms of 'the forest'. The chapter shows that in East Cameroon, autochthony and indigeneity are projected as versions of belonging that conflict with one another. Based on these conflicting versions of belonging in East Cameroon, Chapter 3 explores the ways in which the Baka authenticate their claims to either version of belonging. The chapter focuses on analysing the ways in which the Baka reconstruct their rootedness to the soil so as to authenticate their rootedness in the soil on the roadsides where they now reside. Chapter 4 answers the question of whether or not there is 'groupness' (as employed by Brubaker and Cooper 2000) in the way that the Baka assert their belonging. The chapter highlights and discusses an emerging internal differentiation among the Baka, who have in the past been categorized as being a group of egalitarian indigenous forest people. Chapter 5 analyses how belonging influences the participation of the Baka in development interventions, as well as in community life in the East Region.

Notes

1. For an elaborate understanding of these integrationist stipulations, cf. Article 2 of the convention. Cameroon has also not ratified convention 169. However, it voted in support of the adoption of UNDRIP in 2007 and in '2008, the government decreed official celebrations for International Day of the World's Indigenous Peoples in Cameroon' (IWGIA, 2013: 406).

2. 'Ten Pygmies and One Tall Westerner', by David Mendosa, 2008, Fitness and Photograpy for Fun blog. Retrieved 15.06.2016 from http://www.mendosa.com/fitnessblog/.
3. Sahin Tahir, 'PYGMIES Primitive African People'. Retrieved 27.04.2014 from http://www.youtube.com/watch?v=F721NH20mbg.
4. Some authors have challenged this stance, arguing that dwarfism is a physiological condition that is also visible among other Africans, and it is thus misleading to associate Pygmies with being dwarfs (Dawson 1938: 185).
5. Personal communication with Mentui Samuel of Mballam Baka in East Cameroon. Also see Article 2 of law number no. 5-2011, which promotes and protects the rights of autochthonous populations in DR Congo.
6. Ibid., law no. 5-2011 of the Republic of Congo. Retrieved 10.10.2015 from http://www.iwgia.org/iwgia_files_news_files/0115_Loi_n5 2011_du_25_fevrier_2011_portant_promotion_et_protection_des_droits_des_populations_autochtone.pdf.
7. By cultural marketing, I mean a situation whereby some Baka expressly referred to themselves as being Pygmies, in order to reiterate their perceived mysterious abilities to use tree leaves and skins in treating various aliments. More of this will be discussed in Chapter 6 in the section 'The Baka-Baka'.
8. In Cameroon, this policy existed during colonial times and was a colonial strategy for administrative management. However, at independence, President Ahmadou Ahidjo suppressed it and sought to cultivate a single national identity. For more on this, see Chapter 1.
9. Due to the negative connotations of the colonial term '*indigène*', the English and French versions of the UN declaration respectively refer to 'indigenous peoples', and '*peuples autochtones*' rather than '*peuples indigènes*' (Pelican 2009: 54).
10. The ILO was created in 1919 (ILO: webpage). Retrieved 02.03.2012 from http://www.ilo.org/global/about-the-ilo/history/lang--en/index.htm.
11. Drifts from the etymological meaning to the colonial usage of the term in English Africa, through ILO Convention 107 and finally ILO Convention 169.
12. This is not meant to suggest that grass roots-led development projects are bad, nor that state-led national development is the best model. Rather, it is illustrative of how the concept of autochthony becomes significant in the process of constructing the 'we' boundary and excluding the other, 'them'. As already seen, Cameroon is governed along ethnic lines, which only further strengthens autochthony.

Chapter 1

PYGMIES AMID 'DEVELOPMENT' PRACTICES IN CAMEROON

c∞•∞ɔ

There exists a Pygmy problem in Cameroon. Strictly speaking, it is neither a new question nor a fundamentally specific question. It is an old concern, but which has not yet had the strong echo of other questions … (Logo 2002a: 15; my own translation).

The 'Pygmy problem' in Cameroon, as Logo has pointed out in the quote above, is not a new phenomenon. Rather, it is the extension of an old existing problem of 'Pygmies' in general which the first section of this chapter biefly revisits.

'Being Pygmy': Historically Invented and Reinvented 'Others'

Writing about hunter-gatherers today has to deal with a century of discourses; some rooted in European and African notions of 'difference' and race, others springing from European ideas of "natural man" and all of these are closely bound up in complex discourses that accompanied European colonialism and Imperialism … These ideologically saturated discourses formed an implicit background of unstated assumptions, predispositions and preju-dices. Nineteenth century European settlers in the main regarded the hunter-gatherers with thinly veiled contempt, as incorrigible bandits speaking scarcely intelligible tongues (Lee and Hitchcock 2001: 259).

As Lee and Hitchcock (2001) suggest, the subject of hunter-gatherers, espe-cially Pygmies, has existed in academic, policy and administrative circles for some time. In this subsection I will briefly discuss the various historical inventions about Pygmies, some of which have enhanced a fascination with Pygmies as 'subhumans'.

Pygmies: Apes, Humans or a Myth?

The framing of so-called African 'Pygmies' as essentially distinct and different from other peoples on the continent may be traced back to pre-colonial times when explorers depicted them as humanity's mystery (Mulder 2009). At that time of great exploration and of the discovery of other peoples, explorers – who were mostly from the West – reported on the extraordinary character and physical appearance of 'Pygmies'. These reports in turn made people curious about the nature of Pygmies, which gave rise to various speculations (Mwangi 2008: xvii). The reports also influenced some researchers to engage in finding out whether the so-called 'Pygmies' belonged to the human race. Nonetheless, as Ballard (2006) shows, these researchers tended to focus on showing how different Pygmies were from the researchers ('self') and other black Africans ('others'). The search for such difference thus ended up sowing the unending seed of emphasis on 'distinct difference' as an analytical category in 'Pygmy studies'. This distinct difference has metamorphosed over time, switching between race, culture, ethnicity, identity and most recently belonging. Albertus Magnus (1200–1280) for example, tried to locate Pygmies on a continuum from animals at one end to humans at the other end. Magnus noted that Pygmies and apes shared many similarities at the level of their facial structure. For him, both Pygmies and apes were unable to twist their ears. However, according to Magnus, the major difference between Pygmies and apes was the fact that Pygmies had a language which they used in a very 'primitive' way, such that this Pygmy language could not communicate concepts intelligibly. In a nutshell, Magnus reduced Pygmies to subhumans who were different from apes in some ways, but also very different from other humans. To him, Pygmies did not have a sense of morality or shame, nor did they form regular communities (Jahoda 1999). Four centuries after Magnus attempted to locate the Pygmy in some kind of natural order between apes and humans, the anatomist Edward Tyson (1699) sought to understand whether Pygmies were part of the human race. He opened his classic work titled *The Anatomy of a Pygmie Compared With That of a Monkey* by stating that Pygmies were more ape than human:

> That the Pygmies of the An[c]ients were a sort of Apes, and not of Humane Race, I shall endeavour to prove in the following essay. And if the Pygmies were only Apes, then in all probability our Ape may be a Pygmie; a sort of

animal so much resembling Man, that both the An[c]ients and the Moderns have reputed it to be a Puny Race of Mankind, call'd to this day, *Homo sylvestris*, The Wild Man; Orang-Outang, … the Savage (1699: 1).

Tyson argued that in general, the Pygmy resembled an ape. He noted that 'the Nose of our Pygmie was flat like an Ape's, not protuberant as a Man's, and on the outside of each Nostril there was a little slit turning upwards, as in Apes' (1699: 9).[1] While Tyson framed the Pygmy's identity as being closer to that of an ape, Schweinfurth on his part – considered by O'Hanlon and Welsch (2000) as the forebear of the modern form of the Pygmy 'myth'[2] in the West – shifted from the ape-like racial comparison to human racial comparison.

In his 1874 *Im Herzen von Afrika*, Schweinfurth documented his experiences in the African forest. In this process, he framed the Pygmies' identity as being closer to that of other native Africans. He showed this when he described his encounter with a small man, referring to a Pygmy at the 'court' of Munza, a 'native' king of the Monbuttu (Starr 1896: 415). Schweinfurth reported that Pygmies were humans, but different from other black Africans. This 'discovery' appealed greatly to his Western audience, further raising curiosity about human evolution and the diversity of human races, such that the French anthropologist J.L.A. de Quatrefages de Bréau, dedicated an entire book in 1887 to the Pygmies which he called *Les Pygmées* (Mulder 2009: 47). In this book de Quatrefages, in an attempt to understand the Pygmies, collected passages from writers like Homer, Aristotle and Herodotus, to name a few. From these collected passages, de Quatrefages stated that 'the ancients had information more or less inexact, more or less incomplete, but also more or less true, concerning five populations of little stature, from whom they made their Pygmies' (Starr 1896: 415).

Despite de Quatrefages' publication of *Les Pygmées*, Pygmies continued to be the subject of popular fascination (Dkamela and Oyono 2003). King Leopold II of Belgium for example, exhibited a small group of Pygmies in his Congo display at a colonial exhibition in 1897 (Bradford and Blume 1992). On the same footing, another group of Pygmies, dressed in children's sailors outfits highlighting their innocent primitivity, were exhibited to parliamentarians in the British House of Commons (Jahoda 1999). In like manner, Verner, a missionary caught up by social Darwinism and fascinated with the whole question of the Pygmies, brought Ota Benga, a Pygmy from Congo, and placed him on display at the Bronx Zoo in New York in 1906 (Bradford and Blume 1992):

[In the Zoo, Benga] share[d] a cage with the Bronx Park apes [, and] although [the] director Dr. Hornaday insisted that he was merely offering an 'intriguing exhibit' for the public's edification, he apparently saw no difference between a wild beast and the little Black man; [such that,] for the first time in any American zoo, a human being was displayed in a cage. Benga was given cage-mates to keep him company in his captivity – a parrot, and an orangutan named Dohong (Sifakis 1984: 252–253).

Although Benga's[3] exposition in the zoo was closer to Tyson's ape-like racial comparison of the Pygmies than it was to Schweinfurth's racial comparison with fellow Africans, all three subscribed to biological racial differences. Stanley also subscribed to these biological racial differences and described the Pygmies as diminutive creatures (in Roy 1890). Stanley added that 'despite their insignificant stature, [they make] a formidable foe. They appear to sustain life, like some other savage tribes, on roots and wild fruit ... but their chief dainty is the banana, and their desire for this luxury draws them irresistibly from the depths of their seclusion to the borders of the cultivated spots, where the larger race have shown their superior skill in growing this coveted fruit' (1890: 253–254). Following suit, Barns in his descriptions of the wonderlands of eastern Congo noted that, Pygmies were stunted small people:

> Both my wife and I looked at these sturdy little men with undisguised interest. What need to look further for the Missing Link when he stood there before us! Short legs, long arms, heavy torso; short neck, rounded head, deep set, penetrating, see-in-the-dark kind of eyes; square long lips, protruding jaw. The ape was all there, up to the hair, which was discernible in some cases over the entire body of these dwarfs (Barns 1922: 149).

In the same light, Sinang quotes Trilles, a Reverend Father, writing in the 1940s about the encounter of a 'white' man in the forest who addressed the Pygmies as being the brothers of gorillas:

> You are the brother of a gorilla, one of his descendants ... like him, you climb on trees, you build your house, you carry your little one on your back, you eat the fruits of the forest ... you're black, naked and hairy like it. Where is the difference? You are just a monkey that speaks. In response, to prove his human identity, the Pygmy was silent for a moment, and then lit a fire by rubbing two sticks ('*bâtonnets*') against each other. After lighting the fire, the Pygmy said to the 'white', that's why I'm not a monkey. The monkey does not light a fire, does not pray and will never do so (Trilles 1945: 26; my own translation).

The sustained emphasis on the essential differences of Pygmies from other Africans like Schebesta (1952) argued, made Pygmies so central to the debate on human evolution both racially and culturally, that they have been the focus of extensive research. Bahuchet, one of the prominent contemporary researchers of Pygmies, concluded in his article 'L'invention des Pygmées' that 'in truth, Pygmies do not exist. People who do exist bear the names Baka, BaBongo, BaKola, BaAka, Ba Sua, Éfè, Asua, BaTwa.' Bahuchet asks 'Who knows what they have in common, other than exciting the imagination of Westerners?' (1993: 175; my own translation).[4] Following suit, Ballard says that throughout history, the frame of reference for Pygmies has been earlier myths and instances of encounter that are then themselves re-mythologized (2006: 135).

Despite Ballard's argument, racial stereotypes about Pygmies continue to persist in discourses especially from some Pygmy-neighbouring communities. In discussing the trajectory to citizenship of Pygmies in Cameroon ('*Trajectoires de construction progressive de la citoyenneté des "Pygmées" au Cameroun*'), Logo quotes a Bantu chief who said that Pygmies ought to know their subordinate status within the community, a status that is doomed not to change and can never be likened to that of the Bantu. This is irrespective of whether or not the Pygmies have travelled to Europe, benefited from development aid and/or own cars:

> The Pygmies must know that even if they start to travel by plane and go to Europe or benefit from the aid of NGOs and have cars, they will never reach the Bantu man, nor surpass them in daily life (Logo 2007: 2; my own translation).

Logo further shows that in Cameroon, 'Pygmies are subject to stereotypes, prejudices and complexes built and maintained by neighboring Bantu population without a satisfactory state regulation' (2012: 2). He continues, 'Pygmies are also considered as "things", as despicable and insignificant human beings … they are considered as subhuman beings, slaves, "properties" of some families of neighboring Bantu people … [and] the Bantu call them "Ebaya'a", which means strange beings, inferior beings' (ibid. 2012: 2). In like manner, the recent 2002 controversial exhibition of some Cameroonian Baka 'Pygmies' at the Oasis Nature Park in Yvoir, Belgium (Vinding 2003) suggests a continuation of the emphasis on 'essential difference'. Like Benga, who was 'encouraged to spend as much time as he wanted inside the monkey house [and] even given a bow and arrow … to shoot as part of "an exhibit"' (Bradford and Blume 1992: 180), the Baka were made to build a traditional Baka village 'with some wood and leaves picked up on the spot. They were supposed to show the public their daily activities' (Panapress.com[5]).

Intriguingly, unlike Benga's exposition which was meant for 'tourism' because it was clear that Benga was considered to be of a near animal race, the Baka in the Yvoir exhibition were exhibited for 'development, a humanitarian operation aimed at raising funds to build a school and constructing boreholes in the village of the Baka' (ibid.). This reflects how constructed boundaries in today's worlds of being (Rupp 2011) may sometimes be enveloped in the concept of development. Although it is not clear what the structure of pre-colonial relations between the other 'black African races' and the 'Pygmy race' were, it is clear that the experience of colonization crystallized the manifestations of racial hierarchies between the so-called Pygmies and other African peoples in different ways. These manifestations are either overt derogatory stereotypes as reported by Logo (2012) or covert development assumptions.

Dichotomies: Hunter-gatherers ('Pygmies') Versus Farmers ('Villagers')

In pre-colonial and colonial times, race as a sequence of biological concepts was used to frame and emphasize differences between peoples. Nonetheless, while research in the early 1960s brought biological and cultural racism under immense criticism, its cultural traces were supplanted by studies of ethnicity (Ballard 2006). Thus Turnbull (1961) and Hallet (1973) subscribed to this later school of thought. Both scholars spent considerable amounts of time studying the African Pygmies of the Ituri forest of Congo. However, their hypotheses, approaches and subsequent findings reflected two different schools of thought in Pygmy studies which have respectively marked research and policy on the Pygmies in recent decades. On the one hand, Turnbull in his famous book *The Forest People* raised public interest in the Pygmies. He reductively described them as being the 'real' people of the forest, who have been there for many thousands of years, trusting it to supply all their needs and roaming around the forest at will in small hunting groups (1961: 13–14). He portrayed the Pygmies as 'primitive' people who lived in great harmony with their natural environment without altering it, and who were wholly dependent on hunting and gathering, living in isolation from other African peoples:

> For the Pygmies in a sense, there is no problem. They have seen enough of the outside world to feel able to make their choice, and their choice is to preserve the sanctity of their own world up to the very end. Being what they are, they will doubtless play a masterful game of hide-and-seek, but they will not easily sacrifice their integrity (Turnbull, in Grinker, Lubkemann and Steiner 2010: 183).

On the other hand, Hallet in his book *Pygmy Kitabo* (1973), as well as in his other essays, constructed the Pygmies as the original peoples, remnants of the ancestors of the human race, whose culture is at the verge of extinction and needs to be protected. He referred to biblical stories as being imbibed into Pygmy myths of creation, hence justifying his claim that Pygmies are the remnants of the ancestors of humanity. Writing in a special issue of the magazine *Human Potential*, titled 'To Save a People', Hallet said:

> The Pygmies of the Ituri forest must be saved. They still represent the true human potential for love, peace and harmony, without crime or greed. If people are judged by the quality of their hearts and minds, the ancestral Pygmies are giants of mankind. Yet, our often blind 'civilization' is now responsible for the imminent extinction of these people by systematically destroying their forest (September 1975 issue, published by The Ambassador International Cultural Foundation, no page number).

From these views of Turnbull and Hallet, which seem to have inspired differing conceptualizations of development for 'Pygmy' peoples, the contrast between the findings of Rupp (2011) and those of Pyhälä (2012), who both conducted their research among the Baka of East Cameroon, makes sense. In effect, Rupp challenges the dichotomous categorizations of 'Pygmies', 'hunter-gatherers', and 'indigenous peoples' versus 'villagers' (mostly considered to be Bantus):

> Once interethnic relations in southeastern Cameroon are documented and institutionalized, the stereotype of "Bantu"/"Villager"/Bangando as oppressor becomes a difficult prejudice to overcome. The categories that GTZ's social scientists utilized to frame their research and analysis – Bantu vs. Baka – do more than serve as descriptive modifiers for particular communities. More powerfully still, these simplistic, binary categories provide policy parameters within which administrative objectives and methods are established. As a result of the preconceptions, biases, and omissions embedded in the classificatory models, it is not surprising that studies and development initiatives in southeastern Cameroon tend to privilege the perceived needs of Baka at the expense of a more balanced approach to addressing the concerns of the multiethnic community at large. ... [GTZ's] analyses reinforce and reinscribe divisive social categories (Rupp 2011: 230).

Contrarily to Rupp's view presented in the quote above, Abega and Logo, in a publication on the marginalization of African Pygmies, question why development organizations believe that inserting the Baka into the mainstream is pertinent or better. They question whether it is not necessary to be concerned about the cultural uniformization enhanced by the phenomenon of globalization, and if in doing so 'we' will not be confronted with one of the numerous metamorphoses of the civilizing mission (2005: 25). In like manner, Abega indicates that Pygmies are a culturally distinct group of people with a forest-inscribed culture that needs to be preserved (1998). Following suit, Pyhälä defines the Pygmies as 'an indigenous hunter-gatherer society inhabiting the western range of the Central African rainforests' (2012: 16). Intriguingly, while these scholars (Abega and Logo 2005; Rupp 2011; Pyhälä 2012) challenge approaches to the development of Pygmy peoples in contrasting ways, there has not until now been any research that seeks to understand how the cumulative, yet contrasting development programmes implemented in eastern Cameroon influence the ways in which communities construct 'self' to fit into development or exclude 'others'. The discussions in this book spring from this point and explore how the Baka construct their belonging in a bid to participate in development projects. This is considering that although the Baka live on roadsides with their Bantu neighbours and are engaged in agriculture, they are on the one hand framed as indigenous peoples with a distinct culture, but on the other hand, they are being integrated into mainstream society with some camps being purely agricultural.

A Brief Summary of the Location and Demography of Cameroon

Cameroon is located on the African continent in the Gulf of Guinea and shares boundaries with Nigeria to the west, Chad to the north, Central African Republic to the east, and Gabon, Equatorial Guinea and Congo to the south, as illustrated in Figure 1.1.

Cameroon has a population of about 20.3 million inhabitants (NIS-Cameroon 2012) and occupies a territorial land surface of 475,440 km². Of this land surface, 182,000 km² is covered by tropical rainforest (Molua and Lambi 2013: 7). Administratively, the country is divided into ten regions, three of which (the Centre, South and East Regions) are forested. At a regional level, each region of Cameroon is headed by a governor and is subdivided into administrative divisions, which are each headed by a divisional officer (DO).[6] The divisions of the East Region include the Upper Nyong (largest), the Boumba and Ngoko (second largest), the Lom and Djérem and the Kadey (MINATD). Each division is further subdivided into sub-divisions which themselves are headed by sub-divisional officers (SDO)s. Each sub-division consists of a group of villages. Each village is headed by a chief and consists of quarters and camps (for Bantu villages that have Baka camps, these camps are administratively incorporated into the villages as quarters or subquarters). In the East Region, with the exception of refugee camps (that have developed since 2011 due to crises in neighbouring countries), camps generally refer to Baka groupings/settlements. The dynamics of this appellation will be discussed extensively in Chapter 2.

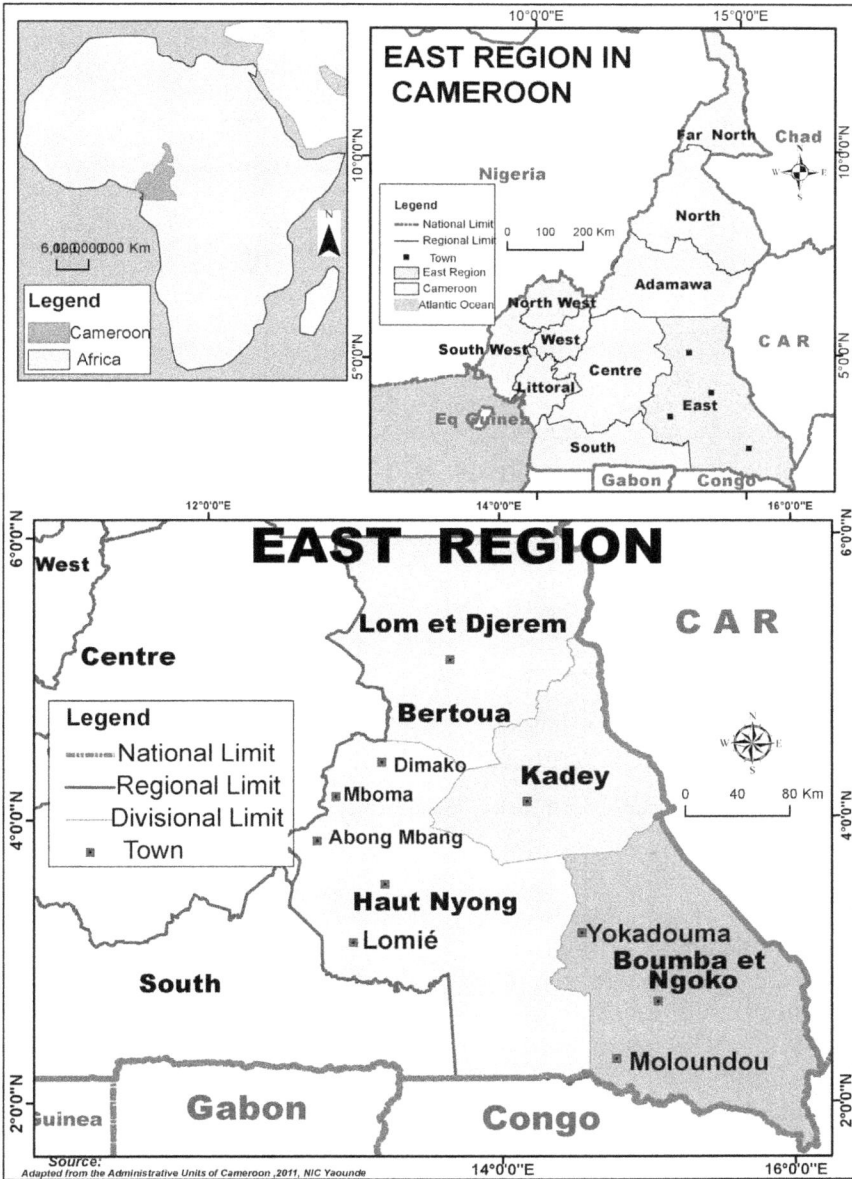

Figure 1.1 Map of Cameroon.
Source: G.M. Lueong

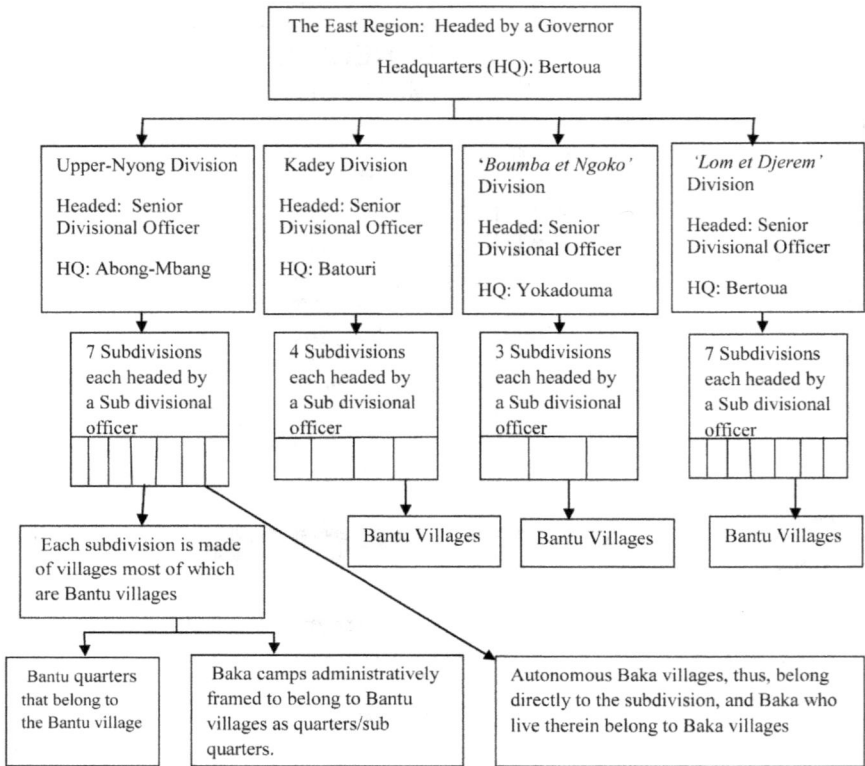

Figure 1.2 Administrative organization of the East Region.
Source: constructed by G.M. Lueong.

A summary of the administrative organization of the East Region is presented in Figure 1.2.

Of the four divisions that make up the East Region, I conducted twelve months of field research in the divisions of Upper Nyong and Boumba and Ngoko. This choice was based on the fact that these two are the largest divisions of the region, and they host the majority of the Baka people. Moreover, the Boumba and Ngoko Division is more forested, while the Upper Nyong is located at the heart of the region with limited forest and a more modern lifestyle. In the Boumba and Ngoko Division, the sub-division of Moloundou was chosen based on the following criteria: its percentage of unexploited forest, the density of Baka population, and the proximity of the Baka to other Pygmy 'groups' in Congo and the Central African Republic. In the Upper Nyong Division, the sub-divisions of Abong-Mbang, Lomie and Dimako were chosen based on the following criteria: exposure to modern facilities such as a tarred road, electricity and water, Baka camps like Bonado which have existed on the roadside for more than sixty years, and the existence of relatively autonomous Baka villages.[7]

The East Region, where the Baka, as well as the Bantu, live is the largest in the country in terms of surface area. It occupies 23.4% of the country's total surface area, but hosts only 4.4% of the country's population. This sparsity gives the East Region the lowest population density in the country (7.1 inhabitants/km^2) (NIS Cameroon 2012). Despite this low population density, the struggle to belong in this region is very salient for the Baka, who were displaced from the forest and made to reside on the roadsides with Bantu sedentary agriculturalists. These struggles are embedded in a series of complex historic and political processes that the country and region have experienced in past decades.

Complex Historic and Political Processes in Which the Problem of Claims to Belonging and Participation for the Baka Are Embedded

Like most African countries, Cameroon has a colonial past,[8] which still leaves some prints and legacies on many aspects of the country's contemporary sociopolitical, economic and cultural realities. These realities are further exacerbated by global processes that the country is facing as part of a global community. Such is the case with the present-day binary categorization and distinction of the population of eastern Cameroon. In this categorization and distinction, some inhabitants of the region are considered to be natives/locals (the Bantu), while others (the Baka, 'Pygmies'), are presented by INGOs, the World Bank and recently the country's Minister of Social Affairs (IWGIA 2014) in a very slippery manner as indigenous forest peoples. This presentation of the Baka aims to fulfil international obligations concerning the global category of indigenous peoples. Intriguingly however, this contemporary presentation of the Baka as indigenous peoples in Cameroon has embedded itself into an ongoing cumulative nexus of three historic and political processes that entangle the Baka in a messy situation. These processes have been captured here as: 1) the post-independence assimilatory processes aimed at cultivating a single national identity, or simply a national unity, agriculture and national development process; 2) the early 1990 multiparty ethnic belonging-participation processes; and 3) the mid-2000s autochthony and indigeneity processes. These processes will be discussed in the next subsections to illuminate the complexities surrounding the Baka's claims to belonging, as well as the various metamorphosed framings and slippery presentation of their belonging.

Pygmies Amid Post-independence Assimilatory Processes

The transformation of Baka into sedentary farmers appears as a process driven from the outside. This is the materialization of a state policy, itself inherited from a cultural uniformization approach. From colonization to an independent state, the primitive became 'the savage', the savage 'indigene', 'the evolved indigene', and the evolved indigene 'citizen'. The citizen must work for the development of the country and the official policy's emphasis is on agriculture … the Pygmy can only engage in this movement by becoming a farmer. This is what permits him to graduate to citizenship. Otherwise, he maintains the status of 'the savage'. And many administrators, even today, use the word savage to refer to non-sedentary Pygmies, as well as all those who refuse to engage in agricultural activity (Abega and Logo 2005: 121; my own translation).

In 1960, the Republic of French Cameroon (the East Region included) gained independence from France. For Cameroon, decolonization either meant defining new values for the new nation state or inheriting colonial values and norms. In either case, it also meant that people constructed by the colonial masters as the 'locals/natives' of the then colony, could become citizens of the newly independent country. Intriguingly, in colonial Cameroon, not all people living within its territorial boundaries were constructed as 'locals/natives' (autochthones). At independence, not all inhabitants could immediately become citizens who belonged in the country. As can be read in the quote above from Abega and Logo (2005), residents of the country were ascribed different statuses, some of which required that they become assimilated into sedentary agriculture in order to be considered as citizens of the new nation state. In this regard, citizenship became a category with implications beyond formal attachment to a nation state, because it was charged with normative expectations towards fulfilling the citizenship role, as well as with rules concerning the distribution of resources and political agency. To this end, the citizenship status and belonging of non-sedentary inhabitants of the country (the Pygmies considered to be hunter-gatherers) were called into question and a series of assimilatory preconditions attached to their path to becoming citizens. These preconditions nuanced questions of nationhood and citizenship with the idea of working for national development. In the present section, I will focus on discussing this nuance by exploring the colonial distinctions that gave rise to the status of 'the natives' or 'the primitive', as well as the requirement for 'the forest peoples' or 'the primitives' to belong to the country via a single cultivated national identity.

In colonial Cameroon, colonial masters referred to all 'non-white people' as being 'natives/locals' with the exception of peoples like the Pygmies, who today constitute the special category of 'forest peoples'. Natives were primarily sedentary subsistence farmers (Boisson 1938), while Pygmies lived in the forest and were mostly mobile 'hunter-gatherers' who had very little contact with colonization/colonial masters (Leclerc 2012: 101). As a result of this, the natives were the targets of colonial civilization and enlightenment. Thus, they interacted more as labourers for colonial masters who were primarily engaged in plantation agriculture, while the 'forest people' were mostly left undisturbed 'in their forest' (Owono 1997; Sinang 2005; Aye Mondo[9] 2013). Since the 'forest people' had very few or no encounters with the civilization and enlightenment projects of colonization, they were often considered by the colonial masters and the natives alike as 'backward', 'primitive' and 'uncivilized' compared to their 'native' counterparts.

With the exception of trading ivory and animal skins with colonial masters through middlemen (native Bantus), the predominantly hunting and gathering-based livelihoods of 'forest peoples' did not rhyme with the needs of the colonial economy, which in the context of Cameroon was mainly plantation agriculture (Sinang 2005). To this end, 'forest people', unlike the natives, were rarely used by colonial masters as labourers; thus, they were rarely displaced from their forest homelands.

However, upon decolonization, the newly independent country grappled with questions of statehood and nation building. In this grappling, questions about which ethnic group would lead the country[10] became more prominent, and ethnicity became a sensitive issue of identification, such that people asserted their belonging to ethnic homelands. In order to manage this dominance of ethnic identification against national identification, President Ahmadou Ahidjo (the first president of the country after independence) and his administrators singled out national unity and national development as core values of the Cameroonian nationhood (Pelican 2006). For the president, all citizens needed to work towards national development, which was mainly agricultural in form, in order to cultivate a single national identity (Takougang and Krieger 1998).

In this frame of national unity and the cultivation of a single national identity, and taking into consideration the multi-ethnic nature of the country, with more than 250 ethnic groups (Mbaku and Takougang 2004: 373; Dorman, Hammett and Nugent 2007: 147), the president branded local ethnic, regional or confessional organizations as politically dangerous. He actively suppressed these organizations in his fight against the idea of a multi-party system. He eventually transformed the country into a single-party state (Pelican 2006). The president's ambition for all Cameroonians to cultivate a single national identity was further reflected in the 1972 constitutional law, which stated that all Cameroonians had the right to freely settle in any place within the country and move freely regardless of their origin (Geschiere and

Nyamjoh 2000: 429). This constitutional provision superimposed itself over ethnic identification processes so that, at that time, national identification gained pre-eminence over ethnic identification.

During this period, agriculture (and especially plantation agriculture) was presented as development and 'superiority' in terms of culture. In this light, taking up agricultural development was justified by both the country's colonial past, as well as the then salient development theory of modernization, which projected agriculture as one of the stages in moving upward on the development ladder (Rostow 1960). Other sectors like forest conservation/exploitation and the development of medicinal plants, which Pygmies specialized in, were left to lie beneath the development dust.

In this regard, agriculture became resounding in the country's concept of nationhood, such that, even in the country's seal, there is a 'coffee branch with two leaves and flanked on the sinister by five cocoa pods' (Point Seven of Article 1 of Part One of the 1972 constitution). Thus, citizens had to work for national development, which was primarily agricultural development (Abega and Logo 2005). The above phenomenon gave rise to a process which I call the agriculture-citizenship-development process, which saw citizens as people who should work for national development by engaging in agriculture. In this process, the Pygmies, who were in general still hunter-gatherers, were far from being considered as citizens belonging to the country. Logo chose to put it that Pygmies were far from being adapted to the uniform and standardized citizenship model developed by the state based on sedentarization:

> The Pygmies are far from adapting themselves to the uniform and standardized model of citizenship developed by the state, based on sedentarization and citizen allegiance (Logo 2002a: 15; my own translation).

In this way, citizenship and belonging was something that non-agricultural inhabitants of the country needed to work for. Thus, the Baka, who until then were non-agricultural forest dwellers, were presented as lagging behind, in a fashion not dissimilar from the colonial construct of 'the uncivilized'. Hence, in a bid to include them in the post-independence national unity, identity and development process, the government and Catholic missionaries introduced a sedentarization process that aimed at 'civilizing', assimilating and integrating the Baka (Bailey, Bahuchet and Hewlett 1992; Pyhälä 2012). As Pyhälä (2012) and FONDAF Cameroun have shown, from the very beginning of independence, Cameroon sedentarized the Pygmies so as to make them integrated citizens who could participate in the national unification process:

From the first days of its independence, Cameroon decided to sedentarize the Pygmies to become full-fledged Cameroonians, the active forces for a country in the process of unification and construction. In 1960, the application of sedentarization began in the East Region (FONDAF Cameroun; my own translation).

Similarly, government officials constructed the Baka 'as a people who are culturally evolving and moving up, a people for whom learning agriculture is the most important and other things will follow; a better diet, health, money to attend school, money for taxes, identity card' (Hewlett 2000: 385). This move, as Abega and Logo have pointed out:

[Was] considered to be towards cultural uniformization [which assumed that] from colonization to an independent state, the primitive became a savage; the savage became an indigene; then the indigene will evolve to a citizen who must work for national development. A process in which agriculture is of prime importance and the 'Pygmy' would only be included in the whole process of national development by becoming a farmer which permits him/her to emerge into being a citizen" (2005: 121; my own translation).

This process of sedentarization and cultural uniformization meant resettling the Pygmies to live on the roadsides with their Bantu neighbours, who were considered to be the host society into which the Pygmies were to become assimilated. This resettlement process was further enhanced by the provision of the 1972 constitutional law, which allowed everyone to live and settle or freely move within the country without any discrimination due to their place of origin.

Nonetheless, not many Baka accepted the move to roadsides. Only a few of them were interested and eventually set up camps on the roadsides. Even so, when they did set up these camps, they tended to combine agriculture, hunting and gathering (Rupp 2011). The forest and its resources were not yet pivotal in boosting the country's economy, and the strong conservation movements that would keep the Baka 'permanently' out of the forest were still incipient. At this time, the Baka mostly saw the forest as their home, a place where they belonged and were in control. They referred to themselves as 'mothers of the forest' (Owono 1997), a trend that continued until 1982 when Ahidjo resigned and the incumbent Paul Biya succeeded to power.

Upon his accession to power, Biya mostly sustained his predecessor's ideal of a unitary state, but promised a more tolerant democracy (Takougang and Krieger 1998: 63–113) albeit still with a one-party system, which he renamed the Cameroon People's Democratic Movement (CPDM). Like his predecessor, Biya stressed national integration over regional, ethnic or religious factionalism. However, just a few years after his taking power, in the mid-eighties and early nineties, the country faced severe economic hardships, which called for a revisitation of the post-independence resource redistribution and development policies. This need led the country in 1988 to adopt the Structural Adjustment Programmes (SAP). In these SAPs, the World Bank and the International Monetary Fund suggested that the country should consider the forestry sector a priority sector, where the Bretons Wood Institution would assist in instituting reforms (Atyi 1998; Amin 2008). Around the same period, the Rio 1992 conference on environment and development was organized, and Cameroon's forest exploitation interests now became combined with conservation interests. These led to an intensive restructuring of the Cameroonian forest and wildlife sectors, which had been managed between 1960 and 1992 by a department within the Ministry of Agriculture (MINAGRI) and a department in the Ministry of Tourism respectively. In 1992, a Ministry of Forestry and Environment (MINEF) was created followed by a forest law, which was enacted in 1994 (Cerutti, Nasi and Tacconi 2008). Since 2004, this ministry has become two separate independent ministries, namely the Ministry of Foresty and Wildlife (MINFOF) and the Ministry of Environment and Protection of Nature (MINEP). This restructuring of the administration of the forest sector brought with it new policy reforms like zoning (better known in French as 'plan de zonage'):

> Despite the emphasis on participation in [this 1994 forest] law, there was no involvement of the rural population and other local stakeholders. The [zoning] plan was produced on the basis of interpretation of air photos and satellite imagery, with no ground inventory. The key issue was the creation of a 'Permanent Forest Estate', exclusively reserved for commercial logging or forest conservation activities, despite their long-standing usage by local village populations (Samndong and Vatn 2012: 215).

This forest reform and many others had noticeable impacts on the Baka, who now began to notice restrictions on their claims to the forest and their obligation to permanently resettle on the roadsides with their Bantu neighbours. Concurrently, at this time the country also witnessed the birth of multiple political parties and the legalization of freedom of association (law 90/053 of 19 December 1990),[11] which until then were actively suppressed. These processes coupled with the economic crises gave the country a new sociopolitical atmosphere, such that the post-independence vision for the cultivation of a single national identity of unity and integration steadily gave way to power rivalries, which were based on ethnic cleavages (Pelican 2006). This ethnically based power rivalry was the birth of another historic and political process which I call the ethnicity-belonging-participation process.

The Ethnicity-Belonging-Participation Process

This process entailed the supplanting of national identity with ethnic identity, and came in addition to the already existing agriculture-citizenship and national development process, in which 'Pygmies' were being sedentarized to fit into the national development and integration machine, in order to become citizens. In this mix, the Pygmies were now faced with the dual challenge of becoming sedentarized peoples, as well as organizing themselves into an ethnic cleavage, so as to participate in the new social life of the country. In like manner, the supplanting of the vision for a single national identity and integration with that of ethnic cleavages gave rise to new striving to consolidate power. This was because the country had now changed from being a single-party system into a multiparty system, in which citizens who belonged to particular ethnic groups were associated with either the ruling party or the opposition parties (Geschiere 2009; Pyhälä 2012).

This process of associating citizens who belonged to certain ethnic groups with specific political parties gave rise to a new emphasis on belonging, which was predominantly based on the 'soil of origin', or at least ancestral origin, and shaped access to state power and resources. In this regard, the old 1972 constitution, which entitled citizens to settle anywhere within the country without discrimination irrespective of their origin became compromised. Thus questions about where the roadside 'Pygmies' belonged gradually started to gain ground, because citizens of the same country were now categorized as 'strangers' and 'natives/autochthones of a given soil'[12] depending on whether or not they were 'sons of the soil' on which they were residing. In this light, the Pygmies, who had no express relationship with any soil, were branded as 'forest people' and/or strangers on the roadsides where they were now residing.

In the same vein, the country, composed of over 250 ethnic groups (three of whom are 'Pygmies'), adopted a regime of ethnoregional elites, which became a leading factor in the politicization of ethnic difference, as it entailed the differential and hierarchical incorporation of groups within the state systems of power (Eyoh 2004). Thus, 'a proof of belonging' became vital in defining identity and asserting rights. Settlers did not have the same political and social rights as people who had ancestral relations with the soil (Geschiere 2009).[13] To this end, the Baka, who had ancestral relationships with the forest rather than with the roadsides, but whose camps were installed on the roadsides either by colonial missionaries or by the government through its sedentarization project, were tagged by their Bantu neighbours as 'strangers' who belonged to the forest despite residing on their (Bantu) native soils.[14]

As time went on, this 'native-stranger divide' between the Bantu and the Baka made the struggle for belonging more resounding, because the introduction of the country's new (above-mentioned 1994) forest laws gradually but eventually made the Baka understand that the laws had stripped them of their claims of belonging to the forest:

> The '*sous-prefet*' [the subdivisional officer] just went into the forest with gendarmes and guns and arrested any Baka who refused to comply, and sent them to prison. So the Baka moved out of the forest and settled in the village along the road (Rupp 2011: 75–76).

As the Baka were made to resettle on roadsides in camps beside Bantu villages, the 'native-stranger divide' and struggles between them heightened. This was especially because most Baka camps were given the names of the Bantu villages closest to them, and were considered to be subquarters of the Bantu village with the Bantu chief being the overall village chief. Interestingly, the Baka and the Bantu speak very different languages, and language is one of the distinguishing features for the construction of ethnicity (villages) in the Cameroonian context.[15] Furthermore, national and international forest-governing organizations, in their policy documents, tend to refer to both the 'Bantu' and the 'Pygmy' as 'forest communities'[16] (Nodem, Bamenjo and Schwartz 2012) without any further distinction whatsoever regarding their ancestral origin.

In the context of policies aimed at benefiting these 'forest communities', this undistinguished categorization of both the Baka and the Bantu as 'forest communities' makes the question of belonging a 'hot potato' for both communities living on the roadsides[17] and engaged in agriculture on different scales. This is because the undistinguished reference to 'forest communities' blurs the boundaries between the 'forest people' who lived and belonged there, having ancestral relationships with the forest (the Baka) and 'the farmer-villagers' (the Bantu) who lived and still live in a forested region. Similarly, the creation of community forests together with a logging policy which demands that 10% of the revenue be given to community forest administrative structures to give back to 'forest communities' in the region makes the issue of belonging one that begs for critical questioning. Who makes the claim of belonging, where, how and why? Who are the 'real' natives who belong to the forest communities (autochthones) who are entitled to profit from forest resources? (Geschiere 2009: 76).

Amid this ongoing 'native-stranger divide' between the Bantus and the Baka on the roadsides, the government, under the global influence of the spread of the category 'indigenous peoples', has blanket coded all Baka as indigenous peoples. This blanket categorization is irrespective of whether or not they belong to autonomous Baka villages on the roadsides, or if they are integrated as subquarters of Bantu villages. This process is what I refer to as the autochthony-indigeneity process.

The Autochthony-Indigeneity Process

Since 2000, in the midst of the ongoing struggles of belonging (the 'native-stranger divide') between the Bantu and the Baka, Plan Cameroon together with the Cameroonian government has initiated a programme to create autonomous Baka villages rather than integrating them into Bantu villages as subquarters. The objective of this new programme is to give the Baka an autochthonous status on the roadsides, where they are currently portrayed as 'strangers from the forest' by their Bantu neighbours, who claim to be the natives/autochthones on these roadsides.

Nonetheless, since 2008 the same government has celebrated the international day of the world's indigenous people, with the the Mbororos and 'Pygmies', among whom are the Baka, being considered as the indigenous peoples on their territory (IWGIA 2014; Pelican 2009). In this context, the 'recognition' of the Baka as indigenous peoples is based on the fact that they are forest peoples who have a distinct culture and livelihood that need to be preserved. This recognition accumulates on the pre-existing cultural uniformization and assimilatory state policies for the Baka. These dual, yet contradictory,[18] processes of autochthonization and indigenization of the Baka leave one with the question of how the Baka themselves assert their belonging.

Amid these contradictory processes, the Baka, now considered by the Bantu as migrants on the roadsides, have to 'prove their belonging' in order to participate and benefit from the 'national cake'[19] or share in the international indigenous peoples' package. However, proving this belonging is a very intriguing puzzle. This is because in contemporary times, the Baka are neither 'sons of the soil',[20] nor 'sons of the forest' from where they were evicted.[21] Moreover, their cultures and livelihoods, instead of being preserved as stipulated by the conventions of indigenous people, are rather undergoing rapid transformations.

From these, it is clear that the Baka are entangled in diverse and sometimes contrasting development policies and interventions. These, among others, include policies and approaches to: 1) 'civilize' and integrate 'uncivilized backward savages' into mainstream 'national' culture; 2) conserve forest and wildlife resources; and 3) preserve indigenous people's rights and cultures on the verge of extinction. These have left Venant and Helen, among other prominent Baka leaders, in a situation where they need to define who they are and where they belong (personal communication with Messe Venant and Helen Aye Mondo, in Bertoua, 27.06.2013). Figure 1.3 is a summary of the major historic and political processes surrounding the framing of the belonging of the Baka.

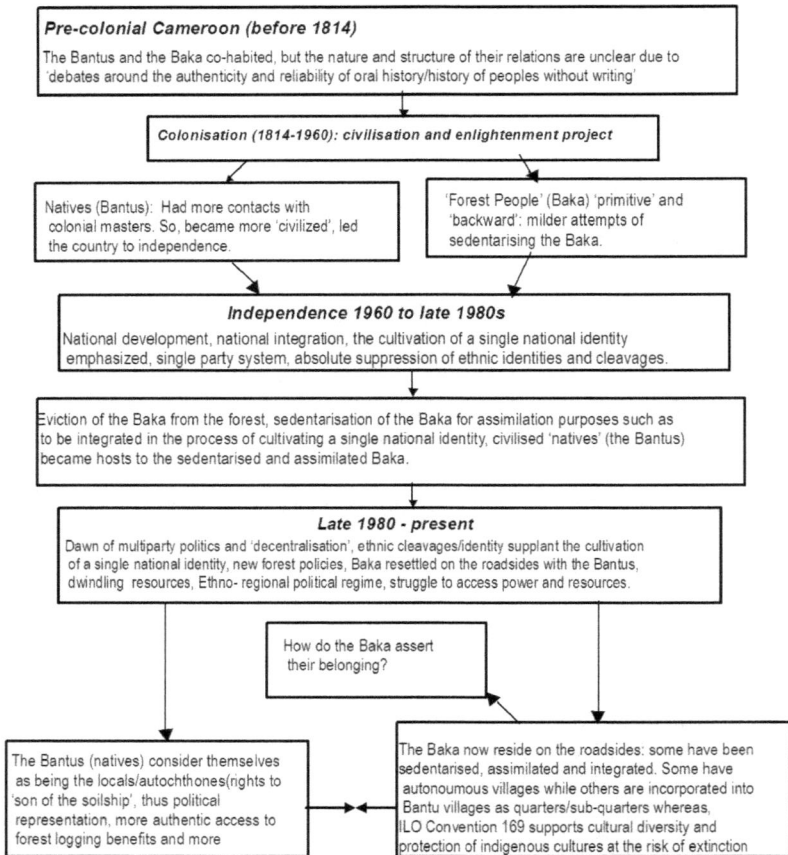

Figure 1.3 Summary of the major historic and political processes surrounding the framing of the Baka's belonging.

Source: constructed by G.M. Lueong.

Notes

1. Although Tyson later said that the specimen he dissected was in effect that of a chimpanzee and not that of a Pygmy as he first believed, the acknowledgement of his mistake did not erase popular imaginations of Pygmies as a 'subhuman' race. Rather, it stirred the curiosity of other researchers to find out who the Pygmies really were.
2. According to O'Hanlon and Welsch (2000), Western narratives about Pygmies can be considered as myths, which originate as far back as the times of Homer's *Iliad*.
3. For a more detailed reading of Benga in the zoo, cf. Bergman (1997).
4. The invention of Pygmies in contemporary times seems to be represented through the media as depicted by the '1988 Hollywood movie *Gorillas in the Mist* [which] portrayed Pygmies as savage gorilla poachers' (IRIN 2006).
5. Panapress.com. PANA Belgium: 'Cameroonian Pygmies Repatriated from Belgium', published online on 25.08.2002. Retrieved 16.11.2012 from http://www.panapress.com/Cameroonian-pygmies-repatriated-from-Belgium--13-461700-17-lang1-index.html.
6. In French speaking regions of the country, including the East, this role is called 'préfet', translated as Divisional Officer (DO) as used in this text. In the two English speaking regions of the country, it is sometimes referred to as the Senior Divisional officer (SDO).
7. Baka villages are a relatively new phenomenon initiated by the governemnent since 2000. In the past, Baka settlements were called 'camps', and administratively incorporated into Bantu villages as subquarters. This is discussed further in subsequent chapters.
8. Cameroon is often considered to be a colony (Ngoh 1996). However, some French writers argue that Cameroon was rather a protectorate and not a colony ('Le Cameroun présente la particularité, parmi les Etats d'Afrique centrale, de n'avoir jamais été une colonie. Il a en effet été, tour à tour, un protectorat allemand (entre 1884 et 1916), un territoire sous mandat (1919–1939) puis sous tutelle (1945–1960) franco-britannique') Nguiffo et Mballa (not dated).
9. Conference presentation, 'Beyond Being Pygmies (BBP): Generational Gaps and the Future of Baka ("Pygmy") Youth in Participatory Local Governance in Bertoua, Cameroon', 27–28 June 2013. Organized by G.M. Lueong and L.F. Nchimenyi.
10. At this time, the country was not yet a united republic. Rather, it had English-speaking Federal Southern Cameroon which was previously a protectorate of the British, and French Cameroon which was under the control of the French. For more information, cf. Fanso 1989 and Ngoh 1996.
11. Often called 'village associations' or 'regional associations', regrouping people (mostly elites) from the same village or who share the same cultural history, who come together to pursue common objectives like village development programmes, lobbying for the appointment of one of the sons of their soil to a post of government responsibility etc., although in theory these associations are said to be non-partisan.
12. For more on this discussion about 'strangers' and 'natives/autochthones', see Pelican 2006.
13. Political priority was given to 'authochthones', meaning members of ethnic groups. Strangers or settlers were instructed to stand as candidates of their home area as they were thought to primarily represent the interests of their group of origin (Geschiere 2009).
14. There are other cases like those between the Baka and the Bangando in Lobeke, which Rupp (2011: 201) reports. She notes that in one instance a Bangando man (Bantu) said that since both they and the Baka live on the roadsides today, they are both villagers

but in another instance, the Bangando are appropriating for themselves the tag 'forest people', so as to gain employment with conservation NGOs and serve as forest guides.

15. I say ethnicity in the Cameroonian context because in Cameroon, 'villages' are mostly referred to as 'ethnic groups'.

16. As Geschiere and Nyamjoh (2000) have argued for other regions of the country, this strategy may well be a conscious manipulation of the regional elite to maximize benefits for their ethnic group while making invisible the existence of other ethnic groups within the region.

17. Where the Bantus claim ownership and belonging while considering the Baka as 'forest people', whom they are hosting on their lands.

18. This contradiction of indigenization is further complicated by the government's categorization of Pygmies as 'marginalized populations' (CERD/C/CMR/19) based on their 'marginal and distinct culture' (personal communication with National Focal Point person, Program for the Development of Pygmy Peoples, MINAS).

19. Since the onset of democratization in Cameroon, only those considered and accepted as 'sons of the soil' are allowed to stand for election in their regions and to lobby for state resources to help their ethnic groups.

20. Not all Baka camps have been transformed into autonomous Baka villages.

21. This is because all forest in Cameroon is government-owned (White and Martin 2002).

Chapter 2

CLAIMS TO BELONGING

Two Conflicting Versions of Belonging in the East Region of Cameroon

⟡•⟡

> A paradox of belonging lies in a basic tension … To belong in the modern world, however, is to talk about home and your sense of place. Time and again, individual and collective belonging has been encroached upon, challenged, fought about, and protected. State rule, market forces, forced displacement, transnationalisation, pluralisation, acceleration of social change, and the widening horizon of human aspirations have rendered belonging contested – from outside and from within. The more it is contested and made explicit, the less likely it is just to be, share, and join in (Pfaff-Czarnecka. 2011: 212).

Albiez et al., in their book *Ethnicity, Citizenship and Belonging* demonstrate with evidence from Latin America that belonging is not given, but fought for, protected and sometimes challenged. In this chapter, I explore how the Baka assert their belonging, given the fact that they now reside on roadsides, while it continues to be ascribed in terms of the forest. By versions of belonging, I am referring to places or categories into which people assert their belonging. The emphasis on indigeneity or autochthony as versions of belonging as opposed to sites of belonging (forest or roadsides, respectively) arise from the fact that state rule, development policy, planning and development interventions in the region are generally organized around indigeneity and autochthony (Schmidt-Soltau 2003). Thus, while sites of belonging like the roadside and the forest are used effectively by people to make claims as to their belonging, these sites are subcategories of indigeneity or autochthony, such that it is difficult to dissociate the sites of belonging from the social categories in which they claim to belong. Structurally, this chapter is organized around four sections. The first section concentrates on the different ways in which belonging is constructed and ascribed in the region. The second section dwells on different on the ground understandings of the concepts of 'indigenous' and 'autochthones' as versions of belonging. The third section discusses the phenomena that threaten belonging, thereby provoking the politics of belonging in the region. The fourth and final section focuses on how the Baka assert their belonging.

Ways in Which Belonging is Constructed and Ascribed in the East Region: Frames and Blurred Boundaries

> People can 'belong' in many different ways and to many different objects of attachments. These can vary from a particular person to the whole of humanity, in a concrete or abstract way; belonging can be an act of self-identification or identification by others, in a stable, contested or transient way. Even in its most stable 'primordial' forms, however, belonging is always a dynamic process, not a reified fixity, which is only a naturalized construction of a particular hegemonic form of power relations (Yuval-Davis 2006: 199).

This section discusses the various spheres within which people in the East Region of Cameroon are constructed to belong. It also shows where these borders are blurred, thereby giving rise to tensions in belonging.

Geospatial and Administrative Demarcation of 'Boundaries of Belonging' in the East Region of Cameroon

In this section, I discuss the ways in which administratively erected boundaries have become frames of belonging into which people are constructed. The basic administrative unit that this section focuses on is a village,[1] which, in itself translates to localness. The concept of a village is tied to a sense of place as a marker of belonging and largely became useful analytically in studies of belonging in Cameroon after the mid-1980s and early 1990s, when ethnic belonging supplanted national belonging. In effect, belonging and territory (Unruh 1998: 89) both intersect at the level of discussions of 'son of the soil'. Thus, administratively demarcated territorial boundaries of belonging play a great role in the ascription of belonging to people who live in these territories. In this regard, an ongoing administrative phenomenon in the region, which entails the merging of Baka camps into Bantu villages as subquarters, becomes problematic. As Pemunta observed in his own research among the Baka:

> The Pygmy communities ... have been in this area since the 1960s, during which concerted efforts were made to encourage them to sedentarize ... The Pygmy communities settled at the outskirts of Bantu villages and their camps are considered as appendices or parts of those villages. Some Bantus even maintain that the camps are transitional, even though the settlement of these Pygmies dates back several decades (Pemunta 2011: 9).

In Cameroon, villages are the basic social units of the social structure. By default, due to the ethnoregional political regime operating in the country, citizens are constructed as belonging to villages (where they have ancestral roots), which then become a marker of their ascribed belonging at the local level. Villages are generally constituted of a 'group' of people who reside in the same geographic location, speak the same language, share the same culture and ancestral myth of origin and who are governed by the same chief (who could be a first-class, second-class or third-class chief, depending on the population and size of the village). All other persons residing therein, but who do not have an ancestral history tied to the village, are considered to be 'strangers' or '*allogènes*'. The village is often rural in nature, and is sometimes used synonymously with the concept of home, where people belong and where they will be buried, as Geschiere (2005) puts it. Van den Berg and Biesbrouck, however, note that:

> Bantu villages are basically administrative units created by German colonial officials with the purpose to get control over Bantu groups who then lived in small settlements dispersed over the forest. The social cohesion of Bantu villages is mainly outwardly directed and most often expressed in boundary disputes with neighbouring villages or conflicts with powerful outsiders such as logging operators (2000: 83).

Most contemporary administrative divisions of the East Region of Cameroon have maintained the names and boundaries given to them by colonial administrators (Sinang 2005). While this history of the invention of villages as administrative units might well be an invention of colonization and interesting for further analysis, the village in the context of this book is considered as a pre-existing socio-administrative and geocultural unit, a place where belonging is engraved and ascribed.

In effect, administratively demarcated villages did not have much bearing on Cameroon's socioeconomic or political life until the events of the early 1990s, when multiparty political struggles caused ethnicity and ethnic cleavages (village associations) to become very important in determining who could make claims to power and resources.[2] In this context, state administrative policies frame some Baka (living in camps) as belonging to Bantu villages, and further refer to this meshing of Baka camps into Bantu villages as a step towards the integration of the Baka and the Bantu. Paradoxically, some other Baka camps were upgraded to become autonomous Baka villages (Mayos, Nkobikon, Lossou, Koumadjab Nomedjo, Bosquet, among others) with their own chiefs. Thus, in the East Region, some Baka are framed as belonging to Bantu villages (what I call 'unusual villages'), while other Baka are framed as belonging to Baka villages.

Taking into consideration the fact that the village conveys a sense of home, belonging and being local for local development purposes, the administrative phenomenon of meshing some Baka camps into Bantu villages (hereafter referred to as 'unusual villages') results in controversies in the way that the belonging of the Baka is ascribed. This is because the Baka, who are administratively framed as belonging to Bantu villages, are constructed by the Bantu as 'settlers' who do not belong to their Bantu villages. Thus, although both the Baka and the Bantu are administratively framed as the 'sons of the soil' at the national and regional levels (East Region), local-level (village level) belonging is highly problematic, as has been pointed out by others:

> The law of the State provides the access to land and forests to 'Pygmies', but it is rather the customary land and forest tenure of the neighbouring Bantu people which constitute a barrier to the effective access of 'Pygmies' to land and forest. At most, in some cases, Bantu tolerate the agricultural use of land by the 'Pygmies', without realization of perennial crops (cocoa, coffee, oil palm, etc.) (Logo 2012: 7).

In 2013, during my time in the field for example, the Baka in Bonado recounted that, depite the fact that they had been residing on the roadsides for more than sixty years and had planted palm trees and other fruit trees on their land as proof of effective occupation (as requested by Article 9 of Decree no. 76–165 of April 1976, which modified the 1974 land ordinance to include the fact that people of Cameroonian nationality could apply for land certificates for land which they effectively occupied prior to 5 August 1974), the Bantu continue to challenge their (the Baka's) belonging in the village by telling them that they are from the forest and still belong in the forest, and that the roadside lands are Bantu ancestral lands.

In view of this, the politics of the ascription of belonging is more heightened at the local level in this region than it is in other regions of the country. Further exemplifying this, Raffaele, an American anthropologist visiting the Baka recounts that:

> Joseph Bikono, chief of the Bantu village near where the government has forced the Pygmies to live by the roadside … glares at me and the Pygmies

[and] demands in French … 'You Pygmies belong to me, you know that, and you must always do what I say, not what you want. I own you. Don't ever forget it.' …. 'You, *le blanc*', he yells, meaning 'the white'. 'Get out of the forest now' (Smithsonian Magazine, December 2008).

In the same vein, Pemunta, quoting a Bantu village head (chief) mentions that:

> One Bantu village head confirmed: 'The Pygmies are my property; they are under my responsibility and control. My parents adopted them and I do not understand why we should keep bickering with them over our land. My brother suggested to them that they should go back to the bush since he wanted to farm on the land occupied by the Pygmies. They refused to go under the pretext that their ancestor's bones were buried here' (2011: 9).

This blurring of boundaries of ascribed belonging, in which some Baka belong to autonomous Baka villages while others belong to Baka camps that have been meshed into Bantu villages, is the springboard for other confrontations and contestations of belonging. This is because blurriness offers legitimacy for erecting 'we'/'us' versus 'them' boundaries, especially in a region where boundaries serve as pre-conditions to development, as well as to access to resources for struggling communities. Figure 2.1 shows the demarcation of administrative boundaries in the East Region of Cameroon. The section in the blue box highlights boundaries that incite the creation of 'we'/'us' versus 'them' conflicts (Barth 1998).

As can be seen in Figure 2.1, contestation of belonging is more profound at the local level. The profoundness of these contestations have led researchers like RASED, writing in *Culture and Traditions of the Baka Pygmies* to say that 'the concept of Pygmy as an ethnic group [at the local level] is gradually disappearing and being replaced by that of the Pygmy as a way of life [indigeneity]' (2006: 7). This framing of belonging based on livelihood and habitat constitutes the next frame of ascribed belonging in the East Region of Cameroon.

Belonging Based on Livelihood and Habitat

> In rural Africa differences in modes of subsistence are widely represented as ethnic differences… and people who consider themselves ethnically distinct often present this as a difference in mode of subsistence (Woodburn 1997: 345, 346)

The eviction of Pygmies from the forest in Cameroon has been followed by a series of administrative measures. Pygmies now belong administratively to

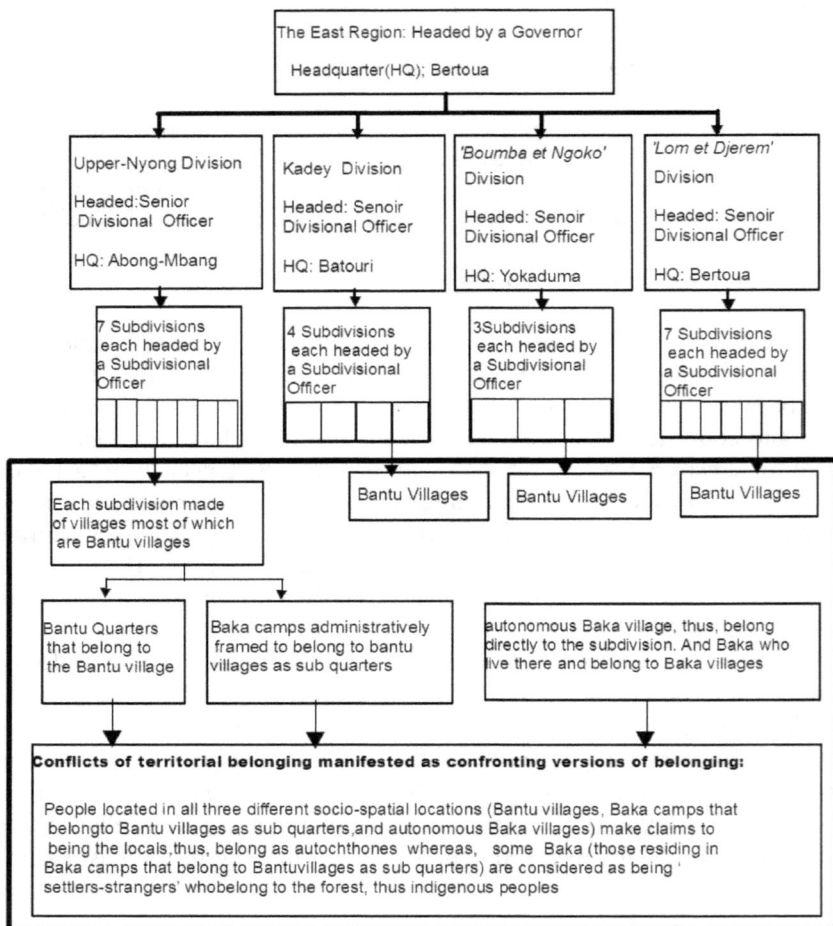

Figure 2.1 Administrative demarcation of boundaries of belonging in the East Region of Cameroon.

Source: constructed by G.M. Lueong from field findings. HQ = headquarters.

both Bantu and Baka villages. However, little has changed in the framing of their belonging in terms of their livelihood and habitat. The Baka's belonging is still framed by their Bantu neighbours, as well as by inhabitants in other regions of the country, as within the boundaries of their mode of subsistence and habitat. During my field research, these framings were common, and even upon my return from the field, a curious friend of mine from the West Region of the country said:

> Tell me, did you really go and see them [the Pygmies]? Are they really Cameroonians? What do they look like? We were taught in nursery school that Pygmies are short people who live in the forest from hunting and gathering (informal discussion with a friend in Germany, Dec. 2013).

From this, it can be seen that while anthropologists have revisited and challenged the presentation of Pygmies as hunter-gatherers who live in the forest (Rupp 2011), the belonging of the Baka remains constructed as such. In this frame of construction, the Baka are considered to belong to the forest. They are mainly hunter-gathers who live in '*mongulus*'[3] (houses constructed from tree branches and leaves), while the Bantu are considered to belong to the villages and are agriculturalists. At the international level, this belonging of the Baka is framed using essentializing terms like 'typical Baka'. The WWF, for example, does this when emphasizing the importance of their Jengi[4] forest conservation project on their webpage, where they state '[to the] Baka people, the forest is mother, father and guardian' (wwf.panda.org). WWF continue further to say:

> Baka Pygmies – the facts: The typical[5] Baka Pygmy will not leave his home in the forest even in exchange for an ultra modern palace in the city. … The Baka are usually very shy when in public. They are friendly and good-hearted especially when one meets them in their abode in the forest (wwf.panda.org).

Thus, despite the fact that today both the Baka and the Bantu live on roadsides and both engage in multiple activities, which make it misleading to construct belonging based on habitat and livelihood, essentialists' frames of belonging are still constructed based on distinctions[6] between their livelihoods and habitats. These fixed framings of the Baka's belonging blur discussions on the belonging of assimilated Baka who are engaged in cash crop cultivation, as illustrated in Figure 2.2.

During field research, I met many Baka families in the Moloundou region who, like their Bantu neighbours, were residing on the roadsides and employed both Baka and Bantu as labourers on their cocoa farms. Mr Bos (a pseudonym), was one of the rare individuals to challenge the former essentialized ascriptions of 'typical Baka who belong in the forest', because he had

Figure 2.2 Baka cocoa plantation.
Source: Oshi 2012. Powerpoint presentation on cash crop cultivation among the Baka Pygmies.

the highest annual produce of ten bags of cocoa in his mixed Bantu and Baka village.

In like manner, the scale of hunting and gathering challenges the essentialized ascriptions of hunter-gatherer and forest-dwelling 'typical Baka'. In general, large-scale hunting/trapping was being done instead by the Bantu, who sell the game to local restaurant owners. During fieldwork, I usually met the Baka with two kills (bush meat). Their Bantu patrons gave them guns and bullets to hunt for them. Pyhälä has also highlighted the same observation made by NGOs and the Baka in the region. She says that:

According to WWF and PERAD (two environmental NGOs working with the Baka in south-east Cameroon), the problem of over-hunting is not due to the Baka but rather a result of outside intruders, including neighbouring Bantu populations, who often give shotguns to the Baka and order them to go and hunt for the Bantu. The Baka stressed this point further: in one community, when asked about how sustainable their forest activities were, a Baka representative responded as follows: 'If all the animals were hunted in the forest, to the very last one, then it would be the Bantus' fault. They cannot come and blame the Baka. For the Baka know very well that one only hunts for one's own consumption, one does not kill a female animal that is pregnant, one hunts only what one needs, and that is not very much. But the Bantu are

Figure 2.3 Engagement in hunting by both the Baka and the Bantu. Left: a Baka man and his catch carried by the researcher. Right: one section of a Bantu man's catch displayed for sale. Both catches were along the Lomié road.
Source: photograph by the research assistant (Dec. 2011).

the ones sending the Baka into the forest to hunt, and to overhunt, to then sell this meat for good money (of which the Baka get a fraction, if anything at all).' Baka representative, anonymous (Pyhälä 2012: 33).

Although previous scientific research on hunting tended to blame large-scale hunting in the region on the Baka, it seems that there is an emerging change in the trend.

Belonging Based on Autochthony and Indigeneity

In Chapter 1, I mentioned that the last of the three historic and political processes surrounding the construction of belonging for the Baka led to the rise of the autochthony-indigeneity divide, whereby the Baka are now presented as belonging to the global category of indigenous peoples, while the Bantu claim to belong to the category of autochthones/locals. In this way, development interventions in the region tend to categorize belonging as either 'indigenous peoples' or locals (who are considered to be autochthones). Rupp alluded to the same phenomenon:

In the contexts of conservation and development initiatives, belonging is defined by NGOs and follows prescriptive categories and guidelines drawn up by global institutions and their representatives. In contexts of forest communities, belonging to the forest is a status reserved for 'Pygmies', 'hunter-gatherers', and 'indigenous people' (Rupp 2011: 53).

Burnham, referring to a World Bank definition of African forest indigenous peoples for example, mentions that the World Bank expressly indicated that indigenous peoples are and can only be Pygmies, with the absolute exclusion of all agriculturalists (2000: 47). RASED describes the population of the East Region using the following terms: 'the local population belong to two ethnic groups: the Bantu, who are the majority, and the Baka ... non-indigenous ethnic groups include the Beti, the Hausa, the Bamileke and the Bassa' (2006: 5). Dyson, in Leohnardt, states that 'in the past the World Bank constructed the identity of a people as a "tribal people". At present, they are classified as an indigenous people' (Dyson 1992: 212, in Leohnardt 1998: 167). From these contrasting definitions by RASED and the World Bank, it is clear that both the Baka and the Bantu belong to the local population as autochthones. But according to the World Bank, the Baka are indigenous peoples in the European and American understanding of the term. This contradiction between RASED's framing and that of the World Bank is suggestive of the confusion and increased blurring of boundaries of belonging in which the Baka find themselves entangled.

What is interesting, however, is the fact that asserting belonging is indispensable for both the Baka and the Bantu in order to access resources in a region that is flooded with development organizations, each having its own criteria for defining belonging, as well as its beneficiaries. Thus, since the focus here is to find out how the Baka assert their belonging amid these frames of ascribed belonging (autochthony and indigeneity), the next section explores whether the Baka and the Bantu understand and employ the concepts of indigeneity and autochthony in the same way as they are framed and understood at the international level. Following on from this, the section discusses the heuristic consequence of this distinction between Euro-American and Baka communities' understandings of the concepts.

Local-level Understandings of the Concepts of Autochthony and Indigeneity in the East Region of Cameroon

Considering that the Baka are having to assert their belonging in a region where their belonging is already externally framed and ascribed between autochthony and indigeneity, it is evident that among the inhabitants of the East Region, autochthony and indigeneity are not understood as conceptualized at global levels (Pelican 2009, Niezen 2010). In this section, I present the various on the ground (local-level) understandings of the concepts as understood by different people in the East Region. In discussing these on the ground (local-level) understandings, I start by presenting the different

Table 2.1 Research sites at the community level (communities visited).
Source: constructed by G.M. Lueong based on field findings.

East Region	Division	Sub-division	Communities interviewed/observed, where intensive research and follow-ups took place (twelve in total)
	Boumba and Ngoko	Moloundou	Banana (Baka)
	Upper Nyong	Abong-Mbang	Bonado[8] (Baka and Bantu)
		Dimako	Mayos[9] (Baka and Bantu), Nkoumadjab (Baka), Lossou (Baka and Bantu)
		Lomié[10]	Cyrie (Baka), Diassa[11], Bingongol[12] (Baka and Bantu), Mendjou, Elanjo, Mballam, Nomedjo

understandings of the Baka based on their status, which ranges from: Baka who were chiefs of Baka villages; to Baka who were camp leaders (with their camps integrated as subquarters of Bantu villages); to simple Baka elders whose ages were approximated[7] to be over sixty years; to Baka who did not own farms but worked for Bantus (those to whom the Bantu referred as 'my Pygmy'); to Baka who owned farms and had children in school; to Baka who worked for INGOs; to Baka youths; to Baka women; and finally Baka who ran NGOs. The different Baka communities in which interviews were conducted are included in Table 2.1.

Table 2.2 presents local-level understandings of the concepts of indigenous peoples and autochthones by the Baka interviewed from the communities in Table 2.1.

From Table 2.2, it is interesting to see how some Baka saw themselves as autochthones while categorizing others as indigenous. According to these Baka, the 'others' whom they categorized as indigenous were not yet 'civilized'. In a similar vein, it is fascinating that other Baka considered themselves indigenous because of self-identification and dispossession (which fits into European and American interpretations of the concepts).

As can be read from Tables 2.2 and 2.3, the local understandings of these concepts, as used by the inhabitants of the East Region of Cameroon, varied greatly. Some Baka, as well as Bantu understand the concepts of indigeneity and autochthony to be synonymous and different to the concept of *allogène*/stranger/settler.[15] Only the Baka and the Bantu who had taken part in meetings or events organized for indigenous people could clearly differentiate between indigenous peoples and autochthones according to their Euro-American constructions. This therefore implies that, unlike in other regions of the world – where the so-called indigenous peoples are fully aware of, understand and have taken up the Western concept of indigenous peoples

Table 2.2 Local-level understandings of the concepts of indigenous peoples and autochthones by the Baka.

Source: constructed by G.M. Lueong based on field findings.

Status of the Baka	Question: Have you ever heard of the term 'indigenous peoples' and/or 'autochthones'? Yes/No.		Question: Are you aware that there is a difference between indigenous peoples and autochthones? Yes/No.	Question: According to you, what does 'autochthones' mean and who are they?	Question: According to you, what does 'indigenous peoples' mean and who are they?
	Those who had heard of the term 'indigenous peoples'[13]	Those who had heard of the term 'autochthones'	Those who were aware of the 'European and American' distinction between indigenous peoples and autochthones	Local understandings of the term 'autochthones'	Local understandings of the term 'indigenous peoples'
Chiefs of Baka villages	One said yes Two said no	All three said yes	One said yes	They said it meant 'sons of the soil' ('*les ressortisants d'ici*')	To the one who had heard about it, it meant Pygmies, because they are still 'primitive' and need help
Elders of Baka camps integrated into Bantu villages	Seven said yes Four said no	All said yes	Five said yes Six said no	To them, it meant the first people who came and settled on the land. According to the majority in this category, the Baka came first but settled in the forest. For them, the Bantu only came after, but settled in the village; yet when the government asked them (the Baka) to settle on the roadsides, the Bantu argued that the Baka are strangers on their (Bantu) land.	For those who were aware, it meant people who were living in the forest. Children/women from the camps are always selected to participate in celebrations for the international day of indigenous peoples.

Elderly Baka (aged about sixty years and older)[14]	Five said yes	All Five said yes	Two said yes Two said no One said they are the same	For them autochthones meant first occupants. To them, they are the real autochthones because their ancestors came first; although, they added, the Bantu claim that they are the autochthones and the Baka are strangers because they belong to the forest.	For them it meant people whom the government first neglected because of their culture, but for whom it now organizes the international day of indigenous people to give them identity cards and some food and non-food items.
	Ten said no	All Ten said yes	All Ten said no	To them, autochthones meant people who discovered the place. Their ancestors discovered it, so they are the autochthones.	
Baka who did not own farms but worked for Bantus	All eight said yes	All eight said yes	Three said yes	For them it meant the Bantu who owned the land. They referred to autochthones as their 'brothers of the village'. They said that it is because they only came to the roadsides some years back. Their parents were not living there and some of them were not even born there.	To them it meant marginalized populations, the reason for which the government, Plan, and many other NGOs are helping them.
			Five said no	For them autochthones are people who were born and bred in the region. Thus, both the Baka and the Bantu are autochthones although the Bantu people think that they are the patrons.	For them there was no difference. Rather, they considered that it is the mindset of the Bantu people who are maltreating them and taking them for gorillas.

Table 2.2 (Continued)

Status of the Baka	Question: Have you ever heard of the term 'indigenous peoples' and/or 'autochthones'? Yes/No.		Question: Are you aware that there is a difference between indigenous peoples and autochthones? Yes/No.	Question: According to you, what does 'autochthones' mean and who are they?	Question: According to you, what does 'indigenous peoples' mean and who are they?
	Those who had heard of the term 'indigenous peoples'[13]	Those who had heard of the term 'autochthones'	Those who were aware of the 'European and American' distinction between indigenous peoples and autochthones	Local understandings of the term 'autochthones'	Local understandings of the term 'indigenous peoples'
Baka who owned farms and had children in school	All ten said yes	All ten said yes	Seven said yes Three said no	For them, autochthones were synonymous with the locals/'natives' of a given village, i.e. people who have their land and do not have any problem with the Bantu. For them the two words were synonymous. Everybody is indigenous and everybody is autochthonous, except for other people who are not from the East Region, like Bamilekes, Hausas and the white people.	To them it meant 'primitive and backward' people. They exemplified this with other Baka, whom they referred to as 'their brothers who are still living in the forest in Moloundou, and are not yet "civilized"', adding that when Plan or another NGO makes birth certificates for their children to go to school, they buy and smoke cigarettes, yet other people just say that Baka people in general are indigenous peoples.

Baka who had worked for INGOs	All seven said yes	All seven said yes	All seven said yes	All seven said yes	For them it meant people who have an agricultural ancestry. People who were rooted in the soil by customs and traditions.	For them it meant people who are dispossessed of their homelands and are left at the margins of society. They used the Baka as an example.
Baka youths	All ten said yes	All ten said yes	All ten said yes	All ten said yes	To them it meant people who are born in a given place, who are 'civilized', go to school and do not wear dirty clothes, irrespective of the kind of house they live in. Poverty makes both the Baka and the Bantu build mud houses. Most of these Baka youths said that they tended not to subscribe to this categorization of autochthonous and indigenous people, arguing that that term 'indigenous peoples' as it is used on the ground seems to be replacing 'Pygmy', which is derogatory.	For them it was synonymous with Pygmies – primitive people, who are running away from school. People who cannot speak French well. It also meant poverty, and could be instrumentalized to get school fees or farm inputs.
Baka who had blood pacts with Bantu families	All three said yes	All three said yes	All three said yes	All three said yes	For them, the meaning of the word has changed. In the past, both the Baka and the Bantu were autochthones by virtue of the blood pacts that made two families become one. Now, autochthones are villagers (the Bantu).	To them it meant people who were living in the forest before entering into blood pacts with village (Bantu) families. It means people who have their own special culture and ways of life that many people do not understand.

Table 2.2 (Continued)

Status of the Baka	Question: Have you ever heard of the term 'indigenous peoples' and/or 'autochthones'? Yes/No.		Question: Are you aware that there is a difference between indigenous peoples and autochthones? Yes/No.	Question: According to you, what does 'autochthones' mean and who are they?	Question: According to you, what does 'indigenous peoples' mean and who are they?
	Those who had heard of the term 'indigenous peoples'[13]	Those who had heard of the term 'autochthones'	Those who were aware of the 'European and American' distinction between indigenous peoples and autochthones	Local understandings of the term 'autochthones'	Local understandings of the term 'indigenous peoples'
Baka women	All nine said yes	All nine said yes	Five said yes	To them, it meant owners of the village land.	To them it meant a special category of poverty, for which there is special assistance available.
			Four said no	It meant poor local people living in villages and camps, unlike city dwellers.	
Baka who owned NGOs (Okani, CADDAP, ASBAK, …)	All four said yes	All four said yes	All four said yes	For them it meant the original inhabitants of a place.	To them it meant people with a distinct culture and livelihood who are pushed to the margins of society.

Table 2.3: Local-level understandings of the concepts of indigenous peoples and autochthones by the Bantu.

Source: constructed by G.M. Lueong based on field findings.

Status of the Bantu	Question: Have you ever heard of the term 'indigenous peoples' and/or 'autochthones'? Yes/No.		Question: Are you aware that there is a difference between indigenous peoples and autochthones? Yes/No.	Question: According to you, what does 'autochthones' mean and who are they?	Question: According to you, what does 'indigenous peoples' mean and who are they?
	Those who heard of the term 'indigenous peoples'	Those who heard of the term 'autochthones'		Local understandings of the term 'autochthones'	Local understandings of the term 'indigenous peoples'
Bantu chiefs	All two said yes	Both said yes	Those who were aware of the 'European and American' distinction between indigenous peoples and autochthones	They associated autochthony with burial grounds of their ancestors. For them, autochthones meant the locals or sons of the soil, very often expressed using the french phrase *'les resortissants légitimes d'une village'*.	For these chiefs, 'indigenous peoples' were a new invention by government and INGOs to discriminate for and help the Baka. Indigenous peoples and autochthones were previously synonymous concepts. They added that in the past, both terms were associated with close ties to the soil. For them the relationship that makes the Baka indigenous peoples was not clear.

Table 2.3 (Continued)

Status of the Bantu	Question: Have you ever heard of the term 'indigenous peoples' and/or 'autochthones'? Yes/No.		Question: Are you aware that there is a difference between indigenous peoples and autochthones? Yes/No.	Question: According to you, what does 'autochthones' mean and who are they?	Question: According to you, what does 'indigenous peoples' mean and who are they?
	Those who heard of the term 'indigenous peoples'	Those who heard of the term 'autochthones'	Those who were aware of the 'European and American' distinction between indigenous peoples and autochthones	Local understandings of the term 'autochthones'	Local understandings of the term 'indigenous peoples'
Elderly Bantu (aged about sixty years and older)	All four said yes	All four said yes	Three said yes	For them, autochthony meant being the first settlers. However, they emphasized that since the Baka were not the first to settle on the roadsides, they are not the real autochthones. They considered the Baka as strangers on the roadsides, but autochthones in the forest, where they first settled.	To them indigeneity and autochthony were in essence the same. Indigeneity was being manipulated by external actors to positively discriminate in favour of the Baka. One of them asked what has happened to the appellation 'Pygmy'/forest peoples. For him, it was better for external actors to clearly say that they only want to help the Pygmies/forest peoples. In that way, the villagers will know that they are excluded.
			One said no	To him, both autochthones and indigenous peoples were the same. He said it means 'resortissants d'ici' (people from this village).	

Bantus who had 'their Baka'	All six said yes	All six said yes	All six said yes	They said they were the autochthones because the roadside was their village and the the government knew them as a village.	They said that indigenous peoples were the Pygmies. People who do not want to do anything for themselves.
Bantus who did not have 'their Baka'	All six said yes	All six said yes	Four said yes	These participants said that the Bantu are the autochthones. However, the Baka people now think that because the government has given them their own autonomous Baka villages, they are also autochthones. They added that the Baka are newcomers ('les venants'), and that is why even their chiefs are only third-degree chiefs.	They said that it is really something new in their community. In the past, it was the same with autochthones, but for some time now, the Baka people go to Abong-Mbang and other places for that day that they call 'journée international de quoi là' (international day of what again). They added that white people come to their community only to help the Baka, as though the Bantu were not suffering, too.
			Two said no	They said that they were all the same people. Only people who do not understand think that the Baka are not humans. They added that the Baka have their own farms and are selling plantains and cocoa, just like the Bantu.	

Table 2.3 (Continued)

Status of the Bantu	Question: Have you ever heard of the term 'indigenous peoples' and/or 'autochthones'? Yes/No.		Question: Are you aware that there is a difference between indigenous peoples and autochthones? Yes/No.	Question: According to you, what does 'autochthones' mean and who are they?	Question: According to you, what does 'indigenous peoples' mean and who are they?
	Those who heard of the term 'indigenous peoples'	Those who heard of the term 'autochthones'	Those who were aware of the 'European and American' distinction between indigenous peoples and autochthones	Local understandings of the term 'autochthones'	Local understandings of the term 'indigenous peoples'
Bantus who had blood pacts with Baka families	Both said yes	Both said yes	Both said no	These Bantus understood autochthones and indigeneous peoples to be the same. They highlighted the points that the Baka were living in the forest and the Bantus on the roadsides. Their parents brought the Baka people to stay on their roadside lands as one family. External actors were responsible for making the Baka stubborn, disobedient and try to say the land is theirs.	
Bantus who worked with INGOs	All seven said yes	All seven said yes	All seven said yes	For them, autochthony meant being local, a native of the local community whose paternal ancestry is rooted in the village.	To them, indigenous peoples were associated with backwardness. They said that the Baka are the indigenous peoples because they are still backward.

Group				
Bantus who had NGOS	All three said yes	All three said yes	All three said yes	For them, autochthony and indigeneity were the same, and referred to the 'sons of the soil'. However, they said that due to differences at the level of education and 'civilization', the Bantu are more autochonous than the Baka, who are typical indigenous peoples (still backward and uncivilized).	
Bantus married to Baka women	All three said yes	All three said yes	All three said no	For them, both autochthones and indigenous peoples were the same. They said that they were all human beings, irrespective of whether Baka or Bantu. To them the difference was situated at the level of people who came from other regions of the country like the West Region (Bamilekes) and the North (Hausa). They considered the latter to be strangers.	/
Bantu youths	All five said yes	All five said yes	Four said yes	For them, autochthony was associated with being the first settler and rootedness in the soil. One of the participants used the intriguing metaphor of the bird and the tree. 'To say there is no difference is like saying that a bird and a tree are the same because they are together. Baka are like birds and we are like	They understood indigeneity as being associated with primitivity and recent settlers. To them, the Baka are indigenous peoples because 'they are still so primitive and really need still have a long way to go in order to meet up with the Bantu.

Table 2.3 (Continued)

Status of the Bantu	Question: Have you ever heard of the term 'indigenous peoples' and/or 'autochthones'? Yes/No.		Question: Are you aware that there is a difference between indigenous peoples and autochthones? Yes/No.	Question: According to you, what does 'autochthones' mean and who are they?	Question: According to you, what does 'indigenous peoples' mean and who are they?
	Those who heard of the term 'indigenous peoples'	Those who heard of the term 'autochthones'	Those who were aware of the 'European and American' distinction between indigenous peoples and autochthones	Local understandings of the term 'autochthones'	Local understandings of the term 'indigenous peoples'
				the trees. This is our village. It is our grandparents who started this village and brought the Baka people here. So, they cannot come to somebody's house and overthrow the house owner.'	
			One said no	For him there was no difference. The Baka and the Bantu were the same. He added that they were even friends, go to school and play football together.	/

to gain a voice, defend their rights and access power at both national and global scales – there is no such consensus among the Baka in the East Region of Cameroon. On the contrary, while some Baka are totally unaware of the Euro-American understandings of the concept, others are aware, but absolutely reject it as derogatory, essentializing and no different from the term 'Pygmy'.

Nonetheless, there are also others who understand the concept in its Euro-American conceptualization, but who tend to focus on its potential instrumentality to enable them to get a voice, defend their rights and participate in development planning and interventions at both national and global scales. These findings tie in with what Pelican (2009) found in her research among the Mbororos (also framed as indigenous peoples) and grassfielders (locals/autochthones) in the Northwest Region of Cameroon. According to her, on the ground understandings of the concepts of autochthony and indigeneity are often incompatible with their Western conceptualizations.

What is outstanding is the fact that although different Baka, as well as Bantus, understand the concepts of autochthony and indigeneity differently, both the Baka and the Bantu associate autochthony with concepts like home and 'being a local'. Nonetheless, the understandings of these concepts vary. In the case of the Baka, this variation gives rise to different ways in which they assert their belonging. Those who reject indigeneity outright assert their belonging as locals (autochthony), whereas those who assert their belonging as indigenous peoples take it up as an instrumental or political category. Different interpretations and claims to indigeneity and autochthony in the region, especially in terms of their association with the concepts of home and 'being a local', are constantly being challenged.

Threats to Claims of Belonging in the East Region of Cameroon

Human displacement and resettlement poses a challenge to claims of autochthony as belonging. 'When belonging is threatened, it is less likely just to be, share[d], and join[ed] in' (Albiez et al. 2011: 212). When belonging is under threat, it becomes articulated and politicized in a manner that 'creates boundaries within the political community of belonging that separates the world population into "us" and "them"' (Yuval-Davis 2006: 204). In this way, belonging no longer only focuses on the unrelenting efforts that hegemonic powers use to uphold and replicate community boundaries, but it also becomes a component of the unending challenges that these political actors pose on the boundaries.

Phenomena That Threaten Claims to Belonging for the Baka

In his framework of analysis for understanding the factors that affect how development or modernization projects result in disasters for the people displaced, Scott showed that, in the quest for greater control over its territory and populations, the modern state has devised numerous schemes which, while ostensibly targeting improved human conditions, have nonetheless 'gone tragically awry' (Scott 1998: 4). According to him, the 'implementation of programs aimed at the simplification of administration of territory and population such as forcing sedentarisation is one of the factors necessary for development or modernization projects to result in full-fledged disasters' (ibid.). Similarly, Brand argues that 'the forced or involuntary movement of people by the state for development related purposes … with the intent of increasing state control have often fallen short of their conceived objectives' (2001: 961). In effect, the majority of those displaced by development projects have tended to fare badly long after such projects are launched (Agrawal and Redford 2009: 3).

In Cameroon, national development,[16] forest conservation/sustainable exploitation[17] and related population displacement/resettlement all took place in the East Region and continue to initiate potential threats to belonging. This is because the process entailed homelessness for the Baka, leaving both the displaced populations (the Baka), as well as the accommodating populations (the Bantu) with a dilemma. This, as mentioned earlier, springs from the recent shift from national development programmes that focused on national citizenship (belonging at the national level) into decentralized local development approaches that emphasize localness (local citizenship), which are often associated with being a 'son of the soil'. In this light, 'being a local' and belonging as a local citizen in the East Region defines access to both power (political participation, nominations and representations at regional and council seats), as well as resources (benefits of forest logging revenues, community forest management and autonomy over land use rights, just to name a few). In this regard, the claim to home (where people can claim to be a son of the soil) is a political instrument and a subtle form of the functionalization of belonging.

Claims to 'Homeland' as a Factor Threatening the Belonging of the Baka

According to Cernea, the risks of development-induced displacement include landlessness, joblessness, homelessness, marginalization, food insecurity, morbidity and mortality, loss of property, services and social disarticulation. The strategy to counter this impoverishment is to provide land for the landless, and shelter for the homeless, just to name a few (2000). Nonetheless, this strategy fails to recognize that providing these lost services does not always satisfy the belonging needs of the displaced populations at the local level, especially in so-called decentralized African societies, where belonging at the local level is the basis upon which people claim and/or have access to resources. As a result, displacement and resettlement inevitably raise the questions of home and belonging, a phenomenon that Couillard et al. have also reported when they say that 'having been dispossessed of their ancestral lands … indigenous forest peoples in Africa today live in extremely vulnerable conditions and experience marginalisation and poverty' (2009: 1).

In the context of the East Region of Cameroon, the displacement, resettlement and assimilation of the Baka is a potential threat to belonging, since, in some instances, the Baka are framed as belonging to camps that belong to Bantu villages, whereas in other cases, they are framed as belonging to autonomous Baka villages. This is because the Baka have a history of displacement from the forest, which is theoretically considered to be their home where they should belong, yet, they now reside along roadsides near Bantu villages, which Bantus claim to be their home. The village and the forest as sites of belonging are no longer just givens, but contested sites of belonging for the Baka. This contest over sites of belonging for the Baka will be discussed using the headings: 'village as home to the Baka' and 'forest as home to the Baka'.

'*Nos frères du village*': Village as Home to the Baka?

> Our brothers from the village maltreat us a lot. They always say that this is their land, that we do not belong here; instead that we are people of the bush (in-depth interview with a Baka camp leader at Diassa, Nov. 2011; my own translation).

The sentiment in the quote above was recurrent among the Baka residing on the roadsides. The first four words, '*nos frères du village*' (our brothers from the village) occurred thirty times from different Baka interlocutors. Intriguingly, most participants who made the statement resided in camps that were administratively framed as belonging to Bantu villages. When I asked them why they used '*nos frères du village*', when they also resided in the village, they tended to say that in the past the Baka lived in the forest. Although they no longer live in the forest, the Bantu still call them '*les gens de la forêt*' (people of the forest). These Baka referred to the Bantu as their 'brothers from the village' not because they felt that the Baka belonged to the forest, but because the Bantu maintained the distinction between them by always calling them 'people of the forest'.[18] To these Baka, calling the Bantu '*nos frères du village*' was a means to maintain the social boundaries which the Bantu constantly erected. In very few cases, some Baka, especially those who recalled having ancestral blood pacts with neighbouring Bantu families, used this statement to reiterate old existing relationships between the two groups.

It is important to mention here that not all the Baka referred to the Bantu as 'our brothers from the village'. There were some Baka who lived in camps that administratively belonged to Bantu villages, as well as others who lived in Baka villages, who argued that they belonged to 'the village'.[19] It was their home, no matter how discriminated against they felt there. During fieldwork, one focus group discussion in Bonado ended in difficulty when one of the participants used the phrase 'our brothers from the village'. After he used the phrase, one of the Baka chiefs, together with other Baka, asked him where his home was. They continued and said that their brothers who still live in the forest (referring to the Baka who live in Moloundou) can say that their home is the forest, but for them in Bonado, their home is Bonado. Their home is the village. They added that referring to the Bantu as 'their brothers from the village' was like taking them back into centuries past.

Mballa, who also conducted research among the Baka, quotes one of her Baka respondents, who insisted that the village is their home and they would not leave it because the forest had been cleared and they are now involved in agriculture:

> We will no longer quit from here because we cultivate cocoa to buy exercise books and textbooks for our children so that they should become people of value tomorrow. They removed the forest, we are out; afterwards, where will we go? (Mballa 2009: 48; my own translation).

From this, it can be said that the Baka consider the village to be their home because there is no more forest, and some of them were born here and will be buried here (as will be seen in Chapter 3). They are now involved in agriculture, which will enable their children to become recognized in the future. Although there is no more forest, Bantu villages accommodating Baka camps prefer to accept that the Baka are only living in their villages, and do not belong to the villages as local citizens. One of the Bantu youths put it in clearer terms when he said that to consider the Baka who live in their village as local citizens of the village was like accepting that the Baka belonged in their village and could one day rule over them:

> Saying that the Baka are from this village is like saying that the Baka could become mayors, to represent who? To say that the Baka live here with us is okay, but not that they are from this village. They remain Baka. It is our grandparents who brought them from the bush (informal group discussion in Abong-Mbang, Nov. 2011; my own translation).

Reading this, it is clear that the history of occupation, migration, displacement and resettlement that surrounds the peopling of the East Region of Cameroon has made the concept of 'homeland' a very disputed and contested one, which threatens belonging and induces a politics of belonging.

Displaced from the Forest and Resettled on the Roadsides: Forest as Home for the Baka?

> You see, we are happy to be living here on the roadside now. We can go to school, travel to Bertoua and Yaoundé. We are no longer primitive like our parents who did not know anything except for hunting. They did not even have clothes to wear. Even if we are still behind in comparison to the Bantu, because they came into contact with education earlier, we are proud that we have our own place here beside the road. Some of our brothers are still there in the bush in Moloundou, and are not yet very well civilized, but we the Baka here in Upper Nyong no longer have much to do with the forest. By the way, where is the forest? Now, the government has helped us to have our own farms and land. We are fine, only poverty troubles us. Today, we cannot begin to think about where we will go, because at least we have a home here in the village (in-depth interview with Bosco of Bonado, Dec. 2011; my own translation).

Across the East Region, not all Baka embrace the essentialist and stable attachments to the forest that most scholars, journalists and travellers ascribe to them. Most Baka living close to the semi-urban areas of the region for example, tended to identify the forest as the home of their parents and ancestors. The then twenty-nine-year-old Baka chief of Mayos village in Dimako sub-division, who was born in their roadside village of Mayos, exemplified the above-mentioned assertion of home in the village and home in the forest by referring to his mother when he said:

> People like mama are not from [in other words, do not belong to] this village [Mayos]; they are from the forest. That is where they were born, and then they later migrated to Koumadjab before coming here to work for a Bamileke man (Nov. 2011; my own translation).

In general, attachments to the forest as home were something that most Baka youths ascribed to their parents. For most Baka youths younger than thirty-five years old, home was where they were born (i.e. on the roadsides). Their parents, in the cases of those who were still alive, were very passive in asserting that the forest was their home. Nonetheless, most of these parents were swift to make claims to the village being home when they used it to refer to how 'civilized'[20] they were. Lebala Justin, the mother of the above-mentioned

Figure 2.4 An illustration of 'civilization' by a Baka woman.
Source: photograph by G.M. Lueong (Dec. 2011, Mayos-Dimako).

chief, illustrated this when she pointed to a cemented house (Figure 2.4) which she built for her family, and added further that she is an international artist who has travelled to France, Ivory Coast, and has featured on national TV with other musicians like Dr Joke, with whom she sang.

When it came to profound wisdom and a mastery of the forest, as well as its plants, older Baka were proud to say that the forest was their home. The same Lebala Justin mentioned above recounted that:

> No Bantu can maltreat any Baka in our village here because they are afraid of me and respect me a lot. They come here to get treatment for many of their sicknesses and bad luck. Only yesterday, I received a man from Douala [economic capital of Cameroon] who came to ask for luck. He came in a Prado car, but when he reached here, he respected me (Dec. 2011; my own translation).

This shifting of the ways in which elderly Baka conceptualize home (home is the village when talking about 'being civilized', but the forest when alluding to fine mastery of medical plants) seems to suggest that conceptualizations of home and belonging among these Baka was based on context and significance. Although these elderly Baka often made claims to the forest being their home, claims to the rights of community forests and the selling of trees located around Baka camps/villages for logging was a source of contention between the Baka and the Bantu, since the Bantu considered that their villages and the surrounding forests belonged to them (Leonhardt 2006). Apart from claims to homeland, another factor that threatens claims to belonging in the East Region is international development interventions.

Foreign/International Development Interventions

In the volume 'Indigenous Peoples of Africa', Sharon Cromer, Senior Deputy Assistant Administrator, Bureau for Africa, United States Agency for International Development (USAID) stated that:

> For the purposes of USAID's policies and programming in Africa, arguably the best characterization might include the concept of 'distinctive social and cultural groups that are relatively politically, economically and/or socially marginalized and therefore vulnerable.' This should include present and former hunter-gatherers, as well as many pastoralist communities. USAID, while recognizing the diversity of indigenous peoples, focuses attention and resources on ensuring all disadvantaged people, including indigenous peoples, are included in development (Nov. 2011).

This distinction made by USAID is not much different from those of other international development organizations, like the World Bank and the WWF discussed earlier in this chapter. These conceptualizations of indigeneity, aimed at balanced development and equal opportunities for those who are considered most vulnerable and sometimes lacking voice within their national political arenas, have sold very well in most parts of the globe. Nonetheless, in the East Region of Cameroon, where poverty is endemic, people tend to use any available opportunity to seek ways of benefiting from these opportunities. The very process of categorizing the Baka as indigenous is seen as a threat to the belonging of their neighbouring Bantus, who sometimes, in turn, assert their belonging in ways that fit into the definition of indigenous peoples. This, for example, was the case of some Bangando youths whom I met during a focus group discussion in Moloundou, and who argued that, when INGOs come to their community and are only looking to help the Baka, they feel 'bitter' and segregated because according to them, they are also indigenous peoples because their ancestors, their parents and even they themselves lived in the dense forested area of Boumba and Ngoko, had never been displaced, were also expert hunters and could serve as forest guides for conservation NGOs. Moreover, these youths argued that it was their grandparents who brought the Baka to live with them together in the village, and when INGOs impose such separation, especially in development opportunities, it can cause 'hatred' and problems between them and the Baka. From this, it may be said that the struggle by some Bantus to be indigenous people in turn threatens the belonging of the Baka as indigenous peoples, such that both the Bantu and the Baka tend to contest each other's legitimacy. An outstanding example of this came up when a Bantu contradicted himself during two different encounters. During the first interview, this Bantu acknowledged that there was a difference between the locals/autochthones of their village and indigenous peoples ('Pygmies'), who had just recently installed themselves on the roadsides and who were still 'primitive' and attached to the forest. However, during a follow-up interview on the subject of special development projects for indigenous peoples, the same Bantu participant said that:

> We are all forest peoples. A Baka is no more of a forest person than me. Some Baka do not even know what I know about the forest. So why should people come and tell me that I cannot serve as a guide in the forest? That is discrimination. In the real sense we, too, are indigenous peoples, because indigenous peoples just means peoples who originally owned the land. I am an indigene of this village (in-depth interview with Pierre, in Moloundou, Oct. 2011; my own translation).

In this illustration, a Bantu participant facing a potential problem of access to resources suddenly adjusted his interpretation of indigeneity and belonging. Taking into consideration his contradictory interpretations, it can be said that the Baka who live in the camp associated with this Bangando village may not by default assume they are indigenous peoples and thus benefit from this, even if they do belong to the category of indigenous peoples. This illustration reinforces Rupp's (2011) observation that in pursuit of employment with NGOs, especially conservation NGOs like the WWF, the Bantu (Bangando) tended to identify themselves as 'people of the forest' who know the forest. Robillard (2010) also showed that 'positive discrimination', a phenomenon whereby INGOs designed development projects entirely for the Baka in the frame of indigenous peoples' development, was a major source of conflict between the Bantu and the Baka of the Boumba and Ngoko Division of the East Region of Cameroon.

I agree with both Robillard (2010) and Rupp's (2011) observation that this 'positive discrimination' tends to initiate conflicts between the Baka and the Bantu. These conflicts have also tended to conflate the struggle to assert belonging to the 'positively discriminated category'. Another phenomenon that threatens claims to belonging for the Baka is representation at regional and local councils.

Representation at Regional and Local Councils

In the East Region of Cameroon, the stipulations of the national constitution became seen as a potential threat to claims of belonging. In Article 55 of Part

X of the 1996 constitution, which focuses on regional and local authorities, it is stated that:

> Regional and local authorities of the Republic shall comprise Regions and Councils ... Regional and local authorities shall be public law corporate bodies. They shall have administrative and financial autonomy in the management of regional and local interests. They shall be freely administered by councils elected under conditions laid down by law. The duty of the councils of regional and local authorities shall be to promote the economic, social, health, educational, cultural and sports development of the said authorities ... The Regional Council shall be the deliberative organ of the Region. Regional Councillors whose term of office shall be 5 (five) years shall comprise: ... representatives of traditional rulers elected by their peers ... The Regional Council shall be headed by an indigene of the Region elected from among its members for the life of the Council.

From this constitutional stipulation, it is clear that apart from the necessity of being an indigene of the region – which translates to belonging to a village in the region[21] – to benefit from political nominations and other development benefits, belonging to a village also gives access to local and regional resources. This is because it ensures both being a representative of the traditional rulers and being the president of the regional council. Both positions grant access to the management of the revenues and resources of the forested region. This explains why the Baka have an interest in asserting their belonging as locals/autochthones and not only as indigenous peoples. An illuminating example of this is the case of a Baka who presented his candidature for the post of mayor and was rejected because he did not belong to the village. In other words, he was not a local/autochthon.

Messe Venant, secretary of the Indigenous Peoples of Africa Coordinating Committee (IPACC), president of REPALEAC and director of the NGO OKANI (which means 'rise up' in the Baka language), is a learned Baka man who was born and bred in a Baka roadside camp in Diang sub-division of the Upper Nyong Divison of the East Region in the late 1960s. His candidature for the post of the municipality's mayor was rejected on the grounds that he did not belong to the village. Messe told me that although he was the first boy from the village to pass the national high school exams, people with whom he grew up and went to school suddenly turned against him and the entire Baka community when he vied to become mayor during the 2007 municipal elections. According to him, the Bantu who contested his belonging said that he was a Baka and not a native of Diang. Messe said that he and his entire community were framed as forest people who had just settled along the roadsides. Curiously, Messe's mother is a Bantu woman from the same region of Diang. Yet his status as 'half-Bantu' could not save him from being rejected. Among the Baka it may be said, as has been shown in the context of other African communities, that:

> Being able to prove that one belongs is … usually the way through which one can access resources, vote and most importantly be voted into power. It will be indeed very difficult for one to seek political office in an area he/she is considered a stranger. One would have to 'be able to point to a home land' or 'home village' to be an acceptable candidate for any political office (Lentz 2006: 1).

As noted by Mballa in her interview with Chief Maya, the Baka chief of Mayos village in Dimako sub-division of the Upper Nyong Division, Chief Maya's autochthony was contested by neighbouring Bantus. The chief succinctly described his experience of getting his official uniform (which showed that power had been legally conferred on him) as a nightmare:

> The divisional officer appointed me here as a third-class chief, yes, but the problem was the uniform. Every other chief's uniform had been sent to Yaoundé. Ours were all measured and our sizes taken in the same way, but everyone else had already received their uniforms. I don't know what the mayor did to me; I went to the office to see the divisional officer. Oh! The secretary told me that I must go hunting, kill a monkey, bring it and give it to the divisional officer before I can see my traditional uniform as a chief. That is how they treated me; up to now, as we speak, I have not seen anything. All other chiefs have had their uniforms, and the measurement of these uniforms started here at my place (Chief Maya of Mayos-Baka in Mballa, 2009: 80; my own translation).

Another factor threatening claims to belonging for the Baka is community forests, as will be explained in the paragraphs below.

Community Forests as a Threat to Belonging

In general, interest in, as well as the scientific literature on community forests and their management in Cameroon (Logo 2002b; Oyono 2004; Oyono 2005a; Logo 2006; Oyono 2007; Nguiffo, Kenfack and Mballa 2008; Mbarga 2013) are huge and diverse, and I will not engage in the many debates surrounding this topic. In this section, I will only touch on aspects of community forests that concern belonging, so as to give a clearer understanding of how, in the context of community forests, tensions around belonging have developed. To do this, I start by briefly discussing community forests in the context of Cameroon's decentralization of forest management, before proceeding to discuss Cameroon's forest zones as foreseen in the country's forest management plan ('*plan de zonage*') as summarized in Figure 2.5 below.

Beginning in 1994 when Cameroon revised its environmental laws, enacting the 1994 forestry, wildlife and fisheries legislation (no. 94/01) and becoming the first country in central Africa to introduce community forestry (Lescuyer 2005), the country was seen, and saw itself, as a regional leader in sustainable forest management (Topa et al. 2009). Indeed, the creation of community forests is the second aspect of Cameroon's decentralization of forest management (Oyono 2004: 98). This 'creation and management of Community Forests consists of a long organisational, decision-making and technical process, involving many different actors (NGOs, the Ministry of Environment and Forests, logging companies and the village communities concerned). [This innovation is, as Oyono argues] aimed at giving village communities responsibilities and powers for the management of their forests and financial benefits accruing therefrom' (ibid.: 99). A core element in the 1994 forest policy was zoning, whereby a national forest management plan (commonly referred to as the '*plan de zonage*') was produced under Canadian supervision (Samndong and Vatn 2012: 215). As Samndong and Vatn highlight, this national zoning plan offers particular recommendations for how forests should be managed. However, despite the emphasis on participation in the law, there was no involvement of the rural population or other local stakeholders. The plan was produced based on the interpretation of air photos and satellite imagery, with no ground inventory. The key issue in the '*plan de zonage*' was the creation of a 'Permanent Forest Estate', exclusively reserved for commercial logging or forest conservation activities, despite their long-standing usage by local village populations (ibid.). According to Pénelon, Mendouga and Karsenty (1998) and Lescuyer (2007), in the '*plan de zonage*' there was also the creation of a 'Non-Permanent Forest Estate' in the form of narrow corridors of secondary forest along the roads, in which diverse forest usages were permitted, including agriculture, community forestry and artisanal logging. As Ngiuffo (2007) and Wily (2011) show, when this '*plan de zonage*' was created, it was said to be provisional, with the possibility that it could be subject to detailed modifications resulting from issues with the reality on the ground. Nonetheless, both authors now argue that no local adjustments have thus far been made, as the plan is already being used to promote the interests of powerful actors in commercial logging.

In Figure 2.5, the blocks in bold indicate areas of interest for this work, which are closely related to claims of community belonging. Who belongs to the council as a local/autochthon? Who belongs to the community? In effect, the creation of community forests, together with a logging policy that demands ten per cent of the revenue be given back to 'forest communities' in the region, make the issue of belonging one that begs for critical questioning. Who makes the claim of belonging where, how and why? Who are the 'real'

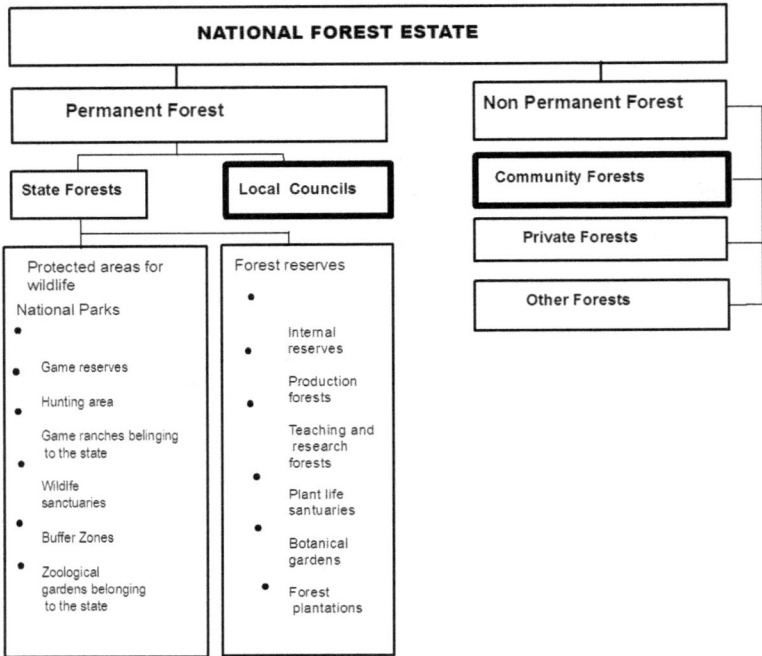

Figure 2.5 Cameroon's forest zones.
Source: Topa et al. 2009: 30.

autochthones who are entitled to profit from forest resources? (Geschiere 2009: 76). Topa et al. (2009: 104) point out that:

'Communities' in the rainforest zone may not fit outsiders' assumptions about communities and how they function. Cameroon's 'communities' are not necessarily stable, homogeneous social entities ... One of the more intractable problems to be resolved, highlighted by many long-term observers, is the poor governance that arises in communities because of conflicts between community members and elites of different ethnic origins and allegiance.

In the light of community forests in the East Region of Cameroon,[22] a community is not neccesarily operationalized as a group of people who live on a given territorial surface as specified by the forest law 94/01 of 20 January 1994. Rather, a community becomes an invention of interested stakeholders who belong there. In this regard, the boundaries of a community as framed by those seeking community forests become very arbitrary and do not even always respect ethnic lines along which other benefits are framed. Topa et al. (2009: 107) noted this when they say that 'establishing a community forest rarely comes from the communities, but rather from all the other actors who have an advantage in the process'. Community forests, they continue, 'often originate through the self-interest of prominent village-orientated individuals with the social capital to gain authorization for a community forest; sometimes these "elites" are urban civil servants who visit the village only rarely'. From this it can be said that claims to belonging are not only important for the 'elite' who establishes the forests to benefit his interests, but they are also important because he has the power to decide who in the community can be included in the community forest management committee. Indeed, as Lescuyer (2005) shows, in Cameroon:

> Community forests provide interesting guidelines on how to commit the local stakeholders into the forest management process. These 'participatory' approaches request an identification and then an 'officialization' of the 'local communities' under the form of constituent organisations (association, committee, …) … The major bias of such formal village organisation is to be built aside from kinship systems that remain the key variable to analyse and understand the forest uses. If local population is to become an essential stakeholder of sustainable forest management, the legal village organisations must be founded on customary socio-political institutions (ibid. 2005: 84).

In like manner, Rupp argues that 'while the legislative guide to forming community forests remains vague on just how such a community is identified and established, NGOs' procedures for collecting data on local communities are premised on categories that identify communities by highlighting differences among them' (2011: 57). These sorts of processes threaten claims of belonging for the Baka, thereby leaving it contested.

Claims to Belonging by the Baka

In today's world, people's belonging can no longer be defined according to a purely geographic notion of place or historical sense of connection. This is because globalization and modernity are likely to disrupt the sense of connection and unsettle the notion of essentialist stereotyping of people within national territories (Papastergiadis 1998). This is the case with the Baka in the context of essentialist stereotypes like forest peoples and indigenous peoples.

Ways in Which the Baka Assert Their Belonging: Confrontations and Contested Authenticities

Yuval-Davis suggests that belonging can be approached from three analytical levels, which include social location, identifications and emotional attachments, and ethical and political values. According to her, social location embodies an intersection of divisions of age, class, gender, ethnicity and sexuality. Identifications and emotional attachments relate to the 'stories that people tell themselves and others, about who they are [as well as who they are not]', which can become very sensitive in times of threat and insecurity. Ethical and political values affect ways in which value and judgement are placed on social locations, identifications and attachments (2006: 202).

In the analysis of how the Baka assert their belonging, it was discovered that there were both general assertions and camp-specific assertions of belonging by the Baka. General assertions were more linked to what Yuval-Davis calls social location, with a stress on ethnicity, while camp-specific claims were more associated with identifications and emotional attachments, as well as ethical and political values.

General Ways in Which the Baka Assert Their Belonging

Faced with multiple external ascriptions of belonging, the Baka are not indifferent to the social processes surrounding them. They are far from being the voiceless, passive consumers of social phenomena in their communities as they are often projected to be. Rather, responses from the Baka on the subject of their belonging indicated that they are social agents with active agency, which was often only suppressed by other social processes, like the injustice and lawlessness which govern their relationships with other ethnic groups within the region (Pyhälä 2012). One Baka interlocutor in Mballam stated that they are proud they are at least being recognized in Cameroon as marginalized indigenous peoples:

> We are proud because, at least, we are already recognized in this country – Cameroon – as marginalized indigenous peoples, and I say at least because we are already enrolled in electoral lists (presidential, as well as municipal) and

also, we have the freedom to speak in front of people. This means that we are fully fledged Cameroonians and there are already NGOs who come to us to lead us and tell us to do this, or not to do that. Well, now let's return to the 'at least' that I mentioned before. We say at least, because it is a condition. It is with a heavy heart that we are telling you this; our leaders are not yet officially recognized as third-class chiefs. Our leaders are still considered as camp leaders or quarter heads as they say. We are totally marginalized, we are only partially recognized by the state … For me, I call this place a village, even if others call it a Baka camp; the word camp must die. This village was created in 1968, but even today, we are still suppressed. There is another word to say that the Baka are nomads; that was our parents – for us, we are not nomads. We have never had the income of the forest (RFA) as Baka people. We are always oppressed. We have never received the community forest assigned to the Baka people. Well, the authorities of that Bantu village decide what happens here with us. We disagree with that (FGD in Mballam, Dec. 2011; my own translation).

In the narration above, some points suggest that the Baka are people with active agency who consciously make claims to their belonging in the East Region of Cameroon. The Baka in Mballam,[23] for example) claimed to belong to the category of indigenous peoples and were proud to belong to this category. Moreover, their use of the term '*peuples autochtones marginalisés*' instead of just '*peuples autochtones*' to refer to indigenous peoples, as do most French-speaking communities, who translate both 'autochtones' and 'indigenous peoples' as '*peuples autochtones*'. These Baka have an in-depth mastery of the distinctions between autochthony and indigeneity in the Cameroonian context. Nonetheless, these Baka were also conscious of the challenges facing their claims to belonging. For them, these challenges are brought about by the administrative demarcation of boundaries of belonging (as discussed above), which merges them into Bantu villages, a process which they argue has tended to erase their autonomy, both as indigenous peoples and as locals. While previous writers have treated the violence and marginalization of the Baka as being perpetrated by the Bantu, who entertain 'colonial-style' relations with the Baka, I point to the fact that this violence and marginalization is the outcome of struggles to legitimate belonging and access to resources in a poor region. One of the many examples highlighted to demonstrate this is the case mentioned above in the section on foreign/international development interventions, whereby, during my fieldwork, some Bangando (Bantu) youths mentioned that the categorization of people in the community as either autochthones or indigenous peoples, especially in the context of development interventions targeted at the Baka (who are considered to be indigenous peoples), was discriminatory against the Bantu (something Robillard

(2010) has called positive discrimination). As these Bantus stressed, such processes could result in violence against the Baka, especially as these Bantus pointed to the fact that their ancestors were the ones who brought the Baka to reside with them in their villages. This struggle to access resources in the region was also observed by Rupp (2011) who says that, in pursuit of employment with NGOs, especially conservation NGOs like the WWF, the Bantu (Bangando) tended to identify themselves as 'people of the forest', who know the forest.

In effect, in making claims to belonging, some Baka assert their belonging to the category of indigenous peoples, whereas others, on the contrary, outright rejected the category. The Baka who reject this category of indigenous peoples tend to argue that accepting that they are indigenous peoples is like accepting that they are 'forest people' who will one day return to the forest and live like their parents did, without education or houses:

> To say that we are indigenous people is to accept that we are people of the forest, as the Bantu say; and also it is to say that we want to go back there in the bush and live like our parents lived without education, without houses and other things. We are very happy to stay here at the roadside. Our parents and grandparents lived there [pointing] in the bush, but today we cannot say that we want to go back there. At least, here we can sell our goods and also go to school like the Bantu, we can read and write French like them, but the problem is that we are only seen as people of the forest, whereas, between us and our Bantu brothers, there is no real difference. If they say that we are people of the forest, then let them leave the forest for us. There, with the support of NGOs such as Plan, we can still build schools, roads and everything. Actually, here at the camp we don't see any difference between us and the Bantu, who see themselves as autochthones (FGD, in Bonado, Nov. 2011; my own translation).

Intriguingly, participants of the discussion from which this quote was extracted mostly used the term 'indigenous peoples' to refer to indigenous peoples, whereas in the quote from Mballam, the globally accepted term 'marginalized indigenous peoples' was used. The question, then, is why some Baka used the term *'peuples indigènes'* while others used *'peuples autochtones marginalisés'*? The answer to this was found at the level of the interactions between different Baka camps with indigenous people-oriented NGOs. It came to light that the participants who used the term 'marginalized indigenous peoples' often had extensive experience (a minimum of two years) with the issues of indigenous peoples, and had already in most cases started their own associations to defend the rights of indigenous peoples. Whereas those who used the term 'indigenous peoples' often mentioned it as the term that the Bantu used to define them, which to them was essentialist, stigmatizing, humiliating and derogatory. Even in cases where the latter category had benefited from indigenous people-specific interventions, they still tended to adhere to the humiliating and derogatory dimensions of the concept as the justification for why they deny belonging to it. From this rejection of the category of indigenous peoples by some Baka, it can be said that while some Baka assert their belonging to the category in a bid to gain political voice and influence, others conceive of the category as having essentializing potential.

In a similar vein, a Baka catechist in Moloundou further recounted that belonging for some Baka has no meaning unless in specific contexts. He said that:

> Today, when a Baka tells you that he is a Baka or a 'Pygmy', it can mean one of the following three things: that he is poor and does not have money, or that he knows traditional medicines, or that he has Baka blood in him. When I say that I am a Baka,[24] I only mean that I have the blood. My parents told me that I am Baka, not that I am poor or anything. I have my large cocoa farm. I also cultivate plantains, cassava and other crops. I am also a Christian and do not do magic. I am a Baka like a Bantu is a Bantu. There is no question of saying I belong to indigenous peoples or whatever, because all those things are the same. It is like pouring wine from an old container into a new one. They [the government] have tossed us here and there until one just does not know what to say (Catechist in Moloundou, Oct. 2011; my own translation).

Other Baka avoid the categories of both indigenous peoples and autochthony. According to them, they are Cameroonians like all other Cameroonians and thus belong as Cameroonians. In other words, these Baka stress their national belonging (national citizenship) over their local belonging (local citizenship). For the most part, these two levels of discourse co-exist but are often used in different circumstances. For example, Lucien, a Baka camp leader in Elandjo, confirmed on one occasion to have participated in the 2011 celebrations of the international day of world indigenous peoples (without exactly understanding that it was an international day of world indigenous peoples, but because according to him, they were told by NGO officials that a very important day was coming up and at the level of the East Region, the day was uniquely for the Baka people to show their culture to the world). However, on another occasion, he composed a song to speak out against the discrimination and subhuman treatment which members of his camp experienced on a daily basis because they were presented as 'backward and uncivilized' indigenous forest peoples. Lucien sings that he is proud to be a Baka, a Cameroonian like all other Cameroonians:

I am proud, I am a Baka, I am a Cameroonian just like others. I am a human being like a Bantu, like an Ewondo. I am proud to be who I am because I'm also a creature of God like everyone else. I speak (Lucien, in Elandjo, Dec. 2011; my own translation).

Koam is another Baka, who asked me to photograph his house and go and show the government that he lives in it because he is poor and not because he is a Pygmy. He went on to add that:

Who as a man will be happy to see his family live in these conditions because he is a Pygmy? They [the Bantu and some government workers] take the name Baka and Pygmies to discriminate against us. We are normal people like all others. We reason and feel bad when we are discriminated against because people think that we are different. That is even why they call us 'peuples indigènes'. They still call us forest people, whereas it was our parents who lived there in the forest. However, the world has changed and so, too, have we, the Baka. Now we want a better life like the Bantu have. When Chantal Biya and Plan were building houses for Pygmies, I thought that they would reach here, but they did not (in-depth interview with Koam, Koumadjab, July 2013; my own translation).

Intriguingly, Pyhälä, who calls for the recognition of the rights of the Baka as indigenous peoples, paraphrases the Baka of Kwamp camp and says that:

When it comes to traditional versus new homes, many Baka still prefer their traditional homes [*mongolou*], saying they 'breathe' better, they are more resistant to wind and rain and extreme weather (both heat and cold), and they are more comfortable. Why, then, should they live in large square houses simply because the latter are seen by others as more 'civilised'? (2012: 18)

From this sharp contrast between the stance of Koam in Koumadjab-Baka camp and that of the Baka of Kwamp camp reported by Pyhälä, it can be said that claims to indigeneity as asserted by the Baka depend on the context. There is no one-fits-all category in which the Baka have a consensus about belonging, based on a common experience of marginalization and discrimination. Rather, as has been seen, some Baka outright reject belonging to the category of indigenous peoples. To them, being labelled with the special status of indigenous people, as well as assigning where they should belong, justifies discrimination, stereotypes and stigma.

In other cases, when the Baka were told by INGOs that they were indigenous peoples, and the Baka saw the potential of benefiting from such categorization, some of them fully asserted their belonging as indigenous peoples.

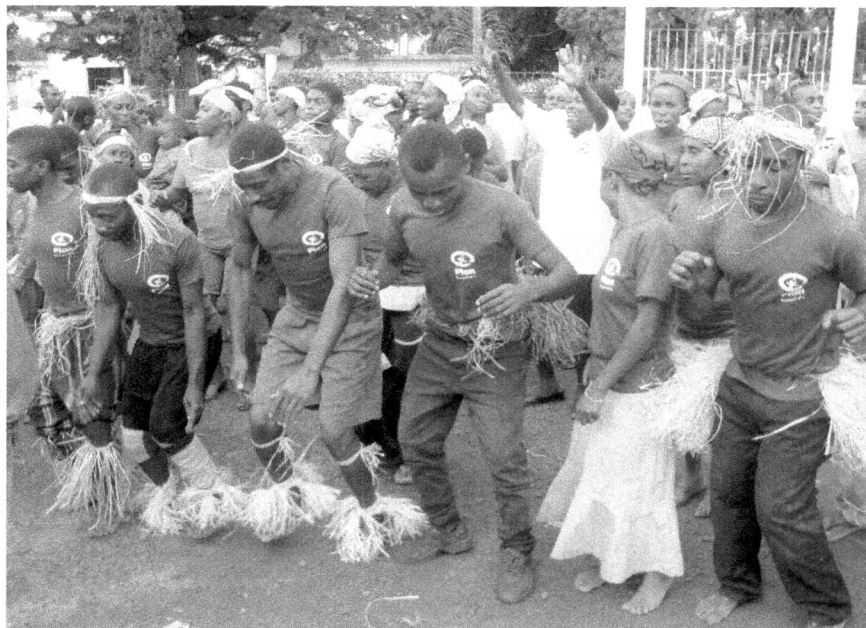

Figure 2.6 Celebration of the international day of indigenous peoples in Abong-Mbang, East Region of Cameroon.
Source: Kinkoh Thomas Ngala (Oct. 2011).

This was the case with some Baka youths and adults who explicitly expressed their belonging to the category of indigenous peoples by wearing blue jerseys given to them by Plan Cameroon, to go and display their traditional dances, as well as other elements of their culture, during events celebrating the international day of indigenous peoples in Abong-Mbang (Figure 2.6). However, when I coincidentally met with one of the participants during one of my interviews in 2011, who was wearing her jersey celebrating the international day of indigenous peoples, and who lived just eight metres away from the Baka cultural centre in Mayos-Dimako (constructed with the help of Plan), she was totally unaware of the whole autochthony/indigeneity debate (Figure 2.7). She was only aware that Plan and other NGOs came to their camp and told them to go for festivities or do some things that would help the Baka. To her, all that was important was making sure that she followed what she was being told because when she followed it, it helped her financially and/or materially. Pointing to the Plan-constructed Baka school in the village, she said 'here we always follow what they say and now we have our own school and some people even have cemented houses. So now our children can also go to school without problems.'

Figure 2.7 A Baka woman from Mayos-Baka in 2011 still wearing her jersey, with the Baka cultural centre in the background.
Source: photograph by G.M. Lueong (Dec. 2011).

Another vivid example is the case of a group of Baka women in Bonado-Doumé (Figure 2.8). This group of women, who won first prize during a competition as part of the festivities of the international day of indigenous peoples, said that Plan had asked that they form a group as indigenous women and go and march in Abong-Mbang. After they had formed the group and danced, they won an award. However, during one of my focus group discussions in Bonado, they refused to respond to any question that had the term 'indigenous peoples' in it. They asked me what use it was for people to tell them that they were indigenous peoples without assistance. For them, this was like using them and their culture to make events appeal to other people. They went on to ask why, since they had been asked to form groups and and dance, and since they had performed so well that they were rewarded, no one was there to promote them (*'qui nous pousse'*)? They were very bitter and did not want to speak. It was only after the assistant camp leader persuaded them that they participated, with reluctance, asking me if I was going to help them to go to places like Yaoundé (the country's capital). In this light, belonging to indigenous peoples meant 'hoping to be assisted'.

From these examples, one would question who among the Baka asserted belonging to the category of indigenous peoples according to the globally accepted criteria. It was fascinating to see that responses to questions like 'Since when did you become indigenous peoples?' or 'Who says that

Figure 2.8 An organized group of Baka women who won a prize during the events marking the celebrations of indigenous peoples' day. 2.8a: Bonado women organized by Plan-Cameroon on International Day of Indigenous Peoples. 2.8b: The same group of women during Focus Group Discussion in Bonado.

Sources: 2.8a - Thomas Ngalla, Plan-Cameroon; 2.8b - photograph by G.M. Lueong, Dec. 2011.

you are/belong to indigenous peoples?', posed to those who asserted their belonging to the category, were overwhelmingly polarizing.

Some Baka said that they only became aware of the category in 2008 during the celebration of the international day of the world's indigenous peoples, when the government, Plan and other NGOs gave them gifts including national identity cards which made the police stop harassing and beating them or asking for game in place of beating them. Since this time, most of them said that they 'felt to be Cameroonians, too'. Thus, being and belonging to indigenous peoples for these Baka was not a matter of self-determination. They were indigenous because they were told so. It conferred recognition for them within the country. In like manner, on the part of the state, this distribution of national identity cards to the Baka falls withing the framework of the Indigenous Peoples Development Programme in the context of the sub-programme *promotion de la citoyenneté* (promotion of citizenship).

Other Baka said that they became aware of their belonging to indigenous peoples during the same celebrations, but what stood out most according to them, was the fact that the minister of social affairs came to them. This meant that the government knew about them and that they were special. For others still, it was during a development intervention, in which the developers asked specifically for Baka peoples. Thus, they felt proud that they were becoming more important than the Bantu, to the point where people came just to help them, without first passing via the Bantu.

In general, only a few Baka who are categorized in this book as 'elites' defined themselves as indigenous peoples. Although they were educated and lived in the city, they belonged primordially to the Baka ethnic group, which suffers marginalization, domination, dispossession and discrimination. Helen, one of these elites, founder and director of Centre d'Action pour le Développement des Autochtones Pygmées (CADDAP)[25] illustrated this when she said that:

> The Baka are indigenous peoples. They have their own culture and are very vulnerable to marginalization, violence and abuse. They have special needs that need to be catered for, because they do not enjoy the same protection as their fellow neighbours, at least in practice although, the law claims to cover everyone (in-depth interview at Abong-Mbang, Nov. 2011; my own translation).

By defining themselves as indigenous peoples and creating their own Community-Based Organizations (CBOs)/NGOs, they were standing up for the rights of their people. Nonetheless, as will be seen in Chapters 4 and 5, the legitimacy of these elites as belonging to the Baka ethnic group (indigenous peoples) was always challenged both by insiders (fellow Baka) and outsiders (Bantus).

Camp-based Differences in Asserting Belonging

It was observed that camps which had obtained the status of a village, like Mayos village in Dimako sub-division, asserted belonging both as locals/autochthones and as indigenous peoples. According to them, this was because although they had the status of a village, which conferred upon them local autonomy, they were still 'backward' and not very 'civilized' compared to their Bantu counterparts. Thus, they were still to some extent indigenous peoples. In this village, it was interesting how the then twenty-nine-year-old chief was swift to point to 'differences' among the Baka based on their level of 'civilization'. To him:

> The Baka do not have one unique identity. We the Baka here in Mayos are different from the Baka in Banana. Even the language is slightly different. Their Baka has more words borrowed from Lingala than our own. Some of them are also still very 'primitive' and attached to the forest. They even call us Bantu. We here in Mayos have already adapted to Bantu things ['*On a déjà adapté avec les choses Bantu*']. We no longer engage in gathering. We can no longer hunt large animals; even hunting has changed and it is difficult with us here where there is no forest. Now the history of the Baka has been erased. We are now also eating foods of the village [i.e. Bantu foods] like kwem, rice, etc. Now we no longer have the exact culture of the Baka. We no longer have grandparents who can teach us those things. Also, we are different because when I was working in Banana in a project called '*photographie de la forêt*', I saw uncivilized Baka and the Bantu did not give them land. They lived behind the houses of Bantu. We do not have such processes here (Chief of Mayos-Dimako, Dec. 2011; my own translation).

On the other hand, the Baka in the Bonado camp, which is a subquarter administratively belonging to the Bantu village Bonado-Doumé, had a divided stance on their assertion of belonging. Since their chief was still considered to be a quarter head and was not yet recognized by the government, some members of the camp were very critical of calling the camp a quarter of the Bantu village (as in Bonado III/Petit Bonado). Doing so meant that they accepted the fact that they belonged to the Bantu village, and thus were sub-citizens under the autochthony of the Bantu. To them, the camp should be called Bonado-Baka until the time when the government grants them the status of a village. On the contrary, other members of the camp held that it was Bonado III/Petit Bonado (a subquarter of the Bonado-Bantu village), because the government said that it was so. This latter group used dispute mediation procedures to illustrate their stance, and one member put it as follows:

> You people who say that we are Bonado-Baka, if we were Bonado-Baka, why is it that the last time the police in Doumé asked us to come back and take the disputed case between Paul and Justin to the Bantu chief, you said it was

a problem among us Baka here in the camp and not concerning the Bantu? Therefore the police said their chief is our boss. It means that the government knows that we are under the Bantu and belong to them. We must just accept it and tell her [referring to me] how things are here. Madam [referring to me], even if our camp leader cannot solve a problem among us here in the camp, we must first take it to the Bantu chief. Only he has the right to send us to Doumé [to the police]. It means that we are under the Bantu chief, right? It also means that we are a subquarter of the Bantu village, right? (Jean, in Bonado, Jan. 2012; my own translation)

This illustration of dispute mediation over belonging came up more than ten times in different Baka camps belonging to Bantu villages.[26] From this it could be said that procedures of dispute mediation engraved into the administrative demarcation of boundaries played an active role in shaping the ways in which the Baka asserted their belonging.

In the same light, Bingongol, another Baka camp located on the Lomié road and created in 1960 portrayed similar camp-based polarization in the assertion of belonging. Like Bonado, the struggle concerned what the camp should be called. To them, what they were called was indicative of where they belonged. The divide between Bingongol-Baka (to mean an autonomous Baka camp) and Bingongol II (to mean a Baka camp that belonged to the Bantu village Bingongol) was so sharp that it resulted in a quarrel (as illustrated in Figure 2.9). Some members of the camp called others Bantus and

Figure 2.9 A quarrel between some Baka camp members in Bingongol-Baka. A Baka woman talking back to a Baka man (who is not visible in this picture) who categorized some Baka women as his 'lazy and coward Baka'.

Source: photograph by the research assistant, Bingongol-Baka (Nov. 2011).

those who were being called Bantus called the others 'slaves' and 'cowards', who had sold their dignity for crumbs from the Bantu.

Conclusion

This chapter underscores the point that the belonging of the Baka can be analysed in two ways: belonging to places expressed in terms of home, and belonging to social categories expressed in terms of locals/autochthones or indigenous peoples. On the one hand, belonging based on the Baka's attachments to a place is often expressed as being their home/homeland and authenticated using the metaphor of 'rootedness in the soil'. On the other hand, belonging based on attachments to the global category of 'indigenous peoples', which, as reinterpreted in Cameroon, refers to people who are in one way or another considered 'not rooted in the soil'. In this analysis of belonging based on indigeneity, the Baka express special attachments to a distinct culture and livelihood, as well as their socioeconomic and political victimization and vulnerabilities. From these two perspectives, it is clear that in the East Region of Cameroon, autochthony and indigeneity are projected as versions of belonging that simultaneously conflict with each other.

In this region of Cameroon, people assert, or are ascribed to belong to, either of the above-mentioned categories, so as to participate in and/or benefit from development interventions and local governance of the region's resources. This is significant, taking into consideration the fact that the East Region is the largest forest region in the country,[27] and it is also endowed with mineral resources including gold, diamonds and copper ore, just to name a few. Nonetheless, it remains the third poorest region of the country (NIS 2012). In view of these facts, the discussion of belonging focuses on a region where two 'categorical communities',[28] 'the poor' (autochthones) and 'the poorest of the poor' (indigenous peoples), negotiate and assert their belonging in order to make claims to livelihood resources.

It is important to mention that although autochthony and indigeneity are widely used within academia, local understandings and conceptualizations of the concepts show conflicts between pre-existing local understandings and the externally imposed meanings (definitions given by development organizations and some state departments) of these concepts. Locally, indigeneity as a version of belonging regroups the following markers and sites of belonging: 'Pygmies', 'forest people', 'hunter-gatherers', people who are not 'rooted in the soil' in the roadside villages and whose claims to homeland on the roadsides are contested, 'discriminated and disempowered peoples', 'people with a marginal culture', 'uncivilized people', 'people excluded from "their"[29] land and natural resource rights', 'marginalized peoples' and 'people who belong to the forest'. Thus, indigeneity as a version of belonging is both ascribed and asserted. In the same light, autochthony as a version of belonging is ascribed, as well as asserted, and regroups the following markers and sites of belonging: the 'natives of the soil', the 'locals', 'sons/daughters of the soil', 'people rooted in the soil', 'villagers', 'agriculturalists', 'civilized people', 'empowered and politically active citizens'. Reading through these local understandings of indigeneity and autochthony against the scholarly constructed interpretations of the concepts, it can be seen that in the East Region of Cameroon, there is a distinction between autochthony and indigeneity.

Other authors writing on this subject of autochthony and indigeneity in East Cameroon have preferred to use the terms 'symbolic' autochthony and 'substantive' autochthony to refer to indigeneity and autochthony (Leonhardt 2006; Geschiere 2009).[30] 'Symbolic' autochthony, referred to as 'indigeneity' in this chapter, denotes people who are recognized as the first occupants of the land, but who do not benefit from any first occupant/son of the soil rights, while 'substantive' autochthony, referred to here as 'autochthony' denotes people who by virtue of their migration history are not the first occupants, yet tend to make claims to and get access to all the benefits that are tied to 'sons of the soil'. Leonhardt, for example, writes that although both the Baka and the Bantu inhabit the East Region of Cameroon, only the Bantu are rooted in the soil:

> While they [the Baka] are very much of the place ... farmer's rootedness in the soil allows them a sense of ownership, collectively and individually. Farmers believe that their fields and surrounding forests belong to them, whereas Baka have access to the hunting territory by virtue of their association with farmer 'patrons' (Leonhardt 2006: 73–74).

From this, it may be said that claims to belonging in the East Region are highly related to struggles to access resources.

The frame of administratively demarcated boundaries of belonging, specifically the phenomenon of unusual villages, was highlighted as a major source of contention and confrontation of versions of belonging. Even when the Baka asserted their belonging as indigenous peoples, their merging into Bantu villages made the Bantu claim that the Baka were locals under their villages. Whereas, when the Baka claimed to be locals, the Bantu contested that they were indigenous peoples who lived in camps as subquarters of their villages. This chapter also pointed to the fact that, contrary to much of the literature which has portrayed the Pygmies (Baka) as being very attached to the forest, with fixed emotional ties to their lifestyles therein, my field findings suggest that depending on the social locations of the Baka, their conceptions of home and belonging vary. The Baka who lived in Moloundou, in the Boumba and Ngoko Division, which is closest to the remaining dense forest bordering the DR Congo, tended to make more frequent references to places in the forest as their home, where they perform their cultural rites. The Baka of the Upper Nyong Division, which is closer to the urban centre of the region with limited forest, tended to reveal very strong emotional attachments to the roadsides as their homes, with an increasing tendency to gradually distance themselves from the forest as their home. In the same vein, the Baka of this division who lived in Baka villages showed stronger attachments to their villages than the Baka who lived in camps that were subquarters of Bantu villages. Also, younger Baka (often below the age of thirty-five) felt more at home on the roadsides than in the forest, and in most cases, tended to associate the 'homeness' of their parents with the forest. In these expressions of home, place of birth was for them a strong identifier of where they belonged. It was also observed that although these youths identified belonging with the roadsides that were their homes, the expression of home as the roadside did not immediately translate into a sense of belonging as indigenous peoples or autochthones.

This chapter demonstrated that most Baka are not very familiar with the international understandings of the concepts of indigenous peoples and autochthones. For the Baka who were conversant with these conceptual categories, asserting their belonging to one or both was always nuanced. Some Baka, who expressed home as being their roadside villages, rejected their categorization as indigenous peoples on the grounds that it was stigmatizing and derogatory. On the contrary, others on the same roadsides asserted their belonging to this category because according to them, their ancestors had been chased away from their forest homeland and they themselves were marginalized in terms of rights and privileges in forest exploitation. Although the different ways in which the Baka and the Bantu respectively emphasize their sense of belonging are always conflicting, both communities tend to intersect when using history, the metaphor of 'rootedness in the soil', as well as the issue of burial grounds, to legitimize their claims to belonging.

Notes

1. In Cameroon, the term 'village' is often used synonymously with tribes and ethnic groups (although sometimes, depending upon the context, an ethnic group may also be used to refer to a group of villages like Bantu, Bamileke, grass fields, etc.). The origin of the word 'village', like that of 'tribe', is highly contested, as will be seen in the following paragraphs.
2. From 1966 until 1990 multiple parties and freedom of association were banned in Cameroon; 'village of origin' and ethnicity did not play a vital role in the quest for

development or its benefits. Firstly, under the one-party system the aim was to cultivate a single national identity, and working for national development was highly commended. Secondly, national development was the reigning model of development against the contemporary targeted and/or decentralized local development models. It was only in the late 1980s and early 1990s, with the arrival of economic crises, multiparty politics, democratization, and local and regional developments that the emphasis on 'home' or 'village' of belonging became more resounding in survival struggles within Cameroonian society.

3. As discussed in previous chapters, these *'mongulous'* are often referred to as huts (Mballa 2009). However, due to post-colonial debates, which consider such appellations derogatory, I prefer to use the terms 'house' and 'dwelling place' interchangeably.

4. The Jengi is the Baka god of the forest and the Jengi project aims to conserve national parks in traditional ways, as the Pygmies did.

5. This concept of typicalness and belonging based on habitat will be further analysed in Chapter 4, where it will be demonstrated that even the Baka themselves use it to justify differentiation between them (The Baka-Baka and the Baka-Bantu).

6. As will be seen later in the book, this constructed distinctions of their livelihoods and habitats is being challenged by the Baka in the ways that they assert their belonging.

7. Their age is approximated because they do not have birth certificates. So, together with them, I used events such as independence and colonization to estimate their ages.

8. Bonado is the main Baka community located along the Abong-Mbang Yaoundé highway, and according to the Baka living there, the 'camp/village' has existed for more than sixty years. However, the debate of Bonado-Baka or Bonado III (to mean Bonado as a subquarter of the Bantu village Bonado) is still very hot and will be discussed later in Chapter 4.

9. The Baka of Mayos have been given a third-class chief and are administratively classified as an autonomous Baka village.

10. All the communities on this main road were interviewed to see if Baka on the same road have similar constructions. These interviews were passive so I have not included a complete list of all the communities in this research.

11. During the discussion a Bantu woman came and interfered and claimed to want to speak for the Baka, because according to her, she knows their culture. Detailed analysis will be made in the following chapters.

12. In this community there is also the 'camp/village'debate between Bingongol-Baka and Bingongol II.

13. In this column, those who had heard of the word 'indigenous' (just hearing the word is enough, irrespect of what it means to them); and in column 4 of the table, those who were aware of the European and American distinction means those who knew that there were European and American understandings of the terms 'indigenous peoples' and 'autochthones'.

14. The ages of the Baka were estimated based on their narrations about the time when President Ahmadou Ahidjo took power (independence). Most elderly Baka do not have birth certificates, thus it is difficult to give their exact ages.

15. *'Peuples autochtones'* and *'peuples autochtones marginalisés'* translate as autochthones and indigenous peoples. Some external actors simply use the word *'peuples autochtones'* in both cases.

16. The use of national development in this context refers to the sedentarization-related displacement of the Baka, which was aimed at fostering national development and enhancing the cultivation of a single national identity, as discussed in Chapter 1.

17. This research uses forest conservation and sustainable exploitation as the motive for population displacement as stated in policy documents without any further critical

questioning of its effectiveness. Nonetheless, I am conscious of the flaws and setbacks of these forest conservation and sustainable exploitation programmes in countries like Cameroon, where corruption is inbuilt in the social system. However, it is not within the context of this work to discuss these flaws and inefficiencies. For a better understanding of such flaws consult Tsing 2005 or Oyono 2005b.

18. This, to me, was a strategy to authenticate legitimacy on the part of the Bantu, as I will argue in Chapter 5.

19. The village is used here not in reference to a particular village, but rather constructed as a site of belonging as opposed to the forest.

20. By 'civilized' here, I am summarizing their words, which included: 'nous sommes déjà civilisés', 'nous ne sommes plus dans les ténèbres', 'nos enfants partent aussi à l'école'.

21. In Cameroon, being an indigene of a region translates to belonging as a 'son of the soil' to one of the villages in the region. In other words, having one of the villages of the region as home, where one belongs.

22. The cumbersome processes of obtaining community forest concessions have not been discussed here, since the focus is on who can belong to the community and not whether communities are able to overcome these cumbersome bureaucratic processes. However, it is important to note that in Cameroon 'collusion and corruption may prove more enduring than any other constraint to community forestry' Topa et al. (2009: 107).

23. It is important to mention here that the interlocutor had started his own local association to defend the rights of Baka peoples as indigenous peoples. He called it 'L'Association pour la défense des droits des peuples autochtones marginalisés de l'Est Cameroun' (Association for the protection of rights of indigenous peoples in eastern Cameroon).

24. Although the catechist referred to himself as an individual, the research did not aim to analyse the ways in which individual belonging was constructed.

25. Refer to Chapter 7 for the founding history of CADDAP.

26. Canadel (2010), writing on the 2010–2014 development plan of Dimako Council, has also mentioned Bantu chiefs as 'Les chefs de villages gèrent la vie socioéconomique de leur communauté et règlent aussi les conflits intra ou inter communautés'.

27. The forestry sector contributes 10% of Cameroon's GDP (Alemagi 2011: 65).

28. By categorical communities, I deviate slightly from Anderson's (1991) definition of imagined communities, and simply refer to the Bantu as a category (the poor) and the Baka (the poorest), with poverty reductively defined as an economic and material lack.

29. 'Their' is used in quotation marks because in the East Region, the legitimacy of the land and resources being theirs is highly contested.

30. As reflected in the publication years of these authors, they wrote at a time when the discussions of indigeneity as an imported global category in Cameroon were non-existent (2006) or relatively early (2009).

Chapter 3

RECONSTRUCTING 'ROOTEDNESS IN THE SOIL' TO AUTHENTICATE BELONGING TO THE ROADSIDES

છ૭·ᏱᏱ

[The] Baka do not have a very strong ancestral connection to the land. They have little genealogical recollection beyond the living generations, and their attitude towards the graves of the dead contains as much avoidance as it does reverence because of the association with loss. Farmers' mastery of the natural environment consists of subduing it to make it humanly productive. Baka mastery of the environment consists of appropriating its naturally occurring resources. Because Baka are not rooted in this way, farmers consider Baka to be wanderers (vagabonds) in the pejorative sense – free and mobile to a fault (Leonhardt 2006: 75).

In its 'traditional' understanding, belonging refers to the historical connections that people have, which establish social spaces by virtue of a protracted history of settlement, a cohesive sense of community and stable social institutions. Thus people belong to a place because they are tied to that place by their ancestry and history of residing there, with the right to exclude others. In other words, belonging invokes a sense of claim to physical space (Gotz and Simone 2003). Studies in human displacement and resettlement, migration and refugees have challenged these place-bounded approaches to understanding belonging. Malkki (1995) argues that such understandings fail to encompass the situation of displaced and resettled people, like the Baka in this case. Rather, they favour a more flexible approach that analyses how people make 'home away from home'. They argue that it is the latter approach that highlights the ways in which people who are displaced from their homelands not only focus on their former roots, but rather invent new ways of creating roots to belong in their new places. The discussions in this chapter subscribe to the latter approach of exploring belonging and focus on the question: How do the Baka authenticate their claims to belonging on the roadsides?

Before diving into exploring how the Baka reconstruct their rootedness in the soil to authenticate belonging on the roadsides, it is important to recall why the Baka have to authenticate their belonging on roadsides. In Chapter 1, it was said that, with the shift from national development approaches to decentralized local development, citizenship and belonging in Cameroon were expressed at two levels: belonging at the national level (national citizenship) and belonging at the local level (local citizenship). In the context of the Baka this could mean either autochthony (belonging as locals on the roadsides) or indigeneity ('strangers' on the roadsides who actually belong in the forest). Moreover, in Chapter 2, it was highlighted that, with the resettlement of the Baka on roadsides, these two conflicting versions of belonging (autochthony/being 'a local' and indegeneity) are either ascribed to people, or self-asserted. It was also demonstrated that each of these versions of belonging was associated with a pool of resources and power. For people to benefit from either pool of resources or power, they needed to authenticate or show proof of their belonging. Nonetheless, while both the Baka and the Bantu now reside on the roadsides, indigeneity as understood in the region is reduced to forest belonging, while autochthony is reduced to relations to the soil and thus roadside belonging.

From this perspective, as indigenous peoples the Baka's claims of belonging to the roadsides were highly contested. In effect, the Baka were often unmasked as 'not really' belonging, or even of being 'fake' autochthones (Geschiere and Jackson 2006: 1). The criteria for belonging were shown to be socially, culturally and historically produced and rendered meaningful, as Albiez et al. argued in their book (2011: 241).

Taking into consideration the above framings, it became clear to the Baka that being 'a son of the soil' or in other words, being 'rooted in the soil' was the major criterion used by the Bantu to contest the Baka's belonging as autochthones on the roadsides. The autochthony and belonging of the Baka were contested and negotiated in ways that were open to various interpretations and reinterpretations. Therefore, the Baka had to find ways of authenticating their belonging on roadsides by showing proof that they 'really' belonged.

To do this, the Baka tended to reconstruct the history of their settlement on roadside lands in ways that proved they belonged as 'members' and not as 'strangers'. The present chapter is grounded in the context of these strategies to authenticate belonging by the Baka. The chapter focuses on analysing ways in which the Baka reconstruct their rootedness to the land. In analysing this reconstruction, the chapter considers how people used their past to enact a sense of what it means to live in a place in terms of intimacy, ownership, usage and displacement or alienation (Brown 2006).

Structurally, the chapter is divided into two sections. The first section briefly captures the phenomena of 'firstcomers', 'first occupants' and 'rootedness in the soil' in the East Region of Cameroon. To do this, the section presents a brief historical narrative about the migration and settling of the East Region of Cameroon. Next, the section proceeds by discussing 'rootedness in the soil' and belonging in the East Region of Cameroon'. Following this discussion, the second section analyses the ways in which the Baka reconstruct their 'rootedness in the soil' as a strategy to legitimize their belonging.

'Firstcomers' and 'Rootedness in the Soil' in the East Region of Cameroon

History has it that Pygmies (the Baka inclusive) were the firstcomers to the Congo Basin, which engulfs the East Region of Cameroon (Logo 1998; Klieman 2003). However, unlike in other parts of the world where 'firstcomers' are automatically considered as being rooted in the land and thus belonging, the case is different for the Baka in the East Region of Cameroon. This is because the phenomenon of rootedness in the land places more emphasis on first occupants than on firstcomers. Hence, according to this emphasis firstcomers may not always be the first occupants and may thus have to prove their 'rootedness in the soil'. Even so, while it is thought that the Baka were authentically the firstcomers though not first occupants, there are still contests about their authenticity as firstcomers. This presents a double task for the Baka in their struggle to authenticate their rootedness 'in the soil' in roadside villages in the East Region of Cameroon. Firstly, they have to authenticate the fact that they were the firstcomers, after which they can show proof that they were also the first occupants. In view of this, the present section will first review the contests surrounding the Baka as firstcomers. Afterwards, it will proceed to discuss the disparity between firstcomers, first occupants and 'rootedness in the soil' as applied to the East Region of Cameroon.

Firstcomers: Contested Historical Narratives

As has been illustrated in the previous chapter, the framing of belonging in Cameroon is centred on the nature of relationship between the so-called 'firstcomers' and the 'latecomers' or 'strangers' (Geschiere and Jackson 2006).

In the East Region of Cameroon the question of who came first is a contested one. This section discusses the subject by reviewing some available historical accounts. In doing so, the following considerations have been made: given the fact that this study focuses mainly on the two broad categories of the Baka and the Bantu (the latter of which is made up of many subgroups), the summarized accounts do not give a detailed history of the migration for each Bantu subgroup in the region. For a more detailed historical account of these, consult Sinang (2005). Also, considering the fact that 'it is difficult to get the pre-history of the forest, [given] that the Baka did not record historical events in writing' (Bahuchet 1992: 30), the history of 'firstcomers' in the East Region of Cameroon as presented here is not one that was written by the Baka themselves.

Lee and Hitchcock make allusion to the fact that it is difficult to describe with certitude who the 'firstcomers' were:

> Until recently, archaeologists assumed that the Pygmies were the 'original' inhabitants of the rainforest where they had lived for millennia as hunters and gatherers before the arrival of agricultural peoples. But current opinion varies on whether humans indeed can live exclusively by foraging the wild products of the rainforest, or whether some form of symbiosis with farmers is a necessary part of the Pygmies' adaptation (Lee and Hitchcock 2001: 261).

In like manner, it has been argued that 'reason' and science question whether it is possible for humankind to survive on foraging (Dunn 1968; Headland 1987; Bailey et al. 1989, Headland and Bailey 1991; Biesbrouck, Elders and Rossel 1999). Biesbrouck et al. state that contemporary 'Pygmies' are not indigenous to the equatorial rainforest (1999: 131). Nonetheless, as Moïse (2014) notes, prior to the 'Bantu expansion', which took place between three and five thousand years ago, Pygmies were the first settlers in the equatorial rainforest. Sinang, writing on the historical relationships between the Baka Pygmies and the Bantu in southeast Cameroon, draws attention to conflicting historical accounts about the firstcomers in eastern Cameroon. On the one hand, he says that a considerable number of myths in Cameroon affirm that the Baka were the first occupants of eastern Cameroon and the Bantu only invaded later, during their migration, which led them to the central African forest. There they met the Pygmies, who served the Bantu as guides:

> Their [referring to the Bantu] fleeing led them to Central Africa right to the Oubangui forests in the seventeenth century, where they met the 'Pygmies'. These [the Pygmies] served them as guides, and refuelled them with fare consisting of honey, yam, meat, fruits and edible termites … The Bangando and the Essel [the Bantu] affirmed that their meeting with 'Pygmies' took place during their migration and that the latter served them as guides in their

progress and sometimes as scouts during the various war campaigns. Despite the absence of archaeological data, these traditions unanimously confirm the pre-existence of Pygmies in the forested region of the Southeast (Sinang 2005: 13; my own translation).

On the other hand, Sinang highlights the contests surrounding the claims of firstcomers when he quotes Eziem, writing on the history of the Congo Basin, who argues that the ancientness of the Pygmies over the Bantu in the Congo Basin is contestable because of similarities in their modes of living. In a similar vein, Sinang adds that the ancient population of the region was of two types: the big men and the small men (Sinang 2005: 17). For him, Bantus and Pygmies in the central African subregion have always lived so close to one another that it is not at all evident who came first. Trilles, a catholic missionary, argues however that Pygmies are the oldest human race living on Earth today and by virtue of this, Pygmies were the first inhabitants of the region (1945).

The Baka strongly agree with this latter assertion and during my fieldwork, some of them even recalled and narrated a myth, which they considered to be their myth of sovereignty in the forest. A Baka myth, very close to the myth that these Baka recounted, has also been reported by Brisson (1999b). These Baka recounted that, according to this myth, the Bantu of today were once Baka who did not respect the laws of the forest. The myth begins that a young Baka man called Zéngélé (who today is the ancestor of the Bantu) was hungry for meat. As a result of this hunger, he went to kill monkeys, but he killed more monkeys than he actually needed, thereby destroying the game that was for everybody. The Baka god, whom they call Komba, was so surprised at this that he transformed this Baka man Zéngélé into the fool of the forest (*'bête de broussse'*), who would later become the villager or *'Kaka'*. *Kaka* does not respect the laws of the forest, its silence, discreetness, moderation in hunting or the fact that Komba makes the game (*'gibier'*) for everybody (Brisson 1999b: 407). Abega and Logo also emphasize the fact that the Baka were the firstcomers, but they allude to the issue of firstcomers and first occupants in the region. They mention that, although the Baka were the first-comers, they were pushed further into the forest by the Bantu,[1] who cleared the forest to such an extent that it is possible for the Bantu to argue that they were the firstcomers on the particular sites that the Baka had left:

> In all the regions that they inhabit, the Baka are presented as the first occupants of the region. This data is recurrent, both in the narrations of the Pygmies themselves, as well as in the traditions of their neighbours. They were sent inwards towards the inhospitable regions of the forest by the Bantu. However, from one place to another, it is possible that the Bantu present themselves as the first arrivals on this particular site. This has important consequences on cohabitation rules (Abega and Logo 2005: 118–119; my own translation).

From these, it may be argued that while there is a majority consensus about the fact that Pygmies were the firstcomers to the equatorial rainforests, there is an intriguing twist to the concept of 'firstcomers' and 'first occupants' in eastern Cameroon. This twist is what I call 'unrooted firstcomers versus rooted occupants'. This is because under the country's formal land law, occupation of land is defined by rootedness in the land, which has an agricultural dimension, as will be seen in the next subsection. Thus, although the politics of belonging in Cameroon is based on the relationship between 'firstcomers' and 'latecomers'/'strangers', the concept of 'unrooted firstcomers' has complicated common sense understandings in the study of belonging. In principle, 'unrooted firstcomers' have become 'latecomers' and 'strangers' while rooted 'latecomers' have become first occupants who belong. This twist of 'unrooted firstcomers versus rooted occupants' is the focus of the next subsection.

'Rootedness in the Soil': How 'Unrooted' Firstcomers Became Latecomers and Strangers

> The metaphor of the 'the soil' is more connected to autochthony than to indigenousness. This is part of the reason that Baka are clearly indigenous but ambiguously autochthones. 'The soil' is an agricultural metaphor; farmers are of the soil (Leonhardt 2006: 71).

In most parts of Africa, control over land is a sign of the extent to which people belong. This is because membership of a specific community is intimately tied to belonging to the land of that community. In this light, the politics of belonging cannot be separated from that of land and land rights (Lentz 2007). In Cameroon, formal law stipulated that Cameroonians occupying or using land as of 5 August 1974 (thirty days after the 1974 land laws were passed) could apply for formal ownership rights to the land. This law defines 'occupying or using lands' in a very complex but reductive way. According to the law, 'occupying or using lands' also referred to as 'man's clear control of the land and evident development' is the exercise of agriculture and/or the construction of permanent houses on the land where people resided. This definition is incompatible with the ways in which most Baka of this era (before 1974) occupied the lands on which they resided. During this era, the houses of most Baka were temporary dwellings and their livelihood was dependent on gathering and hunting. This form of occupation, unlike permanent agriculture, left no marks on the land. Thus, although there is a majority consensus that the Baka were the firstcomers, the law defining land occupancy in Cameroon has transformed the Baka into 'unrooted firstcomers' and thus strangers, while their Bantu neighbours have become 'rooted occupants' who authentically belong. This transformation is further legitimized by the fact that Baka ancestral lands, which the Baka 'occupied' before the 1974 land law, now form part of the state's permanent forest domain today.[2]

Similarly, the Baka did not have any attachments to the burial grounds of their ancestors (RASED 2006). The Baka deserted places (camps) in which they had lost one of their members, whereas often in Cameroon, rootedness and belonging can be authenticated by reference to specific lands on which people's ancestors are buried (Geschiere and Nyamnjoh 2000). In effect, Geschiere and Nyamnjoh demonstrate that one way to test people's belonging in a region or village is simply to ask them to show where their ancestors are buried. In the event that people are unable to show the burial locations of their ancestors in the said region, they are considered not to belong there. To strengthen this point, the authors quote Samuel Eboua, a leader of the political party Mouvement pour la Démocratie et le Progrès (Movement for Democracy and Progress, MDP) in Cameroon who said that 'every Cameroonian is an *allogène* [stranger] anywhere else in the country … apart from where his ancestors lived and … where his mortal remains will be buried' (ibid. 434). Chabal further supports their assertion and adds that 'the link to the ancestors, wherever they are buried … cannot be disregarded' (2009: 29). Paradoxically for the Baka, they did not have the same cultural attachment to burial grounds as their Bantu counterparts:

> As soon as they realized that there was no hope of recovery for the ailing one and that the efforts of the *'nganga'* [witch doctors] had no effect, men, women and children then deserted the *'Balà'* [camps] to settle in another territory. Only two initiated men, who were believed to be 'immunized' against the powers of evil spirits, remained with the dying one. As soon as he expired, they would completely demolish the *'mongulu'* [hut] where the corpse was. After they had hastily completed these operations, the two Baka who had attended to the sick one until the final hours of his life, ran as fast as they could to the new camp (RASED 2006: 18).

From these sources, it is clear that in the Cameroonian sense of the term, even though the Baka are considered to be the firstcomers, they were 'unrooted firstcomers'. In view of this and the fact that proof of 'rootedness to the soil' is essential to authenticating belonging, it was intriguing to understand that the Baka have resorted to reconstructing 'rootedness in the soil' to authenticate their belonging on the roadsides. Although there are discussions in academia about the risks of reducing belonging to 'rootedness' (Malkki 1992), the situation in the East Region of Cameroon presents a special case.

How the Baka Reconstruct 'Rootedness in the Soil' on their Roadside Settlements

As discussed earlier, in the past, the Baka did not occupy the land in ways that showed their clear control of the land and evident development. They did not plant fruit trees nor build houses that lasted. They moved from one place to another and described themselves as 'mothers of the forest' (Owono 1997). Also, the Baka did not have attachments to the burial locations of their ancestors. They deserted their camps each time a member of the camp died. In the same light, the Baka interpreted the meaning of the word 'Baka' as unstable and mobile people who behaved like birds and did not have a fixed location:

> To the question of why they call themselves Baka, they responded that they were like birds that do not stay in one place; they stay for a while on the *'Bakama'* [branch] before flying. This name, therefore, symbolizes the freedom and great mobility that characterize them (Dellemmes 1985: 55; my own translation).

Taking into consideration the Baka interpretation of the word 'Baka' as 'unstable and mobile', it may be argued that the very meaning of the word cemented the 'unrooted' nature of the Baka on the lands which they occupied. However, it is important to clarify here that in the past (prior to the displacement of the Baka to the roadsides), there existed what the Baka referred to as *'Paki'*, which were vast forest territories in which each Baka community lived and migrated within to carry out their livelihood activities. Thus, in those days, it could be considered that the Baka belonged to the forest in the *Paki* where their community resided.

However, as the Baka have migrated from the forest to the roadsides, where their belonging is contested, they are now reconstructing 'a rootedness in the soil' to authenticate their belonging on these roadsides. This subsection analyses this reconstructed rootedness by the Baka. The analysis focuses on four aspects: the reinterpretation of the name 'Baka'; their engagement in agriculture and building of houses; their relation and attachments to burial grounds; and their rejection of the appellation 'camp' in favour of 'village'.

The Reinterpretation of the Name 'Baka' and its Relationship with Being 'Rooted in the Soil'

As noted above, the name 'Baka' in the past was related to a mobile and unstable people within a particular *Paki* in the forest. Defining themselves as

Baka meant that the Baka took pride in their mastery of the forest in ways that did not necessitate road construction, noise, or rupture with the harmonious forest ecosystem of which they were a part. According to some elderly Baka interviewed, being Baka meant that their mastery of, 'intimacy' with and belonging to the forest were such that no outsider could easily predict their exact location and harm them.

According to some Baka whom I interviewed, their mobile nature meant that they really belonged to the forest and mastered 'the rules to live by'. Mobility was considered a strategy of conservation that highlighted their absolute mastery of and belonging to the forest. This, according to these Baka, justifies why their ancestors preferred to be called Baka rather than 'Pygmies', which already had pejorative connotations, even during the time of their ancestors.

Based on this, it can be argued that the Baka enjoyed close sociocultural attachments with the forest, which they considered to be their ancestral territory. These attachments greatly shaped their culture, livelihood and collective belonging to the extent that early anthropologists like Balif labelled them as 'forest experts' and the Baka themselves identified with being 'mothers of the forest'[3] (Owono 1997: 3; Brisson 1999a[4]). Thus, there existed distinct, autonomous and well-defined culturally sustaining connections between the forest and the livelihood experiences of the Baka. At this time the Baka prided themselves on the fact that they were 'doctors of the forest', with an influx of travellers from other parts of the country who came to see and consult these forest experts. These champions of traditional healing used tree skins and leaves and granted success, mystical recipes, power, intelligence and wisdom (Owono 1997). They belonged to the forest in such a way that they said when their forest dies, they will die, too (ibid.). In view of this, it can be argued that, in the past, belonging for the Baka was always a function of rootedness to the forest rather than to the soil. However, since they have resettled along the roadsides where belonging is a function of 'rootedness to the soil', there has been a shift in the ways that they reconstruct rootedness so as to accommodate the changing requirements of belonging on the roadsides. One of these ways is the reinterpretation of the word 'Baka'.

During a focus group discussion in Mballam-Lomié, participants had different interpretations of the appellation 'Baka'. For some of the participants, the word 'Baka', which they wrote as '*BO'AKA*', means '*où est l'homme*' (where man is). For Jean, one of the interlocutors, this translation reveals the embedded nature of the relationships that the Baka people entertain with the forest. To him, the word 'Baka' means belonging to the forest, but not to a specific place inside that forest. Thus, the Baka belong both to the forest and on the roadsides, since the roadsides were once parts of the forest but have been cleared. For others, clinging to the appellation 'Baka' was no longer relevant in today's world, where there are medical doctors everywhere and the Baka can no longer take pride in the fact that they belong to the forest because of their mastery of medicinal plants. According these other Baka, I needed to shift my research focus from 'what the word "Baka" means', to 'what the Baka of today can do'. In almost every camp I visited, the trend to reinterpret the meaning of the word 'Baka' was similar. Additionally, there was a significant shift from emphasis on the word 'Baka' to place of birth as an indicator of rootedness and belonging. This was common among the younger generations of the Baka (born after 1961).

Younger Baka Generations: Emphasis on Place of Birth to Legitimize Roadside Rootedness

There is a new divisive dynamism in the way that the roadside-born younger generations of Baka legitimize their rootedness. Younger generations of Baka claim that they are rooted and belong to the roadsides, because they were born on these roadsides. For them, rootedness is a function of where a person was born. In this light, although the appellation 'Baka' means mobile people, this younger generation claim that they were born after the era of mobility. For them, they were born and raised in permanent camps. Thus, the name 'Baka' as interpreted in the past cannot be used to challenge their 'rootedness in the soil' on the roadside camps where they were born. On the contrary, these younger Baka generations tend to associate their parents' belonging with the forest, because their parents were born and raised in the forest. Moreover, they associated traditional medicine with their parents, born in the forest. The strategy of using place of birth to authenticate rootedness is stronger in younger generations born on the roadside in the Upper Nyong Division, which is closer to Bertoua (the regional headquarters), than in those born on roadsides in places like Moloundou and Yokadouma, where some Baka still identify belonging with the forest (even though they were all born in roadside camps). Having discussed how younger generations of the Baka use their place of birth to authenticate their belonging on the roadsides, the next phenomenon which some Baka used to authenticate their rootedness was their engagement with agriculture and building of permanent houses.

Engagement in Agriculture and Building of Permanent Houses as a Strategy to Authenticate Roadside Belonging

In the East Region of Cameroon, 'the soil' is connected to autochthony. 'The soil' is an agricultural metaphor: farmers are of the soil, and the Baka are clearly indigenous because they are considered non-agriculturalists (Leonhardt 2006: 71). This view is largely shared among inhabitants of the region and was reflected in participants' discussions during my fieldwork. One of the Bantu elders put it this way:

> From time immemorial, the Bantu have always been agriculturalists who are rooted in their lands. This question of who belongs where is not one to be debated. We all know that the Baka only moved to the roadsides a few decades ago. Before even the whites came, they were forest peoples, and they still are. To debate about where the Baka belong is like saying mosquitoes belong to the house. So why should the government now sow disorder in the community by taking our lands to give to them? The only thing is for the government to allow them to hunt and gather as they want. After all, that's how they lived, and we – the Bantu – still came and met the forest intact. I think the main problem is not us [the Bantu]. The problem is these logging companies which have made the government chase the Baka out of the forest (Bantu elder, Banana, Nov. 2011).

Such strong assertions of 'rootedness in the soil' and the devout feeling towards it as constructed by the Bantu 'seems natural to sedentary agricultural people' (Tuan 1977: 156). As discussed in Chapter 1, in the early 1960s, agricultural production and national identity were inseparable phenomena in Cameroonian life. The Baka were forced to engage in agriculture in order to belong as national citizens. During this time, government administrative officials, assisted and advised by village chiefs, distributed land to some Baka families to enable them to cultivate cocoa:

> The administration launched an operation known as 'operation thousand feet' aimed at developing cash crop production among the Baka and to grant them a place on the roadsides. The divisional officers and agricultural monitors, assisted and advised by village chiefs of the 'villagers', were responsible for redistributing land to Baka families so that they could cultivate cocoa, as well as providing them with identity cards (Robillard 2010: 119; my own translation).

In some cases, like in Ekom, Catholic missionaries bought land, titled it and gave it to the Baka (Abega and Logo 2005: 119) to consolidate their belonging. In this light, sedentarized and assimilated Baka became 'ambiguously autochthones' since they became farmers of the land (Geschiere 2009). However, since both the Baka and the Bantu are now engaged in agriculture to varying degrees, the scramble for rootedness is no longer negotiated based on who is a farmer in relationship with the soil and who is not. Instead it is based on: Who came first? Who discovered who? Who brought who to the roadsides?

In discussing these narratives, both the Baka and the Bantu tend to reconstruct different histories, all of which rely on the interplay of memory and history to authenticate their rootedness on the roadsides. Although the reliance on the interplay of memory and history to authenticate belonging may be contested on the grounds that memory rarely carries back more than three generations, unless refreshed by writing or shrines and rituals (Gillet 2002: 22), ongoing struggles over material resources in the East Region of Cameroon have reshaped the way in which the Baka make sense of their rootedness and belonging on the roadsides (Baker 2012: 26). In reconstructing rootedness, both the Baka and the Bantu highlight two major narratives, which are invasion/non-occupancy and being brought to the roadsides by the Bantu or by missionaries.

Invasion/Non-occupancy

On the one hand, the Baka reconstruct a history that reveals an invasion by the Bantu. On the other hand, the Bantu reconstruct a history of non-occupancy by the Baka and argue that:

> When [the Bantu] started to build [our] villages, the forest was empty. There were no other people. We knew that the Baka lived there too, but we never saw or felt them ... When we first saw the Baka, they had no clothes. But we ... already had clothes and salt (Rupp 2011: 79).

Rupp further argues that the statement 'the forest was empty' highlights the point that the initial Bakwélé (Bantu) perceptions were that the Baka were invisible, generally insignificant people lacking basic elements of social decency. Additionally in Rupp's analysis of social insignificance is the issue of 'selective forgetting'. Indeed, during my fieldwork, most Bantus hardly recalled anything about their own migration into the East Region of Cameroon, yet they could remember accounts which said they were the first to settle and occupy the roadsides. Garbutt, studying the local settler authenticity in Australia, reports similar narratives of selective forgetting when he mentions 'the status of the locals and the born-and-bred settler Australians as pre-eminently belonging in place depends on selectively forgetting settler migration while, paradoxically, maintaining a memory of first settlement' (2011: 5). In this regard, it may be argued that mechanisms which transmit ideas about the past could be manipulated by wielders of cultural and political power (Innes 2009). On the part of the Baka, they recalled that it was the Bantu who cleared the forest inwardly to meet them:

> The Baka did not come out to meet the Bantu; rather, the Bantu came in to meet us by constantly clearing the forest to set up their plantations (Baka elder, Banana, Oct. 2011).

The version of this Baka seems to have some historical evidence taking into consideration that, according to Moïse, the Bantu peoples first encountered 'Pygmies' in the forest during the 'Bantu expansion', when the first peoples to migrate into the equatorial forest from the north, speakers of Bantu languages, moved from their homeland in the Nigeria/Cameroon borderlands across most of the continent south of the equator (Moïse 2014: 90–91). Nonetheless, sedentarized Baka seem to have a different narrative of reconstructing rootedness, which I have called the narrative of being brought by the Bantu or by missionaries to the roadsides.

The Bantu Brought the Baka to the Roadsides Versus Missionaries Brought the Baka to the Roadsides

The Bantu construct a history according to which they brought the Baka to the roadsides to teach them agriculture. However, the Baka have reconstructed a history which shows that missionaries, illness and the government made them resettle on the roadsides and engage in agriculture. According to Libala Justine, the mother of chief Nouchtegenou of Mayos-Dimako village, the Baka of Mayos came to reside on the roadside without any Bantu intervention. In the early 1970s, they migrated from another nearby Baka camp called Nkoumadjab. The reasons advanced for their migration were that a Bamileke[5] man who traded in timber employed them to serve as plank transporters from one forest around Mayos to his plank mill, which was located in Mayos. The distance from Nkoumadjab, where they previously resided, was a long way from Mayos and there were many pregnant women transporting these planks. Taking into consideration the long distances and the pregnant women, the Baka decided to start a new camp in Mayos to shorten their trekking distances. Thus, according to Libala, there were no grounds on which the Bantu could claim that they had brought the Baka to the roadsides to engage in agriculture. A Bantu elder from the Mayos region claimed that his grandparents told him that they were the ones who gave the Baka of Mayos the land on which they now reside.

In like manner, in Abakoum-Lomié, the Bantu elders said that the Baka of Abakoum had been the slaves of their grandparents, and were given the land on which they now resided. These elders recalled that as kids they were always sent by their parents to go and call their slaves (referring to the Baka). According to them, it is inconceivable that the 'Bayah' (a pejorative word used by the Bantu in this village to remind the Baka that they are slaves, with animal ancestors and that they belong to the forest) begin to claim rootedness on the roadsides today (interview with Jean, Oct. 2011).

According to these Bantu elders (whose views did not necessarily represent the views of the majority of Bantu elders who I interviewed), the Baka were discovered and brought to the roadside by their ancestors. The Baka have no rootedness to speak of, because no matter how engaged they are in agriculture, they remain strangers ('*allogènes*'). For these elders, phenomena like the construction of the road, the arrival of 'the whites' and interventions by development organizations were to blame for what they called a brutal change in the course of history. One of the Bantu added that in view of this trend, nothing would surprise him – including if one day the Baka stand to say that they want to be the paramount chief of the Bantu village. Cheekily, he said that 'it happened with President Obama of the USA, so why not with their Baka. In the world of today, everything is becoming possible'. Intriguingly, during the same interview with these Bantu elders, a young Bantu child of about twelve, listening to his father, suddenly said 'when I grow up I will chase away all those *Bayah* people. They should go back to the forest if they do not want to obey' (Bantu boy, Abakoum, Dec. 2011). When I asked him why he thought the *Bayah* (Baka) should go back to the forest, he said because they came from the forest and his parents gave them the land, yet they are not obedient. This discussion by the Bantu in this community is not far from what Pemunta observed and quoted a Bantu village head (chief) as saying:

> The Bantu village head confirmed: the Pygmies are my property; they are under my responsibility and control. My parents adopted them and I do not understand why we should keep bickering with them over our land. My brother suggested to them that they should go back to the bush since he wanted to farm on the land occupied by the Pygmies. (2011: 9).

Rene, a Baka elite and treasurer of Association Baka (ASBAK) from Abakoum-Baka, however, recognized the above-mentioned pejorative word '*Bayah*' and added that, to him, it is intimidation aimed at reinforcing the hegemony of the Bantu. For most Baka, the Bantu do not only refute their rootedness on the roadsides. The Bantu go even further to reinscribe the 'unrootedness' of the Baka across generations using intimidating words like '*Bayah*', '*les Gorrilles*' (gorillas), '*nos gens là*' (our people) and '*les gens de la forêt*' (people of the forest) to instil in the minds of younger Baka generations the sense of being owned by the Bantu and not really belonging on the roadsides. To challenge this intimidation, which the Baka sometimes referred to as a pejorative oral falsehood transmitted across generations, Rene said that he had taken it upon himself to educate younger Baka about how the Baka came to settle along the roadsides, so that no Bantu man could intimidate them by saying that they do not belong. Rene added that all his children in the camp now know that Abakoum is their home and there is no second home. The forest is where they go to look for food, just like their Bantu neighbours do. From this, it is clear that with dwindling resources and the struggle for belonging in order to access these resources, the authenticity of rootedness is not only constructed, but also transmitted across generations. It can be argued that for the Baka 'home and movement are not necessarily directly or neatly opposed; people's identifications with and relationships to place are, rather, much more complex than either "rooted belonging" or "rootless mobility" … places must be understood … as flexibly constructed by people through their own attachments' (Baker 2012: 26).

In the process of reconstructing rootedness on the roadsides, the Baka of Abakoum recalled that their village came into existence in 1960 and was founded by missionaries. They mentioned that since the founding of their village, they have been involved in agriculture and have built permanent houses. For these Baka, they belonged in ways that ought not to be contested. According to them, the only advantage the Bantu had which enabled them to contest the rootedness of the Baka was the fact that the Baka did not have any elites[6] to enlighten them on how to register their lands. Thus, they did not benefit from the 1974 Land Act. In this light, the real challenge to their roadside rootedness was not their 'unrootedness' but rather their lack of elites, whom they frequently referred to as torch-bearers. One of the Baka elders in Abakoum stressed that:

> No Bantu man brought us to the roadside here. We came to settle here through some white missionaries who were walking in the forest and found my great grandfather very sick, to the point of death. So they told him and other members of the camp to move out of the forest and to come and settle on the roadside here, so that if he fell sick again, it would be easy for us to come to their hospital (Baka elder, Abakoum, Dec. 2011; my own translation).

This elder's narration is closer to what Robillard (2010: 117) noted when she quoted a source from the Catholic Archives in Bertoua which mentions that a Baka was sent to go and look for other Baka in the forest so that they could settle on the roadsides:

> A Baka well-known among his people was asked to go and look for his brothers, wherever they were scattered in the forest, so that they should come and settle on the roadside (letter dated 29 May 1973, Archives of the Diocese of Bertoua; my own translation).

To further support the narrative that nobody brought the Baka to the roadsides, another Baka elder in Bigongol recalled that his grandparents were the first people to settle on the roadside where they now reside. He recounted that his grandfather told them it was a group of Baka women who founded their village even before the Bantu arrived. For this Baka elder, their rootedness on the roadside is based on the fact that his parents, like their Bantu neighbours, occupied the lands on which they resided by planting palms and food crops. From this it can be said that some Baka tend to use their engagement in agriculture and building of houses as a strategy to authenticate rootedness and roadside belonging.

Intriguingly, the Bantu in Bingogol argued that the Baka are 'unrooted' because they migrated from the forest to meet the Bantu on the roadsides. One of the Bantu elders added that they obstructed the Baka from applying to become an independent Baka village because 'it was impossible for immigrants to form a country in their host country'. According to these Bantu, the Baka are just immigrants camping on part of their lands. They are not rooted in any way and this is why the Bantu call it a Baka camp, which is the same as saying a subquarter of their village. This contestation has tended to cloud the 'firstcomer'/'latecomer' relationship between the Baka and the Bantu of Bigongol, such that even among the Baka there was an internal divide as to whether they were a camp that belonged to the Bantu or a village (Bingongol-Baka) that has not yet been recognized by the government.

In this divide, some Baka argued that they belonged to Bigongol-Baka, because they are autochthones and do not belong to any Bantu village. However, others argued that they belonged to Bingongol II – a subquarter of the bigger Bantu village. The Baka who claimed that Bingongol was a Baka village refuted the appellation 'Baka camp'. For them, calling Bigongol a camp meant that they were temporary, not rooted, not at home, not belonging and thus would one day leave. This argument about what the appellation 'camp' insinuated was raised by many other Baka elders. Helen, a Baka activist and elite further added that:

> We must ban that word 'camp'; when people continue to call our dwelling places camps, it is a way of saying that we do not belong here. More so, it makes the Bantu understand that one day we will leave. This is why I tell all my brothers to use the word 'village'. As such, with time, people will really understand that we belong here just like others (Helen during BBP conference, Bertoua, June 2013; my own translation).

Authors like Abega and Logo (2005: 225) have also alluded to the same issue when they say that:

> The creation of third-class chieftaincies of Pygmies is one of the questions that raise the recognition of citizenship of the Pygmies in Cameroon and the securing of their land rights (my own translation).

On the contrary, the Baka who said Bigongol was still a camp argued that they were parasites in the Bantu village that welcomed their grandparents. Thus, they were a subquarter belonging to the bigger Bantu village. These Baka were promoters of the phenomenon of '*nos frères du village*' (our brothers of the village), which I highlighted in Chapter 2. It was fascinating to listen to these Baka who now reside on the roadsides with their Bantu neighbours refer constantly to their Bantu neighbours as '*nos frères du village*', whereas the Bantu constantly refer to the Baka as 'people of the forest' or '*les gens là*' (those people). In view of this '*nos frère du village*' phenomenon among some Baka, the question was whether or not belonging for these Baka has remained place-bounded, despite their moving to the roadsides. Since the Bantu were the first to have contact with the colonial masters, they are more rooted in the land and there is no need for Baka 'who just came out of the forest' to claim that they belong and are rooted like the Bantu. According to these Baka, the Baka are not agriculturalists and will never be, irrespective of how hard they try. One of them went further, to add that:

Just as the Baka master the forest and its laws, so, too, do the Bantu master the land and its laws. Baka people do not have any secret tradition or norms about the soil; they have no god of the soil. How do they want to claim authority when they cannot communicate with their ancestors? (Bingongol, Jan. 2011; my own translation).

To these Baka, rootedness is not a function of agricultural cultivation but rather a function of intimate secret relationships with the land. This comes close to what Paradies calls 'essentialized indigeneity', and argues that it 'coalesces around specific fantasies of exclusivity, cultural alterity, marginality, physicality and morality, which leave an increasing number of indigenous people vulnerable to accusations of inauthenticity' (2006: 355).

Most intriguing in this 'intra-camp' divide at Bigongol was the fact that the Baka who said Bigongol was a village and not a camp were all farmers with their own cocoa and plantain farms, whereas those who said it was a camp decried their exploitation and torture by the Bantu. This suggests that for the latter category of Baka, rootedness and belonging are fixed and place-bounded concepts. This defies the fluidity of rootedness and belonging exhibited by sedentarized Baka, who have a progressive conception of home and rootedness.

Until now, I have been discussing how the Baka reconstructed the history of their engagement in agriculture as a means to authenticate rootedness to their roadside dwellings. Throughout the discussion, three major points were highlighted. Firstly, that rootedness, just like belonging, for the Baka is a very fluid and contested concept, which creates divisions among the

Baka. Secondly, that even Baka residing in the same roadside camps reconstructed the history of their settlement differently. Thirdly, that with dwindling resources and the struggle for belonging, both the Baka and the Bantu have invented narratives to authenticate rootedness, which they cautiously transmit across generations through oral narrations. In view of this, it may be argued that among the Baka, the reconstruction of history is not the same at all levels. 'It is shaped by specific social and historical imperatives. At the local level [of the village/camps] it is driven by both internal needs and external forces. As such, two levels of history can be observed: a history closely related to its internal social and political structure on the one hand, and another closely related to the globalising influences of the colonial experience and nation state building on the other' (Vubo 2003: 598).

Baka Relations and Attachments to Burial Grounds as a Means to Authenticate Rootedness

Many communities in Africa emphasize burial grounds as the basis for asserting rootedness to the soil where one belongs (Ojwang and Mugambi 1989; Cohen and Odhiambo 1992; Geschiere and Nyamnjoh 2000; Page 2007). Funerals and burial places are viewed as pointers of where one actually belongs (Geschiere 2005: 47). In most parts of Cameroon, the funeral is the ultimate moment of confirming a person's origin and also the belonging of his people (ibid.). In a study among the Bamileke (western francophone region) of Cameroon, Geschiere and Nyamnjoh (2000) highlight the pertinence of burial grounds as a pointer to rootedness and belonging in Cameroon. They refer to the case of a Bamileke politician who in his desperation to belong went as far as exhuming his deceased father's body. They say that this Bamileke politician was born and bred in the anglophone region but was rejected by the Bamileke community because his deceased father had not been buried in Bamileke soil. In his struggle to belong, the politician disinterred his father's remains, purchased a piece of land, and reburied him among the Bamileke, chiefly because people belong where their ancestors are buried and where they themselves will be buried. Following the same pattern, in the East Region of Cameroon, the Bantu attach a lot of importance to graves and burial grounds as indicators of belonging. In general, graves are dug in front of the compound, as may be seen in Figure 3.1. As one of my Bantu interlocutors recounted, 'some Bantus in this division prefer not to eat properly, only to save money and cement/tile a grave, because then people will know that the deceased person existed and belonged to that family and village' (interview with Emile, Doumé-Abong-Mbang, Upper Nyong Division, Nov. 2011). Indeed, during my stay in the

Figure 3.1 A Bantu grave in front of the house.
Source: photograph by the research assistant (Aug. 2013, Bertoua).

field, especially in the Upper Nyong Division, I noticed that most graves are either cemented or tiled, even when the houses that the graves belong to seem to be very traditional (made of mud and sticks and roofed with thatch).

Historically, the Baka did not have such close attachments to the burial grounds of their ancestors. Burial grounds were deserted and new camps started. In this light, the Baka, unlike the Bantu, did not associate their 'rootedness in the soil' with the burial grounds of their ancestors. According to the Baka chief in Mendjou, they were 'masters of the forest' not because they buried their ancestors in the forest, but because they understood the divine rules of the forest:

> We were the patrons of the forest, not because we buried our ancestors there, but because we mastered the divine rules of the forest. You see, the Bantu tell us to go into the forest because our ancestors were buried there, but a Baka man has never operated like that. We have our ways of doing things and they have theirs. For example, they reverence graves to the point that they do not only bury their dead in front of their houses, but they take pride in putting tiles on these graves, whereas their own houses are not cemented. The Bantu man has always attached great importance to graves (Baka chief, Mendjou, July 2013; my own translation).

Indeed, the Baka had relations with their ancestors but not with the burial grounds of their ancestors. However, since the Baka settled on roadsides, their relationship with burial grounds has changed. RASED (2006: 19) highlights that 'due to their settlement, death no longer causes panic and the desertion of the "*Bala*" [camps]. The Baka now bury their dead. They dig the grave and manufacture bamboo coffins' (RASED 2006: 19). This switch to burying their dead in graves inside the camps/villages where they live may be explained by the fact that land has become scarce and they are obliged to live in fixed places. What is intriguing about the new relationship the Baka have developed with burial grounds is where they bury their dead, who can bury dead where, and where home is. These aspects reveal the new ways in which the Baka make sense of their 'rootedness in the soil' and belonging on roadsides.

During a focus group discussion in Bonado, one of the first Baka road-side settlements located on the Yaoundé-Bertoua highway, members of the camp animatedly pointed to a grave (Figure 3.2) in front of their camp as a signifier of the fact that they are rooted in the soil and belong to the 'camp/village'.[7]

In view of this, the question that comes to mind is why do the Baka, who in the past avoided the burial grounds of their dead and ancestors, now bury their dead in front of their camps/villages? Common sense would have it

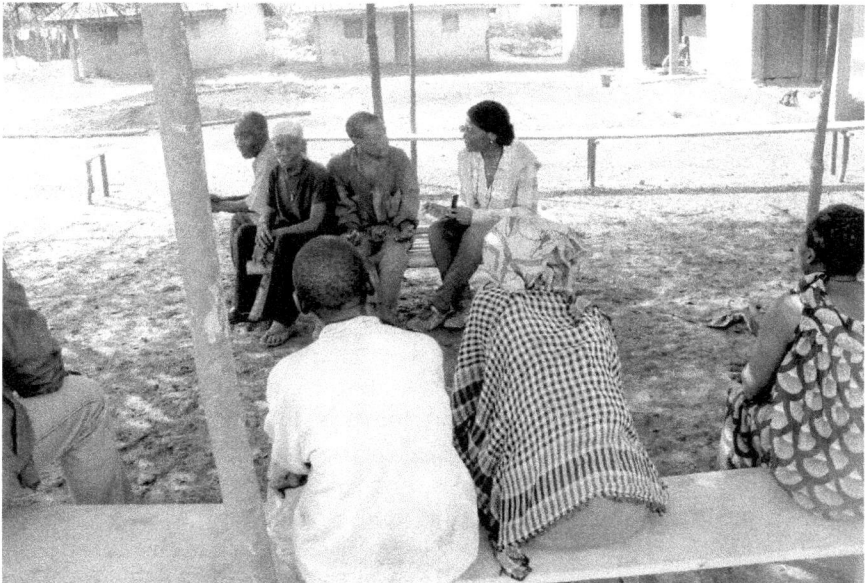

Figure 3.2 The grave of a Baka camp member in Bonado. In the picture, the grave is the pile of soil behind the three Baka men.
Source: photograph by the research assistant (Nov. 2011).

that since they are now forced to settle permanently on roadsides, where land is scarce, they would bury their dead behind the camps since it is in their background to avoid graves. The answer to this question, discovered through fieldwork, was tricky but fascinating. An aunt of the deceased boy said that the boy's grave was dug in front of the house, like the Bantu do, because the Baka belong to the roadsides:

> Look at the grave of our son. You can see that it is also in front of the house like that of the Bantu, right? This is because we belong here and will go nowhere else. In the past, our ancestors abandoned the camps when a member was dead, but today, things have changed. If we abandon it, where will we go? More so, when we bury our dead in front of our houses like this, the Bantu can no longer threaten us that we should leave (Bonado-Doumé, Nov. 2011; my own translation).

From this quote, which highlights burial in front of the house, it is clear that the Baka not only bury their dead in front of the camp/village, but also in front of the house where the deceased person belonged. Moreover, burial is now done in front of houses instead of behind them for two reasons. Firstly, to let the Bantu know that their dead have been buried in the camp and they can no longer move (which may be interpreted as a way for them to claim their land rights and relationships to the soil). Thus, even if they were to be evicted forcefully, nobody would occupy their camps/villages because there are graves right at the entrances. Pemunta also alluded to this explanation when narrating an eviction dispute, during which the brother of a Bantu chief wanted the Baka to go back to the forest where they belonged. He quoted the Bantu chief who said that 'the Baka refused to go under the pretext that their ancestor's bones were buried here' (2011: 9). A second reason advanced for burial in front of the camps was for the spirit of the dead to watch over the camp.[8] What I find interesting about the Baka burying their dead in front of the house was the fact that in general, only camps/villages which did not have their own land title insisted on burial in front of the camps. In other camps, where the government had recognized their land occupation and/or granted them the status of a village, camp members were not very keen on burying their dead in front of the house as a strategy to authenticate their rootedness in the soil.

Among the Baka, burial grounds and rootedness in the soil were not only framed along the lines of belonging to the roadsides against Bantu contestations. It extended into the internal dynamics of Baka society. In one of the Plan International constructed Baka villages, some Baka said that when Plan Bertoua selected their village to benefit from its building project, some Baka from other camps quickly came and set up '*mongulus*' (traditional Baka houses) in the camp, thinking that they would benefit from the construction programme. However, the Baka of this Plan-assisted village rejected them, because the parents of the other Baka were buried in a different roadside camp, and thus they belonged to that camp.[9]

In a similar vein, the Baka in Elandjo village described a chieftaincy conflict between big Elandjo and small Elandjo. The Baka in small Elandjo recounted that their parents had died and were buried in small Elandjo. Pointing to a place in front of their camp, these Baka said that the bones of their parents were there. Thus, they could not leave the bones of their parents and migrate again to another place. For them, they belonged to small Elandjo. Even if the Bantu disturbed them, they added, it would be a waste of time because the Bantu cannot farm on the graves of people who they do not know.

To further stress this emphasis now being laid on burial grounds by the Baka, these Baka of small Elandjo referred to their brother who was enthroned chief but who had left the camp with other camp members and started the big Elandjo camp. Two of his children had died in small Elandjo, and he thought that another camp member was responsible for these deaths. The Baka of small Elandjo said they could not go to big Elandjo to swear allegiance to their chief because the chieftaincy ought to be where the remains of their parents were laid to rest.

In view of the revelation about the relationship between burial grounds and rootedness for some Baka people, it may be argued that although 'advocates of indigenous rights have strengthened the impression that indigenous societies are powerless in the face of the unrelenting force of non-indigenous expansion' (Coates 2004: 18), the Baka are not as powerless as they are projected to be. An analysis of different strategies used by the Baka to reconstruct their rootedness on roadsides makes me side with authors like Malkki (1992) and Ojong and Sithole (2007) who argue that rootedness is a fluid concept and depends upon context and advantage.

Conclusion

This chapter highlighted the different ways in which the Baka reconstructed 'rootedness in the soil' in a bid to authenticate belonging on the roadsides. According to the discussions in this chapter, once land became valorized during and after colonization, 'rootedness in the soil' and the belonging of the Baka became reconstructed and manipulated in different ways, depending on the need in question. In this regard, reconstructed historical accounts by both the Baka and the Bantu are conflicting. On the one hand, some Bantu make their case that the Baka were 'non-existent' and only moved out to meet them in their villages. Whereas on the other hand, some Baka argue that the Bantu cleared the forest to meet them inside the forest, while others claim that it was the missionaries who brought them to the roadsides. The chapter also highlights two major loci around which 'rootedness in the soil' are reconstructed. The first is how the dynamics of ancestral burial grounds as justification for 'rootedness in the soil' have changed among the Baka, who previously abandoned the lands on which their ancestors were buried, as cursed places. The other highlight is on how the Baka reinterpret the meaning of the word 'Baka' (which was formerly associated with wandering) to fit the contemporary needs of 'being rooted in the soil'. What is intriguing about these reconstructions are the frames within which the Bantu construct the 'non-existence' of the Baka and the frames within which the Baka construct the 'invasion' of the forest by the Bantu to legitimize their belonging.

The chapter also underscores the fact that, as the Baka moved from the forest to settle on the roadsides, their narratives about rootedness and belonging have changed to adapt to the prevailing situation in the roadside communities. In the past, for example, the Baka took pride in asserting belonging to the forest, something they authenticated by referring to themselves as mothers of the forest. In the same light, they interpreted the appellation 'Baka' to mean birds, who only settle on a branch of a tree to rest, eat and then to take off to the next destination. They saw themselves as typically mobile people. During this time (before 1960, when most of them were still living in the forest in their *Paki*), they never had any close attachments to the burial grounds of their ancestors. However, upon their resettlement on the roadsides where 'the dramatic reconfiguration of wealth and want ... has produced extreme levels of uncertainty about the legitimacy of established identities, rights and claims' (Broch-Due 2005: 1), the Baka have now adopted new ways of negotiating and authenticating their rootedness and belonging. While on the roadsides where emphasis on 'rootedness in the soil' is indispensible to authenticate local level belonging, the Baka have begun to establish different relationships with the soil from those in their ancestral past. The Baka reconstruct their history to fit into the current narratives of being legitimate 'sons of the soil', something which the government is also encouraging through autonomous Baka villages and appointing traditional Baka leaders whose jurisdiction corresponds to precise spatial boundaries (land surface) within which the Baka can legitimately assert belonging.

The discussions in this chapter also reveal that resettlement on the roadsides and the development of new relations with the soil do not initiate a total rupture with forest belonging for Baka people. As the Baka move from one place to another and try to make sense of home and belonging, they retain memories of their previous belonging to other places. This discovery ties with what Albiez et al. suggest when they say 'belonging comprises both spatial and social dimensions; individuals belong to particular places and social layers at once. The spatial dimension of belonging is reinforced through the historical and memorial dimensions' (2011: 241).

Notes

1. This phenomenon of pushing the Baka deeper into the forest is frequently held in the region to mean that in the early days of Bantu migration into the then forest, it was the Bantu who were agriculturalists, clearing the forest for farming. This process of clearing the forest caused the Baka, who then were primarily hunter-gatherers, to move deeper into the heart of the forest.
2. For more on land tenure processes and dispossession of the Baka, cf. Nguiffo, Kenfack and Mballa (2009). Retrieved 02.03.2014 from http://www.forestpeoples.org/sites/fpp/files/publication/2010/05/cameroonlandrightsstudy09eng.pdf.
3. When Obam Meyissa, an aged pygmy from the village of Nkó Wa Womba, said 'We are the mothers of the forest' (Owono 1997: 3).
4. 'Si la forêt meut, nous mourrons aussi, car nous sommes le peuple de la forêt [a Mombuti said] … Vous voulez notre mort, alors que nous ne voulons que l'ombre de la forêt' (Brisson 1999b).
5. Another Cameroonian from the West Region of the country.
6. This discussion of elites and participation in develoment will be elaborated on in Chapter 5.
7. As discussed in Chapter 2, members of this camp had a divided view on what the camp should be called. For some, the camp should be called a village. For others, it should be called a camp. Similar observations were observed in Bingongol II and Mballam, just to name a few.
8. This research will not go into the details of relationships between the dead and the living among the Baka. However interesting the subject may be, it falls outside of the scope of this research.
9. This research did not find any historical literature on intra-camp mobility among the Baka. Thus, it is hard to tell whether this rejection of Baka from other camps is a new phenomenon or that already existed.

Chapter 4

INTERNAL DIFFERENTIATION AND INEQUALITY AMONG THE BAKA

ᴄᴀᴏ·ᴏᴅ

Although people come here and say that there are Baka and there are Baka, those of us inside know how things function here. There are Baka who, when you meet, you immediately know that these are Baka. There are also others who, when you meet, you immediately see the behaviour of the Bantu in them. They struggle only for their stomachs, spend most of their time mixing with people from the government and even these white men who come here. My children in the camp here call them 'Bantus' because there is no difference between them and the Bantu. As I am telling you, our community has become a totally different thing. Everyone wants to survive and no one cares to share again like our parents did in the past (Baka elder, Koumadjab, Dec. 2011; my own translation).

In this work, it has been shown that the East Region of Cameroon is highly multi-ethnic and socially differentiated in composition. The region is inhabited by diverse Bantu groups, the Baka and settlers from other regions of the country. Differentiation in the region has often been approached as an ethnic Bantu and Baka phenomenon in which the Baka occupy the lowest stratum in the social hierarchy. This ethnic differentiation conveys a strong message about the homogeneity of the Baka, such that the state and other development actors tend to categorize the Baka as a homogenous community in terms of ancestral habitats, capabilities, vulnerabilities, livelihoods and stereotypes. Such projected homogeneity among the Baka can be misleading on several grounds.

Indeed, different Baka people have tried as much as possible to define themselves as being distinct from others. It was observed that the Baka who resided in camps closer to the city and who were engaged in agriculture for example, considered themselves to be 'civilized' and 'superior' to their non-agricultural counterparts. A similar stream of difference is reflected in younger generations of the Baka, born on the roadsides, who differentiated themselves from their forest-born parents, even when the latter were living with them in their roadside camps/villages. They claimed to be more 'superior' and 'civilized' than their forest-born parents. On a similar footing, the Baka who lived closer to the denser forest in Moloundou neighbouring DR Congo and the Central African Republic considered the Baka who lived in the vicinities of Dimako and Doumé (closer to the regional capital, Bertoua) to be Bantus.[1] According to the Baka from Moloundou, the Baka of the Upper Nyong Division had lost the essence of being Baka. Also, some Bantus alluded to the above-mentioned differences among the Baka by using the terms 'uncivilized' Baka and 'civilized' Baka. In view of these distinctions, this chapter explores whether there is any 'groupness' in the way that the Baka construct their belonging.

Unlike other sociological studies, I will not approach social differentiation from the perspective of gender, race or ethnicity, rural versus urban, or aboriginal versus other citizens. Rather, I will focus on social differentiation within a supposedly 'social' category. Thus, rather than using the more classic approach to differentiation, which is based on societal heterogeneity, the chapter will use the 'more modern perspective which indicates unequal access to power and the resources of power, [a] perspective [that focuses on] inequality' (Lee 2003: 207). This is because, here, the focus is to understand the social dynamics of belonging as expressed by the Baka, who, by virtue of their social position as the lowest social stratum within the East Region of Cameroon, face numerous challenges in accessing livelihood resources, as well as power to influence decisions that concern their lives in the community.

Structurally, the chapter is divided into four sections. Section one briefly presents the traditional structure of Baka society; section two discusses the changes that have occurred in the structure; section three discusses differentiation as narrated by the Bantu; and section four discusses differentiation as framed by the Baka themselves. Section four also highlights an emerging elitism among the Baka. Behaviour has not been elaborately discussed here given its psychological underpinning. I will rather highlight internal contests and infighting among the Baka with a substantial emphasis on what I call the 'Baka-Baka', the 'Baka-Bantu' and the elite.

Differentiation in the Traditional Baka Society

In the East Region of Cameroon, terms such as the 'Baka-Baka', the 'Baka-Bantu' and the elite are at the heart of differentiation among the Baka.[2] To discuss these differentiations, it is important to briefly summarize how traditional Baka society was organized. This is especially important because, in the past, the Baka as a hunter-gathering community was described as being acephalous and egalitarian (Woodburn 1982; Marlowe 2005; Gray 2011). The focus here is whether the Baka society was a differentiated and stratified one prior to their roadside settlements, where there are struggles regarding belonging.

Throughout history, Pygmies (the Baka included) have always been considered as an egalitarian and achephalous society. Duffy summarizes the egalitarianism of Africa's hunter- gatherer Pygmies in the following way:

Try to imagine … a way of life where land, shelter, and food are free, and where there are no leaders, bosses, politics, organized crime, taxes, or laws. Add to this the benefits of being part of a society where everything is shared, where there are no rich people and no poor people, and where happiness does not mean the accumulation of material possessions. Put all this together and you have part of the traditional life of Africa's hunting and gathering Mbuti Pygmies (Duffy, 1984: vii.).

From a similar perspective, Gray narrates that:

The hunter-gatherer version of equality meant that each person was equally entitled to food, regardless of his or her ability to find or capture it; so food was shared. It meant that nobody had more wealth than anyone else; so all material goods were shared. It meant that nobody had the right to tell others what to do; so each person made his or her own decisions … It meant that group decisions had to be made by consensus; hence no boss, 'big man', or chief (Gray 2011: no page reference[3]).

Indeed, according to Boehm, egalitarianism is in effect a hierarchy in which the weak combine forces to dominate over the strong. Egalitarianism is established and maintained by a strong social ethic. The entire community is constantly vigilant against those who attempt to usurp authority over others, wielding various levels of ostracism to discourage would-be despots. Thus, he characterizes egalitarian societies as community-led, rather than lacking a leader. The dominance of the entire community is strongly maintained and ever-present (Boehm 1993, 1999).

For her part, Robillard argues that being acephalous does not mean that these societies lived in anarchy or that there was no order (Robillard 2010: 84); rather, in these acephalous societies, there existed different types of power defined by people's age, hunting ability and mystical capabilities to heal ailments. The egalitarian ideology refuted the concentration of these different forms of power on one single individual. Thus, unlike in Bantu society, where power was conferred on the traditional ruler, the traditional Baka society as it was organized did 'not allow headship' (RASED 2006: 20). Rather, the Baka considered as chief an individual whom they called '*Nkumou*', but also refered to as '*Nkunkuma*'; a collaborator with other notables, whom they also referred to as wise men. These collaborative relations forbade autocracy and inequality. Moreover, unlike in contemporary times when the government, in a bid to create stable Baka communities, is appointing Baka camp leaders and village heads, the traditional process of selecting a chief was thorough and involved an encounter with the death of the previous leader, acceptance by the ancestors and a welcome by the Baka. This process was aimed at ensuring that the new leader became a selfless carer, rather than the divisive, egoistic and self-centred Baka leaders that the government is appointing today (Baka elder, Cyrie, Nov. 2011).

As Doko Emile, the chief of Nkolbikon-Baka, narrated, some traditional Baka chiefs like his late father (who did not have 'wicked' mystical powers) chose their successors while they were still alive and informed the rest of the camp members about their decision. However, he said that most traditional Baka chiefs have what he called 'complicated mystical powers', and upon the death of such a chief, the wise men and some other camp elders make the late chief's prospective successor spend a night in the same room as the corpse of his deceased predecessor. This process, he said, aims at ensuring that the deceased chief transfers all his 'complicated mystical powers' to his successor. Doko went further, to add that the process was not as simple as he described, but that he could not provide a more systematic description of the process, because as a Baka chief, it was forbidden for him to expose sacred aspects of the Baka culture (interview with Doko Emile in Nomedjo, Jan. 2016). RASED has, however, provided a systematic report on the process of chosing a successor for a traditional Baka chief. According to RASED (2006), upon the death of a reigning Baka chief, his assistants, called '*Boklaks*', meet with the heads of clans, called '*Bigambis*', to choose his successor, usually one of the deceased chief's sons. The choice is guided by the son's bravery before ferocious beasts, his physical and psychological strength, as well as his respect for Baka traditions. This son (hereafter, the prospective chief) also needed to have a good measure of charisma.

After choosing which son would be the new chief, the chief's assistants, together with the clan heads, took the chosen one into the house where the corpse of the dead chief was laid out and made him lie on the same bed with the dead chief, face to face. The chosen son was then left alone in the house while the chief's assistants and the clan heads left and closed the door. Both the dead chief and his successor spent the night together, while the chief's assistants and clan heads kept watch outside. Early next morning, one of the clan heads would push the door open from a distance so that the physical and psychological condition of the prospective chief could be considered. For the door to open required that a snake totem, which symbolized the approval and confirmation of the choice of the new chief by the ancestors, proceed out of the door first. If a snake did not come out in the morning, the assistants and clan heads had to wait until the afternoon, because when they respected the selection criteria closely, it was certain that the snake would appear. Once the snake came out and the door opened, the prospective chief could come out. If the prospective chief's eyes were almost blood red, it further confirmed that he had acquired the power of his predecessor. Thus, he had the special ability to communicate with the cosmos, the living and the dead.

After having gained this ability, the chief had to work in collaboration with the wise men or '*Boklaks*', the hunting specialists or '*belombe*', the '*bigambis*' or clan heads, the blacksmiths, the '*nganga*', and the traditional birth attendants. The wise men helped the chief to urge people to respect the Baka tradition, as well as transmit it to the younger generations. The hunting specialists were specialized in hunting big game like elephants, leopards and gorillas. It was believed that these specialists had the ability to transform themselves during the most dangerous hunts by invoking the god of the forest, whom they refer to as '*Edjengui*'. It was the responsibility of these hunting specialists to supply camp members with meat. The clan heads were the notables or representatives of families or clans before the chief. They served as intermediaries between the chief and the clans. It was through these clan heads that the chief communicated with the people, and vice versa.

The blacksmiths were responsible for producing hunting tools like spears ('*mbenga*'), axes ('*kopa*') and knives ('*mba*'). They were responsible for ensuring that no family lacked weapons. It was also their duty to produce all weapons used during the hunting initiation of youths. The '*nganga*', whom some call sorcerers today, were the specialists in traditional medicine. It was believed that they had supernatural powers that enabled them to diagnose and treat mystical diseases. It was also their responsibility to find and denounce witches, who were considered to be responsible for untimely deaths in clans. They were often solicited by the chief to carry out mystical autopsies. Finally, the chief worked in collaboration with the traditional birth attendants, who were responsible for attending to deliveries. They were considered to be experts who could delay a delivery in case there was an emergency that required long-distance trekking from one camp to the next. In a similar vein, it was believed that these attendants could treat some cases of infertility and limit or completely stop births if a couple desired to do so.

The endowment of skills and expertise among the chief and his collaborators created a sense of interdependency. Thus, although the Baka were egalitarian in their structure, there existed some form of differentiation and specialization within their society. This differentiation and specialization as narrated by the Baka and authors like RASED (2006) was functional (here-after referred to as horizontal differentiation, to imply the lack of hierarchical differentiation in social functions). However, upon the resettlement of the Baka in a hierarchically structured society, where capabilities and livelihoods play a great role in determining where people belong in the social hierar-chy, there were significant changes in their social organization. The reported traditional functional differentiation (which appeared to be horizontal in nature) has changed in a way that has given rise to an emerging vertical differentiation among the Baka.

Vertical Differentiation among the Baka

In Cameroon, the differentiated approaches to the development of the Baka people have not only resulted in contested belonging. They have also nurtured Baka who now have different livelihoods and capabilities, thereby creating a stratified differentiation among the Baka. Unlike in the past, where differen-tiation among the Baka was functional and more horizontal, with minimal inequality, there is a clear, unequal stratification among the Baka today.

In narrating the experience of his roadside-born Baka assistant with a forest-born Baka who was a cousin of his assistant, Leonhardt (2006: 75) alludes to this emerging differentiation and distinction among the Baka. He describes the experience of his roadside-born Baka research assistant meet-ing a forest Baka cousin of his and asking for the traditional Baka firelighter. Intriguingly, this forest Baka cousin of his assistant refused to give the lighter because he did not consider Leonhardt's roadside Baka assistant a Baka (even though his cousin). Thus, he could not extend normal Baka courtesy to some-one he did not consider part of his Baka social world. The present section focuses on discussing such distinctions and differentiation among the Baka.

Differentiation among the Baka: A Bantu Perspective

Although most literature on the relationship between the Baka and the Bantu portray the Bantu as the lords who exploit the Baka as their servants (Abega and Logo 2005; Leonhardt 2006; Pyhälä 2012), the Bantu do not consider all Baka as potential servants. Based on the finding of this book, the Bantu classify the Baka into two categories: the 'typical Baka' and the 'civilized and intelligent' Baka. According to most Bantus, the 'civilized and intelli-gent' Baka are at the topmost end of the Baka internal social hierarchy. This categorization is based on the degree of assimilation of these Baka, as judged by the Bantu. However, some Bantu considered the 'typical Baka' as being on the top of the hierarchy. For these other Bantus, the 'typical Baka' were still experts in traditional medicine and could mystically give people luck and success in their life's endeavours. A further analysis of these categorizations and classifications revealed more complex phenomena. This revelation suggests that the discussion of differentiation among the Baka from a Bantu perspective deserves more attention than the few lines above.

'Typical Baka'

The Bantu distinguished between the 'typical Baka' and 'civilized' Baka. Indeed, the ways in which the Bantu residing in different geographical areas of the East Region of Cameroon identify, differentiate and classify the Baka are quite fascinating. On one hand, the Bantu who reside in Moloundou and Yokadouma (closer to the region's natural forest) tend to pay attention to the Baka who are becoming 'civilized' and exercising their agency. Whereas the Bantu who reside in the Upper Nyong Division (closer to the regional capital), pay more attention to the disappearance of those whom they call 'true Baka'. Thus, unlike their counterparts in Moloundou and Yokadouma, these Bantus in Upper Nyong tend to categorize their Baka neighbours as not 'true Baka'. One of the Bantu chiefs in the Upper Nyong Division mentioned that in contemporary times, it is pretty difficult to find 'true Baka' in Dimako-Upper Nyong Division. According to him, the Baka in Dimako are almost like the Bantu because they are assimilated, 'very civilized' and are sometimes more intelligent than the Bantu:

> Nowadays, it is really difficult to find the 'real' Baka here in Dimako. The Baka here are almost like the Bantu. They are already assimilated and sometimes even wiser than the Bantu. They are very 'civilized' and no longer practise too much witchcraft. In short, one cannot compare them with those at Moloundou. Those are the 'real' Baka. Our Bantu brothers there still enjoy very cheap labour because, with just a tuber of cassava, they can have some of those Baka in Moloundou as a workforce for a whole day. The Baka from here already know about money and even negotiate when solicited for labour (Bantu chief, Dimako, Jan. 2012; my own translation).

RASED also says something on this differentiation: 'the typical Baka is gradually disappearing, [whereas] the Baka history and rich cultural identity … have not been documented or preserved in any other manner for present [and] future generations' (2006: 3). In general, most Bantu use the term 'true Baka' to refer to those whom development actors in the region call 'typical Baka'. I prefer to use the term 'typical Baka' because it is softer than 'true Baka', which I find judgemental. Based on the categorizations made by the Bantu, the Baka who live near the Cameroon–DR Congo border in Moloundou are typical Baka because they are 'uncivilized', offer their labour for free, and practise 'sorcery'. For some Bantus, such Baka are rare to find among the Baka living in the vicinity of the East Region's capital, Bertoua. One Bantu woman in Bonado Doumé (near to Bertoua town) said that if someone wants protection and/or luck (through mystical incantations from the Baka, who are considered to be experts in giving luck), s/he should not waste time in going to the Baka who live around Bonado. According to her, these Baka do not know anything. To her, 'true Baka' are those who live around Yokadouma and Moloundou:

> If you want luck [in life], or protection, do not waste your time with the Baka here. They know nothing. The 'real' Baka are there towards Yokadouma and Moloundou. Those ones are strong (Bantu woman, Bonado, June 2013; my own translation).

It was fascinating to discover that the 'typicalness' of the Baka, as categorized by their Bantu neighbours in the Upper Nyong Division, is associated with expertise in traditional medicine and with the geographical location of the Baka. In my view, such place-bounded categorizations are essentialist, and strategically framed to further enforce distinct differences between the Bantu who do the categorization and the Baka who are categorized.

'Civilized' and Intelligent Baka

In Moloundou, where the Baka constitute about sixty per cent of the division's entire population, it was interesting to observe that unlike in the Upper Nyong Division, where the Bantu paid more attention to distinguishing 'typical'/'true' Baka, emphasis was laid instead on the 'civilized and intelligent' Baka. The Bantu in Moloundou frequently referred to these so-called 'civilized' and intelligent Baka as '*les Dualas et les Obamas*' (people from Douala, the economic capital of Cameroon, and Obama, referring to President Obama of the USA). In view of this, the questions that came to mind were: Why was emphasis not laid on the 'typical Baka', as was the case in the Upper Nyong Division? Why was the distinction based on the concepts of '*les Dualas et les Obamas*'? These questions guide the analysis and discussion in this section.

In Moloundou and Yokadouma, it was commonplace for some Bantus to refer to the Baka as 'their people' ('*nos gens là*'). However, the Baka who did not comply with being '*les gens des Bantu*' were considered to be distinct, and given the names '*les Dualas*' and more recently '*les Obamas*'. These appellations, '*les Dualas*'[4] and '*les Obamas*', were metaphorical and compared to the arrival of 'civilization' in Cameroon. As one of the Bantu narrated, civilization came to Cameroon through Douala, when the white colonial masters first sailed there. Civilization entered Cameroon through the Duala people, who became civilized upon their encounter with the colonial masters, and later on, spread this civilization to other parts of the country. To these Bantus, referring to some Baka as '*les Dualas*' is the same as saying that the Baka who have come into contact with civilization are the vectors of civilization to their Baka brothers.

This appellation '*les Dualas*' is gradually being replaced by that of '*les Obamas*'. For these Bantus, this replacement started when Barack Obama was elected president of the USA in 2008. According to them, the very vocal and outspoken Baka could be compared with President Obama, the descendant of a 'slave' who has become vocal to the point of ruling in the land where his ancestors were oppressed. For these Bantus, the Baka whom they referred to as '*les Obamas*' were distinct in that they seemed to have forgotten their background and dared to go into social spheres reserved for their masters (the Bantu). According to most Bantus in this region, this category of Baka was very small in number, but they were considered to be potentially very 'dangerous' to the peace and stability of their cohabitation, which was based on patron-servant relationships. For the Bantu, these Baka exercised their agency without fear of intimidation or torture.

Interestingly, there is mixed appreciation of these categorizations of '*les Dualas*' and '*les Obamas*' among the Baka. On the one hand, some of the so-called '*Dualas*' and '*Obamas*' do express a sense of pride and happiness to be categorized thus. Some of these Baka mentioned that they had a dream to one day rule the Bantu. From their perspective, they were determined never to depend on the Bantu for subsistence. Rather, as one of them, a cocoa farmer, said during the cocoa picking season, he always ensured that he had one or two Bantu boys working as labourers in his cocoa farm. On the other hand, however, there were some Baka families who considered Baka girls who were categorized as '*les Dualas*' or '*les Obamas*' to be prostitutes and 'unreal Baka' because according to them, these girls frequented nightclubs and bars in the region, which was not normal in the Baka culture.

Differentiation among the Baka: A Baka Perspective

The margin of differentiation among the Baka as framed by the Baka themselves is complex. This is because some Baka categorically refer to others as 'Bantus', whereas those often referred to as 'Bantus' refer to the former as 'their lazy and backward brothers'. This rift in categorization has resulted in social stratification among the Baka. Based on categorizations made by the

Baka, the different strata include the 'Baka-Baka', the traditional ruler, the 'Baka-Bantu', and the elite.

The 'Baka-Baka'

Earlier on in this chapter, I mentioned that there is a geographical divide in the ways that the Bantu categorize and differentiate the Baka. In effect, the Bantu who live closer to the DR Congo paid more attention to the 'civilized and intelligent' Baka (whom they called '*les Dualas et les Obamas*'), while the Bantu who lived closer to the capital of the East Region highlighted the 'typical' Baka (whom they called '*les vrai Baka*'). This geographical margin was also used by the Baka to differentiate between themselves. During three different focus group discussions on the subject conducted with a total of twenty-one elderly Baka (aged about sixty and upwards) living closer to the DR Congo (in Moloundou and Yokadouma), sixteen of them considered themselves to be 'typical' or 'true' Baka. According to these Baka, they are at the helm of the Baka cultural hierarchy because they are the only remaining 'true' guardians of the Baka culture and retainers of its mystical strength. One of these Baka elders from Banana camp further highlighted during an in-depth interview that there are Baka who are Baka because they have Baka blood, but in reality they are not Baka. According to this elder, a 'true Baka' is one who has the blood, the culture and the behaviour of Baka people:

> There are Baka who are Baka because they have Baka blood, but in reality, they are not Baka. One can rather say that they are Bantu who were born into Baka families. The real Baka is the blood, the culture and the behaviour. This is why you may hear some say that this person is the real Baka, that is to say, he's 'Baka-Baka', meaning Baka by blood, culture and behaviour (Baka elder, Banana, Oct. 2011; my own translation).

Although the Bantu, as well as most Baka, recognize that being Baka is primordial and a status obtained through lineage, according to some Baka blood relations are not enough for a Baka to be considered a 'real' Baka. This latter category of the Baka say it takes more than just being born to a Baka family to be considered a 'real' Baka. This was indeed an outstanding and new discovery, considering that among their neighbouring Bantus and even the rest of the Cameroonian ethnic groups, there is no such distinction if one is born to parents who both come from the same ethnic group. This sort of distinction was striking because, until now, many of the social phenomena observed among the Baka were micro-level replicas of what is going on in Cameroonian society more broadly. This observation raised the following analytical questions: Is such a striking internal differentiation among the

Baka the result of differentiated approaches to the development of Baka people? Or is it the result of an increased demand for traditional medicines, as well as a high demand for forest guides by tourists and conservationists, both of whom need the expertise of the Baka as forest peoples?

In effect, both the differentiated approaches to the development of Baka people and an increase in the demand for traditional medicines and a high demand for forest guides contribute to the emerging internal differentiation among the Baka. However, each of these phenomena contributes differently. On the one hand, some Baka differentiate themselves as Baka-Baka because they want to gain the market for traditional medicine and forest guides. These were the Baka-Baka who emphasized that being a 'real' Baka was conferred not only by birth but also by culture and nature. On the other hand, there are also some Baka who differentiate themselves as Baka-Baka because they want to show proof of their desperation, vulnerability and the need for help from indigenous peoples' INGOs. This latter category of Baka-Baka live mostly in '*mongolous*' (traditional Baka houses) and some go as far as renting out their farms, so as to appear helpless and marginalized, thus appealing to INGOs, who often target such typical Baka. In some cases, the Baka who live in camps that are relatively more dispossessed make fewer claims for aid than their counterparts who live in camps that have access to land. In this context, some NGO officials[5] consider the Baka to be a highly manipulative group of people. Mballa alludes to this manipulative tendency of the Baka by describing how some Baka sent their children to school because they wanted to benefit from products of the World Food Programme (rice, flour, milk and beans). However, after they got these products, they withdrew their children from school and took them hunting (2009: 136). A closer analysis of the Baka's own version of this presumed manipulative tendency, however, reveals a form of Baka agency and initiative amid multiple and contrasting development interventions. The Baka chief of Lossou further illuminated this when he said that the Baka are not as stupid as they are seen to be. Over the years, they have learnt to play their cards well with development officials (BBP conference, Bertoua, June 2013).

This initiative by some Baka-Baka to present themselves in a way that is perceived as vulnerable and deprived suggests that the marginalization of the Baka people needs to be discussed with care and keen attention. Azarya (in Abega and Logo 2005) argues that self-marginalization or absolute dependence on the state and other international organizations by the Baka is not an entirely state-provoked phenomenon. Although 'state actions [have pushed the Baka] to the margins of society by restricting [their] culturally accepted opportunities for advancement, damaging their sources of livelihoods and self-respect or disadvantaging them *vis-à-vis* rival groups' (ibid.: 23), the emergence of a Baka-Baka category among the Baka is not entirely due to state action. From my point of view, it is also a result of agency and initiative among the Baka.

While this distinction of the Baka-Baka might be interpreted as a result of their quest to affirm their identity, my field findings mostly pointed to the fact that the distinction was motivated by two things: the quest for social recognition and the quest for social assistance. At the level of social recognition, social power is a major component. The Baka-Baka who considered themselves to be the retainers of mystical might claimed to have the highest authority within their camps. Nonetheless, it is important to recall that these Baka-Baka claims of authority do not necessarily translate into their ability to coerce other camp members to listen and obey their orders. In a few cases, as chief Doko of Nomedjo village recounted, such Baka-Baka are able to use 'complicated mystical powers' to harm other camp members who do not give in to their demands to share hunting catches and/or food. In one of the camps where there were Baka-Baka, some of them mentioned that their Bantu neighbours were afraid of harassing them because of their mystical might, which the Bantu respected. In her own book, Rupp touched on the subject of social power, but focused on social power based on ethnic parentage, as indicated in Figure 4.1.

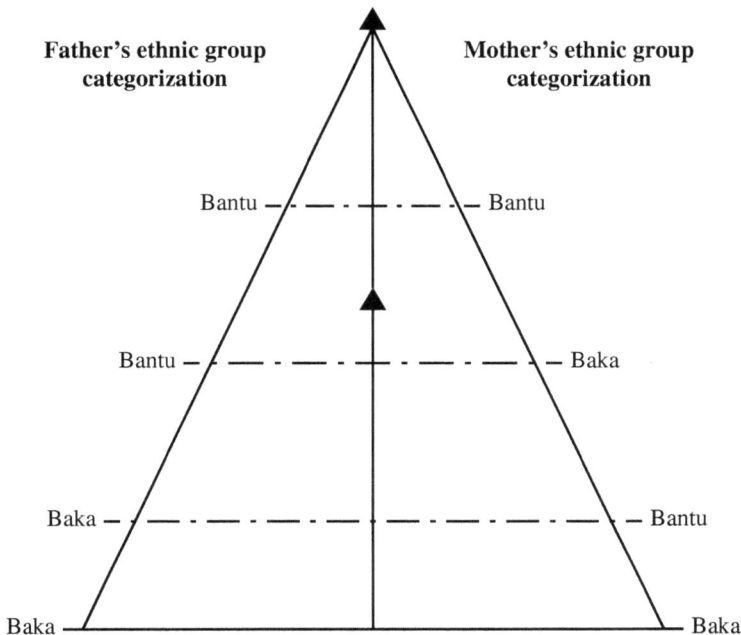

Figure 4.1 Relative degree of social power based on ethnic parentage.
Source: constructed by G.M Lueong with inspiration from from Rupp (2011: 125).

According to Rupp's study, children born to purely Baka families had the least social power relative to those born to mixed Baka and Bantu parents. What Rupp seems to suggest is that all Baka born to purely Baka parents had the same social power. Nonetheless, as I have discussed, there is also a hierarchy of social power among Baka born to purely Baka parents. This social power is based on blood lineage, geography, capabilities and behaviour. In effect, most Baka who considered themselves to be typical or 'true' Baka tended to demean the other Baka, whom they did not consider to be 'true' or real Baka. For them, the latter were Bantus and did not deserve to be served the normal Baka courtesy, as was the case with Leonhardt's roadside-born research assistant (Leonhardt 2006). The process of the government appointing Baka leaders is also a source of distinction among the Baka. The Baka also make distinctions between the 'traditional leader' and the 'traditional ruler'.

The Traditional Leader Versus the Traditional Ruler

As discussed in previous chapters, in early 2000 INGOs like Plan International, together with the government, initiated a process of creating Baka villages and appointing third-class Baka chiefs to head these villages. The move aimed to crystallize the belonging of the Baka in their roadside settlements, since it gives the Baka rights over the land on which they reside. Before being halted indefinitely, the move drew strong support from both researchers and policy makers, who argued that it was the only way forward to consolidate the belonging and citizenship of the Baka. For example, Logo, in his paper titled 'Citizens in Quest of Rights? The Citizenship Odyssey of the Pygmies of the Rainforest of Cameroon' states that:

> The establishment of community chiefdoms, to have decisive and sustainable impacts over the citizenship of 'Pygmies' and their access to land, must ultimately lead to the creation of third-class chiefdoms and the securing of the land rights of 'Pygmies'. It is an important transitional phase and a significant evolution in the relations between the State and the 'Pygmies'' communities and between the latter and the neighboring Bantu people (Logo 2012: 8).

Interestingly, while this move was highly recommended as a way out for the Baka in the East Region of Cameroon, my field observations among the Baka suggest that the move has also left the Baka struggling with a great deal of internal rivalry between the Baka rulers and the Baka traditional leaders. Traditional Baka rulers are chosen with customary scrutiny, while the traditional leaders were appointed by the government. These traditional leaders could be legally recognized third-class chiefs governing Baka villages or camp leaders serving as quarter heads under the leadership of Bantu chiefs. What is unique about traditional leaders is the fact that they exist for all Baka camps and villages. On the contrary, the traditional ruler is appointed by the council of notables, and could coordinate a number of Baka clans. In most cases, the traditional leaders appointed by the government are the traditional rulers chosen by the Baka council of notables. This was the case of Chief Nouchtegenou Dieuvonne, third-class chief of Mayos-Dimako. However, since there are no traditional rulers in some Baka camps, only government-appointed traditional leaders prevail. In these cases, the government-appointed leaders appear arbitrary to the Baka.

To most Baka, the traditional ruler is superior and of higher standing than the traditional leader. The classification of this superiority again depended on whose perspective you consider. For the Baka-Baka, the traditional ruler was the most superior and was considered to be a Baka-Baka, while the traditional leader was considered to be inferior, a Baka-Bantu and a 'traitor'. Even when the leader was the ruler, the Baka tended to distinguish his functions. During an interview with one of Chief Nouchtegenou's camp members in Mayos, the interviewee said that:

> When those Plan people[6] come and give him his money, he thinks that he can just give people orders. He [i.e. the chief] said we should not go and work for the Bantu. Will he feed our families? If he is telling me about an initiation ritual, I will listen because there he has the power to tell me what to do (Mayos, June 2013; my own translation).

This may reveal the difficulty of introducing new administrative structures and governance systems to groups of peoples. This difficulty will not be explored in this book in further detail. Rather, I will discuss the 'Baka-Bantu' and their views on traditional leaders and rulers.

The 'Baka-Bantu'

> We the Baka here in town are very different from those who still live in the bush out there in Moloundou. Those Baka are not yet 'civilized'; they even call us the Bantu (Baka participant, Mayos, June 2013; my own translation).

In Chapter 2, I analysed how the Baka also framed differentiation along geographical lines. I mentioned that the Baka living closer to Bertoua (capital of the East Region) tended to classify those living in the regional border areas like Moloundou (which borders Central African Republic and DR Congo) as more 'primitive' and still in the bush. In this discussion, it was mentioned that the so-called more 'primitive' Baka (Baka-Baka) had their own definition of who was a 'real' Baka. For them, being a 'real' Baka meant being Baka by blood, culture and behaviour. Thus, the Baka who were only Baka by blood, without the culture or behavior, were considered to be 'Baka-Bantu'.

In this regard, geography became a margin of differentiation only if it could influence the culture and behaviour of the Baka. One of the Baka from Moloundou (the more forested region) recounted that one day he had gone to visit his family in Bonado (closer to the city, along the Yaoundé-Bertoua highway). While in Bonado, he discovered that the Baka who lived there behaved in ways that were totally different from theirs in Moloundou. The Baka in Bonado, according to him, were very greedy, and every person cared only about his (nuclear) family. For him, these Baka could no longer be called Baka-Baka because they were already 'Bantus'. In the same light, there were intra-camp differentiations whereby some camp members considered others as Bantus because the latter did not embrace the 'irrational sharing'[7] that was expected of them. Interestingly, while these Baka were referred to as 'Bantus' because 'their behaviour was similar to that of the Bantu', they only referred to the other Baka as 'lazy idiots', or as not sufficiently advanced. Vincent of Mendjou village emphasized that:

> My brothers here in the camp are absolute idiots! When you tell them to work their own farms and stop working like slaves for the Bantu, they will form their own groups in the camp and begin to call you a Bantu. In the camp here you have Bantus and Baka, even though we all are Baka. When they see a car pass like you people [referring to me and my research team] they will all run and wait for you to give the money that you have brought. They are not willing to do anything. When they are hungry, they go and work like slaves for the Bantu and get a tuber of cassava and crude alcohol and that is it. They are fine. When people like us now harvest our plantains and cassava, they will want us to share with them. When we don't, they call us Bantus (Nov. 2011; my own translation).

Following suit, some Baka in Mayos recounted that although their other Baka counterparts called them 'Bantus', they were not Bantus. They were Baka who were learning to become 'civilized' and to be free from slavery by doing what the NGOs were teaching them to do.

These narrations and others suggest that being a Baka-Bantu is a transformative process,[8] in which some Baka are considered by others to behave in a way that 'contrasts strongly with the Baka's customary sharing of food, especially the sharing of meat that occurs in hunting camps, where hunters distribute the hunted meats equally among all participants of the camps' (Bahuchet 1990; Kitanishi 2000; Hayashi 2008, all in Oishi 2012: 126). However, to authenticate their belonging to the Baka community, especially in camps like Bonado and Lossou (both in the Upper Nyong Division), most of these Baka-Bantu mentioned that they still held to their cultural rituals, but did not often go hunting or gathering because the forest was no longer close to their camps; it took hours to reach a nearby forest, and getting a catch was not always guaranteed because, according to them, animals were becoming more scarce in the forest in the Upper Nyong Division. For these Baka, change and adaptation were indispensable and were something they had to learn to live with. The changes in forest-governing regulations which keep them out of the forest will never be repealed, since everybody is on the road to progress. According to these Baka:

> Time has changed and the truth is that you will not see any Baka who really want to go and stay back there in the forest as our parents did. However, not wanting to stay inside the forest does not mean that we have become different people. Even the president of this country, who has gone to all places in the world, knows that he has a home and always goes there. He does not stay there but goes there for traditions and other things. So if we want the forest, it is not to stay there, it is because we want to keep what makes us Baka, that is to say, a place where we can go and do our cultural rituals (focus group discussion with Baka youths in Mayos, Dec. 2011; my own translation).

It was interesting to observe that these Baka-Bantu alluded to home when talking about the forest. This is because the Baka who resided on the road-sides, like those in Mayos, tended to reconstruct 'rootedness in the soil' as a strategy to make a sense of home on the roadsides. This double view of home in the forest and home on the roadsides therefore suggests that as the Baka moved from the forest to the roadside, they made new meanings of place. Thus, although the Baka-Baka refuted the belonging of the Baka-Bantu, the latter attempted to legitimize their belonging in the Baka community by linking their ancestry to the forest, which the Baka-Baka also claimed to be experts about.

Among the Baka-Bantu, there were also special categories who were Baka-Bantu not only because of their neglect of Baka culture and behaviour, but also because of their mixed blood. This category of Baka-Bantu was made up of children born to Baka men who were married to Bantu women. Such Baka-Bantu were not so common.[9] However, although they were few, they faced a harder time asserting their belonging, even to the other Baka-Bantu. Messe, one such Baka, said that it was a dilemma which he, his siblings and his own kids were facing and had to deal with every day of their lives. Prior to meeting Messe, many participants had talked to me about him.

During one of my interviews with a Baka camp leader, for example, he told me that Messe was not a Baka. Rather, it is his mother who is a Baka. Yet, because there is money in the *'affaires Baka'* (Baka business), Messe had become a Baka overnight and was intruding into Baka issues. To put it in the words of this Baka camp leader:

He forces himself into our issues because he is 'drinking' money from it. Actually, he is not a Baka! His father is a Bantu. Only his mother is a Baka, but we do not know on what he is counting to say that he is a Baka (Baka camp leader, Moloundou, Oct. 2011; my own translation).

In the same municipality where I interviewed this Baka camp leader, a Bantu who was running an NGO said that Messe cannot be considered a Baka man because it is his mother who is a Baka. According to this Bantu man, Messe had given up his Bantu identity to hunt for money in the Baka NGO business. The man added that Messe travels everywhere and even has a car and a very big house. Intriguingly, when I met Messe, his version of the story was different. Messe recounted that his father was the first ever Baka man to marry a Bantu woman. Thus, contrary to what the other Baka and some Bantus had told me, Messe's father is a Baka and his mother is Bantu. Messe is also married to a Bantu woman, but emphasized that he constantly felt embarrassed by having to justify the fact that he was a Baka. In another interview with Mballa on the same subject, Messe mentioned that he has experienced rejection even at the level of the local community where he grew up:

I cannot say that I have not experienced this phenomenon. I have really experienced it, the phenomenon of rejection. Even at the village level, given my intellectual capacity, it is sometimes really [hard for villagers to believe that I am a 'Pygmy' who is capable of doing what I am doing] … whereas, I do not even consider myself as such..... I am the one who ensures that the family's needs are met (Mballa 2009: 63–64; my own translation).

In terms of hierarchy and social power, the Baka-Bantu considered themselves more superior, 'civilized' and advanced, relative to their Baka-Baka brothers. They based their superiority on the fact that they were able to do the things that the Bantu (their 'former masters') did. The troubling thing in this ranking is the fact that 'civilization', as expressed by the Baka-Bantu, is considered to be a function of education, engagement in agriculture and ability to interact with government officials. Thus suggesting that for them, assimilation was equal to civilization. In most cases however, officials of some INGOs and the government tended to laud these so-called Baka-Bantu for their level of progress and engagement in development projects. This understanding of 'civilization' as education, engagement in agriculture and ability to interact with government officials by the Baka-Bantu is intriguing, considering the fact that one of the specific objectives of the current Pygmy People Development Plan of the Forest and Environment Sectorial Programme (PPDP/FESP), funded by the World Bank, is to 'preserve the identity and enhance the cultural values of these peoples'. In this document, some of the recommended activities highlighted as adopted by the government include 'equal cultural opportunities [whereby the government undertakes to] sensitize the Baka … on the risks of the development process, assist IP [Indigenous Peoples] associations in capacity building to preserve traditional knowledge, culture and livelihood patterns'.[10] This logic of preserving the culture and livelihood of the Baka amid ongoing assimilative agricultural promotion activities for the Baka to my point of view is not only confusing for the Baka but may be considered as one of the factors sustaining differentiation among the Baka. This is because one version of these contrasting approaches to the development of the Baka is presented as superior and more relevant to society than the other.

The 'Elite'

It has been observed that there are 'elites' among the Baka. However, unlike the Baka-Baka and the Baka-Bantu, the 'elite' as a social category has received broad scholarly attention. Marx, in his time, wrote about the 'elite' as a social class. Mills (1956) however dissociated the concept from that of social class and associated 'elites' with the social category at the epicentre of administrative power ('the power elite'). In the Cameroonian context, Biya, the president of the Republic of Cameroon, writing on communal liberalism (1986), subscribed to Mills's stance and strongly denied the existence of social classes in the Cameroonian society:

> In the Cameroon of today, there are no social classes, strictly speaking; maybe they are in gestation, but I do not subscribe to the thesis that there exist already sharp social classes in our country (Biya 1986: 129; my own translation).

Although Biya refuted the existence of social classes in Cameroon, the existence of the 'elite' as a social category is widespread within the country. In effect, elitism is knitted into almost every aspect of the country's sociopolitical, economic and cultural life. In the domain of development and access to resources, 'elites' are perceived to be the vehicles of both local and national development.

Authors like Ela (1982), Foudouop (1997) and Ngandjeu (2000) have written extensively on the role of the 'elites' in local and regional development in Cameroon. For Ela, elites constitute a force of Africa in peril. He sees 'elites' as those who have the responsibility to build and advance the country, as well as the entire continent. To him, 'elites' ought to put their ingenuity and energy towards leading the continent out of poverty and underdevelopment. He goes further to add that elites not only possess the capacity and the means, but are also more enlightened and informed about the nature of the multiple challenges facing the continent. Foudouop (1997), for his part, considers the elite as a vector of local development in Cameroon. By defining elites as the vectors of local development, Foudouop refers to people from a locality, people who bring something to their localities and who are able to lead their localities to development, people on whom the community can count for the good governance of their affairs. Ngandjeu (2000) sees elites in a similar light to Foudouop.

The emergence of an ethnoregional political regime in Cameroon has further enhanced a growing pressure on elites 'to act as facilitators and manipulators with respect to the state. [To do this, they form] elite development associations, [through which] they lobby foreign agencies and NGOs to provide their home villages or regions with new sources of wealth and livelihood' (Nyamjoh 2010: 63). As Kah puts it, 'when your brother dey for on top plum tree, you too go chop black plums' (2010: 21). Kah uses this statement in Cameroonian pidgin English to mean that if your brother is on top of a plum tree, then you too can eat plums. In the Cameroonian context, this is often used to mean that if you are in a position of administrative and/or political authority, then your family relatives or members of the same village can benefit from state and non-state livelihood resources, state-sponsored/co-sponsored development projects, as well as job promotions (if they are employed), among others.

This trend of elitism, whereby communities rally behind their elites to bid for their own share of the national cake (Monga 2000) was also observed among the Baka. A cross-section of the Baka, especially the Baka-Bantu, mentioned that it was only through their elite that their current oppression and exclusion could be averted. Michel, a Baka youth in Mballam, remarked that there is already a difference between Baka camps. According to Michel, Messe[11] was an exemplary Baka elite, and he added that the Baka in Mballam are still swimming in the dark because they do not yet have elites like Messe. In his words:

> There is already a difference between the different Baka camps. In some camps, where parents knew earlier of the importance of education, there are elites who fight for them. The Bantu do not dare threaten them, whether in regard to forest revenue management, land use or many other things. You see someone like Messe Venant, he is one of the examples that have been cited. With us here in Mballam, we have no elites. So, we always swim in the dark because of that (Baka youth, Mballam, Dec. 2011; my own translation).

The Baka 'elites' (like Messe Venant and Helen Aye Mondo, among others) consider themselves to be the bringers of development to their communities. Interestingly, most of these elites had founded and are running local NGOs.

However, unlike Ela (1982), Foudouop (1997) and Ngandjeu (2000), who considered elites as people who work for the development of their communities, there is much more to learn about elitism and leading one's community into development among the Baka than has been described by these authors. This will be elaborately discussed in the next chapter, where I talk about the participation of the Baka in development projects. At the moment, I will limit the discussion to differentiation and levels of social power among the Baka, which may be summarized as in Figure 4.2.

In Figure 4.2, elites are considered to be at the top of the social hierarchy, based on their level of interaction with the rest of Cameroonian society. However, if the ranking were done from the perspective of being a 'typical' Baka (blood, culture and behaviour), the Baka-Baka would be at the top. It was observed that the ranking of social power among the Baka varied depending on who did the ranking. While I have attempted to present this ranking in a neat hierarchical order, I recognize that when it comes to magical might (engagement with activities like mastery of traditional healing and giving luck to people from within and external to the Baka community), the classification cannot be as neat as it is sketched above. This is because while the Baka-Baka prided themselves on such abilities and skills, there were also Baka elites who had similar skills but who did not emphasize them.

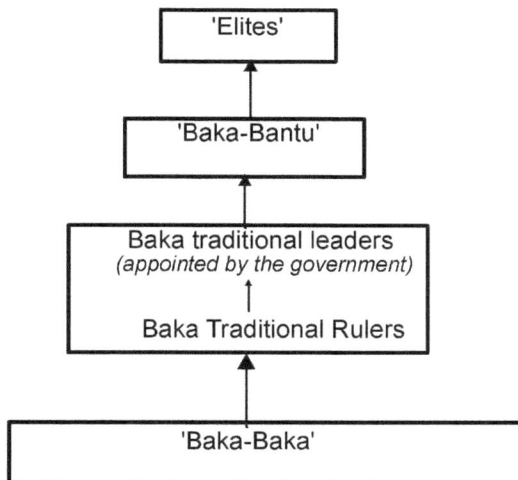

Figure 4.2 Social stratification and power among the Baka.
Source: constructed by G.M. Lueong.

Although there is social stratification among the Baka, there exists social mobility across the different strata. Based on field observations, there was significant social mobility among 'les Dualas et les Obamas', who emerged from Moloundou (a predominantly Baka-Baka region). The determination of the latter to one day lead the Baka out of oppression (thus becoming elites) could be quoted as one factor among many revealing indications of social mobility.

NGO Intervention Reinforces Stratification among the Baka: A Hypothesis

> That woman, she is a typical Baka. You see that wound on her face; it is her drinking that caused it. Even though she has travelled to many places in the world, what makes her different from those real Baka in the forest is that at least she lives in a well-constructed house and can read and write (development worker in Bertoua, July 2013; my own translation).

In the East Region of Cameroon, different development organizations have different philosophies and approaches to the development of the Baka people. As Messe, a Baka elite mentioned, development organizations rarely work in collaboration and each development organization has its Baka (BBP conference presentation, June 2013). Some of these organizations state that they work with 'typical Baka' and others, like the WWF, go further to list the characteristics of 'typical Baka'. WWF state: 'Baka Pygmies – the facts: The typical Baka Pygmy will not leave his home in the forest even in exchange for an ultra modern palace in the city' (WWF, the Jengi Project). Such statements suggest that there are 'untypical Baka'.

Such categorical distinctions made by development organizations seem to contribute to the ongoing differentiation process among the Baka. This is because being a 'typical' Baka means being 'primitive', backward and 'uncivilized' when compared to others. Similarly, most Baka youths who could read and write strongly dissociated themselves from being 'typical' Baka. For them, 'typical' Baka were those who could not read or write, but rather spent most of their time in the forest. In this ongoing distinction process it was not clear whether the Baka youths had picked up the concept of 'typical' from development organizations or whether it was their own invention, which just happened to coincide with the discourse of some INGOs operating within their communities.

Nonetheless, it was very clear that the phrase 'typical Baka' had become very recurrent, even among the Baka when they framed 'in-group' distinctions. During the arguments that occurred in Bonado and Bingongol camps on whether the camps should be called Baka villages or Bantu subquarters, participants frequently used the phrase 'typical Baka' as a way to insult the ingenuity of their fellow Baka campmates. In view of this, it may be said that with the intensity of the struggle between the so-called 'typical' Baka (Baka-Baka) and the Baka-Bantu, the ongoing differentiation may, with time, become sharper and more conflictual. The camp leader of Mballam-Baka alluded to this when he mentioned that '*parmi les Baka, il y a aussi le patriotisme, le racisme, la haine, la discrimination et les rancunes*' (Nov. 2011) (among the Baka, there is also patriotism, racism, hatred, discrimination and grudges). By '*patriotisme*', this leader was referring to infighting, power struggles and inequality among the Baka.

Infighting, Power and Inequality among the Baka

The Baka have always been portrayed as the victims of inequality in the East Region of Cameroon. However, in analysing social stratification and the struggle for resources among the Baka, it can be argued that the Baka also perpetuate inequality through infighting, which results in discrimination. This infighting was predominant among the Baka elites who had started and were running NGOs. They strove against each other to the point that some were unable to cooperate on different development programmes. Some of them resorted to forming cliques, and forbade the NGOs of other Baka elites from intervening in particular Baka camps. Messe reported a similar situation in his work with the NGO OKANI. Messe, secretary of the Indigenous Peoples of Africa Coordinating Committee (IPACC), president of the Réseau des Populations Autochtones et Locales pour la Gestion durable des Ecosystèmes Forestiers d'Afrique Centrale (REPALEAC) and director of OKANI, recounted that Baka elites who run NGOs in other divisions of the East Region had told him not to extend his activities to their divisions. He said that he was told to limit his activities just to Dimako, where he is based, because extending his activities to places like Yokadouma and Moloundou would enable OKANI (his NGO) to emerge as a regional NGO. This would overshadow the visibility of the other Baka elites and their own organizations. This 'territorialization' of elitism among the Baka has had different effects on different Baka communities, since some Baka NGOs have access to more resources than others.

Since these NGOs served as channels for resource distribution among the rest of the Baka communities, infighting among the leaders of the NGOs prevented some of them from intervening in certain divisions and camps. This ended up leaving some camps without any assistance. As some members of a Baka camp in Moloundou mentioned, they do not know whom to believe in, because their own leaders, who are their Baka brothers, create a lot of confusion by telling them not to collaborate with some particular local Baka NGOs:

> Ultimately, we no longer know whom to trust. Our leaders, our very own Baka brothers, come here and tell us that if this or that association comes to you to get information, do not give it. We obey them and only later on do we see how those associations [that we were told not to give information to] are assisting others, while we are just here. Whereas those who came to tell us not to give away information do not even return to us to say do this or that. In the end, we are the losers (Baka camp, Moloundou, Oct. 2011; my own translation).

This struggle was also observed at the level of circulating information. When a communiqué about funding opportunities, conferences or seminars was sent to the region through some Baka-run NGOs, others never received it. Those NGOs that formed 'cliques' expressed their fear that one of the renowned Baka NGOs in the region would soon become a regional NGO and then they would be unable to secure funding for their own activities.

Conclusion

This chapter explored the specific question of whether there is any sense of 'groupness' in the way that the Baka construct their belonging. It revealed that while the Baka have been projected as one group with the same vulnerabilities, capabilities and attachment to the forest, they are in fact greatly differentiated, with an internal hierarchy that I have broadly categorized into the 'Baka-Baka' or 'typical' Baka, the 'Baka-Bantu' or 'civilized' Baka, and the 'elites'.

The chapter also shows that while Baka society has often been portrayed as acephalous (Abega and Logo 2005: 258) and egalitarian (Tchoumba and Nelson 2006), there exists some level of functional differentiation. Indeed, the introduction of different and contrasting development interventions among the Baka, together with the introduction of traditional rulers (chiefs), which seeks to legitimate Baka villages as autonomous administrative entities on the roadsides, has led to vertical differentiation and stratification among the Baka such that there is stuggle and infighting. To this end, it can be said that although in most development programme documents Baka culture is depicted as 'established on an egalitarian society based on the concept of sharing, the prevalence of free will, the conservation of the community values based on the principle of nomadism and mobility' (Cheumani 2012: 14), Baka society is more dynamic than presumed.

Most importantly, the ways in which these contrasting development interventions present themselves as being important and relevant to the society play a role in the interpretation of 'civilization' and classification of social hierarchy among the Baka, such that some Baka consider themselves to be more 'civilized' than others. In like manner, it can be hypothesized that the categorization of some Baka as 'typical' by some INGOs is enforcing the differentiation process among the Baka. This is especially so because those not considered to be 'typical' described themselves as being 'already civilized', whereas those considered to be 'typical' were presumed to be 'uncivilized', with civilization generally being defined as assimilation into agriculture. The chapter also shows that unlike other forest peoples,[12] who rejected development interventions and prided themselves on their mastery of traditional medicine skills, as well as forest-dependent livelihoods, most 'Baka-Baka', who in general are considered to be the 'typical Baka', are not reluctant when it comes to development interventions.

Taking into consideration the differentiation observed among the Baka, it is understandable that even though most Baka experience exclusion, marginalization and violence, all of which are unfavourable conditions in which 'most ethnic movements develop' (Simo 2006: 64; Lewellen 2003: 161), there is 'to date no organised social movement on indigenous peoples' rights in Cameroon (unlike in South America, for instance, where the movement has gained strong ground)' (Pyhälä 2012: 17).

Notes

1. A similar process is observed among other ethnic groups in the country. For example, people living in towns use the pejorative term '*villageois*' to describe their parents/relatives living in villages. However, my field findings did not provide me with significant backing to argue that both processes may be related.
2. The information in this section was collected from in-depth interviews conducted with Baka chiefs as well as a close reading of RASED (2006).
3. This quote was retrieved online on 01.03.2014 from http://www.psychologytoday.com/blog/freedom-learn/201105/how-hunter-gatherers-maintained-their-egalitarian-ways.
4. While there is a Baka community in the Boumba and Ngoko Division of the East Region called Douala, the use of '*les Dualas*' in this categorization of the Baka has nothing to do with the Baka of this community unless they happen to fit into the categorization.
5. The then Plan Community Development Facilitator for Lomié.
6. By Plan people, she was referring to Plan International, because it is very active in the region. In most cases when people see a car in their area, they take it to be Plan even when it is not.
7. The use of the phrase 'irrational sharing' is used here not as my own invention, but rather as a summary of what the Baka-Bantu in question said. They tended to say that it is not possible for them to invest their energy and time in their farms and their lazy brothers expect that they will share their produce with them. They can sell it to meet their other financial obligations, like paying for their children's school fees.

8. Oishi has shown that, due to cocoa cultivation and access to the market economy by some Baka, 'considerable economic inequality has emerged among individuals, causing a conflict between self-interest (economic gain) and existing egalitarian ethics' (2012: 115).

9. This category of Baka-Bantu was not common because generally only Bantu men marry Baka women. Their children are considered to be Bantu, because among the Bantu, family identity is patriarchal.

10. Retrieved 06.03.2014 from http://www-wds.worldbank.org/external/default/WDS ContentServer/WDSP/IB/2004/06/01/000012009_20040601150518/Rendered/PDF/ IPP86.pdf.

11. Messe is the Baka whom I referred to when discussing rejection of the so-called 'Bantu-Baka' earlier in this chapter.

12. 'You *napëpë* [whites] talk about what you call "development" and tell us to become the same as you. But we know that this brings only disease and death. The forest is our life and we need it to fish, grow food, hunt, sing and dance and have feasts. It gives life for all. Without forest, there is only sickness' (Davi Kopenawa, in Sarawak 2007). This quote reflects the views of some forest peoples in the Amazonian forest. Davi Kopenawa is a Yanomami leader from Brazil.

Chapter 5

DEVELOPMENT PARTICIPATION AMONG THE BAKA IN THE EAST REGION OF CAMEROON

❧◦☙

The Baka community has become a development laboratory; everybody wants to do something for the Baka. However, we the Baka people have a proverb that says, 'he who claims to do something for us without us is doing it against us' (Messe Venant, secretary of the Indigenous Peoples of Africa Coordinating Committee (IPACC), president of the Réseau des Populations Autochtones et Locales pour la Gestion durable des Ecosystèmes Forestiers d'Afrique Centrale (REPALEAC) and director of OKANI, BBP conference, Bertoua, June 2013; my own translation).

During my fieldwork stay among the Baka, one Baka youth alluded to these multiple and sometimes contrasting development interventions when he said that they are tired of different development interventions that come and urge them to engage in different activities that end up conflicting. He said that once the Baka start to have an understanding of the activities of one project (or 'start to progress', to use his words), other development projects come and initiate different activities, such that the Baka find themselves stopped in the middle of what he called 'progress'. This challenge of being stopped in the middle of 'progress' has made most Baka devise means (i.e. use their agency) to deal with the different development actors in the region. This Baka youth went on to add that:

In the past, we the Baka were being told to do this, to do that, to stop that, but now we have stopped. We have already stopped, we have tried to stop. But now, I do not really know what to tell you my brothers, my sisters and my older brothers; I do not know what I'll say to you now. Open your eyes, since we have been urged to stop and we have not refused to stop. Truly we accepted the point that we should stop. Well, what I still have to ask is this: since we were told to stop, when can we do anything of our own? ... But I've seen this for a long time; it's not today that we started coming to attend meetings. How will this meeting that we are assisting in now benefit us? (Baka participant, BBP conference, Bertoua, June 2013; available online, my own translation[1]).

From the perspective of the development actors,[2] Baka people as 'Pygmies' have similar abilities, skills, and qualities and behaviour. In this regard, their participation in development interventions, as well as in local governance (at the level of municipal councils) was often reported in a categorical way without further differentiation. Their participation, as reported by some state officials and development actors, is bundled in statements like 'the Baka do not want to participate', 'a Baka man does not want to involve himself', 'the Baka are so attached to their culture' (personal communication with the National Focal Point Person, Programme for the Development of Pygmy Peoples of MINAS, and with a community development facilitator, Plan Bertoua). However, as already mentioned above, there is differentiation and stratification among the Baka. In view of this, the question that comes to mind is whether and how this differentiation and stratification is reflected in the participation of the Baka. This chapter focuses on how claims to belonging influence the participation of the Baka in development projects in the East Region of Cameroon. Structurally, the chapter is organized into two sections. The first section describes some development projects and interventions in which the participation of the Baka was observed, while the second section discusses the ways in which the contested belonging of the Baka influences their participation in development interventions.

Development Projects and Interventions in Which the Participation of the Baka Was Observed

The participation of the Baka was observed both in development interventions that saw them as indigenous peoples, as well as in those that saw them as assimilated integrated Cameroonians (locals/autochthones). In both cases, local, national and international development organizations were consulted. In total, three Baka-initiated NGOs, one government initiative and one INGO were observed. These five initiaves were chosen from more than one hundred active development initiatives in the East Region of Cameroon. This selection was based on their relative popularity in the field. A non-exhaustive list of development organizations working with the Baka in the East Region of Cameroon has been included in the Appendix of this book. For now, the focus is on the projects in which the participation of the Baka was observed, as well as how the participation was effectuated.

Projects by Baka-initiated NGOs

As mentioned above, the participation of the Baka was observed in projects initiated by three Baka NGOs. I will briefly describe these NGOs, their activities, as well as some typical scenes to illustrate how participation was effectuated. The three Baka NGOs observed were OKANI, Centre d'Action pour le Développement Durable des Autochtones Pygmées (CADDAP) and Association des Baka du Cameroun (ASBAK). OKANI in the Baka language means 'rise up', and aims to train the Baka to take the initiative in their own development issues. It is a membership organization with about sixty active members based in different sub-divisions of the East Region of Cameroon. It was created in 2004 by a group of Baka people. It is chaired by Messe Venant, who also holds positions of responsibility at the Indigenous Peoples of Africa Coordinating Committee (IPACC) where he is secretary, and REPALEAC where he is the subregional president. According to Messe, the founding president of OKANI, the main goal of the organization is the empowerment of the Baka for the emergence of Baka elites. 'The direct activities of the organization include the diffusion of a simplified leaflet in the Baka language on human rights, promotion of participative videos on Baka culture, teaching Baka culture to children at schools and to teachers, and a project on "participative cartography"' (Valtonen 2009: 17). Prior to founding OKANI in 2004, Messe had been working with AAPPEC, a Catholic NGO that previously operated using the name PPEC, Programme Pygmées de l'Est Cameroun (AAPPEC, 1969–2001) that operated in the East Region of Cameroon to promote the social inclusion of the Baka people.

CADDAP was created in 2002 by Helen Aye Mondo who is also the national president of REPALEAC. CADDAP seeks to combat violence, abuse and torture used against the Baka. It also works to defend the land rights of the Baka, as well as 'the promotion of citizenship and other rights, like support for children's education, promotion of agriculture … handicrafts, traditional medicine, hygiene and health, and non-timber products' (ibid.). Prior to starting CADDAP, Helen said that she got inspiration from the blatant discrimination that she saw her people subjected to, even during international conferences. She said that in the past she had worked as a local project assistant for an ILO project that aimed to combat the marginalization of the Baka people. She recounted that in the late 1990s, while working for this project, the ILO and other government ministries organized an international conference in Yaoundé to discuss issues regarding recognition of the human rights of Pygmy peoples in Cameroon. She said officials of the ILO, top government officials and local Baka people were invited to take part in this conference.

However, when it was time for reception and refreshment, Helen said she was shocked by the sharp difference in the quality of food that was served to the Baka participants as opposed to other conference participants. She said that on the table where other participants and top officials, including herself, were served, there were plenty of delicious meals available throughout the event. She was surprised to see, however, that the Baka were asked to line up in front of another table where the food was a mixture of rice, fish and ground-nut paste that was half-cooked, as though it was 'food meant for dogs'. When she questioned why such food was being served to the Baka, those serving the food, not knowing that she was a Baka herself, said they served the Baka different food because the Baka are 'Pygmies' and are not used to modern foods.

At this point, Helen said, she took her plate from the table reserved for officials and went and sat with her Baka brothers and sisters because, according to her, it was inconceivable that a conference could be organized to recognize the human rights of a group of people who are not recognized as humans during the conference. This action raised some alarm in the hall, and it was only after this that the Baka were served the food that had been reserved for the other conference participants. After this event, she said that she decided to start her own NGO, where she would fight for her brothers' and sisters' rights, but back then, she needed more experience and skills. So she continued to work with different NGOs in different capacities until 2002, when she received the 'last straw that broke the camel's back', to use her words.

According to her, this was when, during events marking the 2002 celebrations of international women's day in Abong-Mbang, the chairwoman of the occasion told Baka women that they would not be allowed to participate in the march because, according to her, the Baka were 'dirty' and would 'stain and dirty the scene of the occasion'. She recounted that the chairwoman insisted that since the occasion was being televised by the national Cameroon Radio Television (CRTV), to be broadcast live across the country, the appearance of Baka women would make the whole occasion 'ugly'. Helen, who was one of the Baka elites attending the occasion, said that she stood up and told the chairwoman that if the Baka women are not allowed to march, she would create a scene by taking the situation to the international media. According to Helen, these two situations, among others, led her to start her own Baka NGO, CADAAP, with the intention of fighting for the rights of Baka people.

ASBAK was created in 1999 by a group of Baka people who previously worked for an international Baka development project.[3] According to Rene,

ASBAK's treasurer and one of its founding members, they founded the organization because they had discovered that their previous employers had limited mastery of Baka problems and realities and did not want to recognize that the Baka mastered their problems better than outsiders. Schmidt-Soltau, writing on ASBAK, however, says that:

> ASBAK was founded by former SNV extension officers of Baka origin. The key group of actors is quite limited (not more than 10) and is perceived by SNV as an 'elite-association', with 'little or no relation to the ordinary Baka...'. While most Baka interviewed were quite positive towards them ... ASBAK was conceptualized by some Baka informants as 'hyper-kokoma' – a link to the outside world, without a say on internal affairs (Schmidt-Soltau, 2003: 15).

Dkamela's (2003) study 'Associations, argent et exercice du pouvoir chez les Pygmées Baka de la région de Lomié (Est-Cameroun)' mentions that the challenges faced by ASBAK as a Baka association arise from institutional prescriptions by law, which involve hierarchical structures that appear to have accelerated the unravelling of traditional egalitarian Baka social norms and processes. He alludes to conflicts of leadership and distancing between the leaders and the base as some of these challenges. Nonetheless, infighting among Baka elites is a struggle for visibility on local, national and international platforms.

Throughout the description of the Baka NGOs above, one phenomenon seems common to the motivation for starting a Baka NGO. This is the fact that the founders of these Baka NGOs were Baka who had previously worked for other development projects or interventions before starting their own NGOs. In like manner, these Baka considered themselves to be the elites of their communities and the bringers of local development, to borrow from Foudouop (1997).

In the next paragraph, I will describe a typical scene of participation which I observed in a Baka-initiated NGO during my stay in the field. For the purposes of anonymity, a pseudonym will be used to identify the NGO. The observed Baka NGO event was a consultation meeting aimed at selecting which Baka communities would benefit from a livelihood development programme that one of the international development organizations operating in the East Region wanted to sponsor. The event took place during November 2011 with the Baka communities in Lomié. I was told by the representative of this Baka NGO that the INGO had subcontracted the selection of its project beneficiary communities to this Baka NGO with the following aims: *'dynamisme social et participation des communautés bénéficiaires prospectives'* (social dynamism and participation by the prospective Baka communities). During my time observing the process of community selection, the Baka

NGO organized a meeting at its head office and invited twenty Baka from the communities. During the meeting, the NGO representative explained the project and its sponsors to the Baka participants. After this explanation, he asked the particpants present whether their communities would commit to the project's requirements.

In response, some Baka immediately said that their communities would participate in the project. Others said that they had to consult with other community members before giving their response. A third group of Baka participants asked for more clarity on the project and its funders. They asked who exactly in the Baka communities was to benefit from the project and what long-term effects the project would have, because they were tired of short-term projects. The Baka NGO representative noted down the names of the communities where participants responded positively to his question.

For the Baka who said they needed to consult with their other community members, he gave them a deadline to do so and get back to him with their responses. For the third group of Baka who had asked for further clarity on the project, this repesentative said quite little. He basically said that if they were interested in participating in the project they would all benefit as a community, but if not, another community that showed interest would be chosen, because there were many Baka communities eager for such an opportunity. Once he presented the project as an opportunity, these Baka became enthusiastic about being listed as beneficiary communities.

Nonetheless, when I conducted follow-up interviews with these Baka, some of them mentioned that they had enlisted in the project because by participating in it they would learn how things worked, and then start their own NGOs so that INGOs could also subcontract projects to them. They referred to another Baka in Mballam who had participated in a project and learnt how it functioned, and had started his own NGO; now he also works with INGOs.

Reflecting on how the Baka elites above got the motivation to start their own NGOs, it may be said that although the Baka are often presented by some officials as passive participants during meetings and projects, some Baka in fact use their agency in ways that are not so visible to development actors and researchers, who spend a relatively short time in the field. This is because when Baka participate in projects, it takes a significant amount of time before they can withdraw and start their own NGOs. In this regard, a project official or researcher who can feasibly only observe the participation of Baka in project consultation meetings may tend to conclude that the Baka are passive and without agency of their own. Whereas the sudden proliferation of Baka NGOs in the East Region, as can be seen in the Appendix, suggests that the Baka do have some form of active agency and participation.

This said, I will discuss the national and international initiatives in which the dynamics of participation by the Baka were observed.

Government Initiative

One government initiative was observed. The Indigenous Peoples Development Plan (IPDP), best known by its French appellation, Plan de Développement des Peuples Pygmées (PDPP), which is a subsidiary of the national programme of participatory development (Programme National de Développement Participatif, PNDP). This programme was launched in 2003 and ran until 2015. It aimed to mitigate the marginalization of the Baka by providing national identity cards and creating autonomous Baka villages, among other things.[4] The other programme observed was civic participation in local governance at the level of municipal councils and parliament. The dynamics of Baka participation in these initiatives will be discussed in detail in later sections of this chapter.

International Initiative

The international initiative observed was the Baka Rights and Dignity (BRD) project, coordinated by Plan Bertoua. The Baka Rights and Dignity project is best known by its French appellation, Projet Droits et Dignité des Baka. The project began in the East Region of Cameroon in 2003 (then using the name Pygmy Rights and Dignity), with funding assistance from Finland's Ministry of Foreign Affairs. 'The BRD project is essentially about children (Baka and Bantus), and about the Baka as an indigenous group' (Valtonen 2009: 24). It engages in a number of activities such as sponsoring the establishment of birth certificates for Baka children and the establishment of national identity cards for adult Baka to enable them to participate in elections. The BRD also build modern houses for some Baka communities, drill bore holes to provide water to some Baka camps, promote the domestication of non-timber forest products (NTFP) by the Baka, do capacity building for some local Baka NGOs, and provide sponsorships for Baka children in school. Figure 5.1 illustrates a Baka Rights and Dignity project sign placed in a Baka community that benefited from the project. In the East Region of Cameroon, Baka communities that benefit from the BRD project all have a similar sign identifying them as beneficiaries of the project.

As mentioned above, the BRD promotes the domestication of non-timber forest products. Figure 5.2 is an illustration of one of the sites where the BRD promotes this domestication. In the figure, a BRD community development

Figure 5.1 A Baka village that benefited from the Baka Rights and Dignity project of Plan Bertoua.
Source: photograph by the research assistant (Nov. 2011).

Figure 5.2 Baka being shown how to tell when a seedling is mature enough for transplanting.
Source: photograph by the research assistant (Oct. 2011).

facilitator is demonstrating to some Baka men how to know when seedlings are sufficiently mature for transplanting.

Not all Baka were interested in or participated in this non-timber forest domestication activitiy of the BRD.[5] Follow-up interviews with some Baka who had participated in this activity and already had seedling farms revealed that these Baka aimed to become 'civilized', like their Bantu neighbours. According to these Baka, organizations like Plan and GIZ, just to name a few, had the know-how to help them become 'civilized' by teaching them how to engage in revenue-generating activities. In this section, I have called this process guided participation. By guided participation, I mean participation in which the Baka were actively taking part in projects designed either by the state and/or other development NGOs/INGOs. In this form of participation, the projects were most often designed externally, and the Baka considered the project designers to be experts who had the goodwill to help the Baka escape the traps of vulnerability, discrimination and violence. From this perspective, some Baka actively engaged in such projects and believed in the guardianship of the good-willed expert who would help them improve their living standards. These Baka went further to add that some of their Baka counterparts who had learnt agriculture in the early 1960s, when the government was forcing all Baka people to become farmers (in its post-independence national development vision for the cultivation of a single national identity), have mastered agricultural practices. Today, these Baka are sufficiently rich that they do not suffer from any marginalization by the Bantu. Taking into consideration the fact that these Baka, engaging in what I call guided participation, were emulating the examples of their fully sedentarized Baka counterparts, one may argue that guided participation among the Baka is a camouflaged practice of what Antonio Gramsci (1971) calls hegemony. This is hegemony defined by the domination of one group over others, and is brought about by the active compliance of those groups who are actually disadvantaged in the framework of an ideologized conception of a common good like 'national development'. In the context of this book, it was observed that the Baka who were framed by other Baka counterparts as 'Baka-Bantu' engaged in this form of participation. The latter believed that they were on their way to development and 'could reach development'[6] if they learnt from others.

These Baka consider their participation as a learning process through which they could become like the Bantu. They actively participate in micro-projects like cocoa cultivation and marketing, the domestication of non-timber forest products and Baka school construction projects among others. These Baka argue that the initiators of such projects understood how the Cameroonian system functioned and were in a position to help them become 'civilized' and catch up with their Bantu neighbours. According to them, the secret way out of what they called 'their plight' in the East Region of Cameroon is learning from and copying what NGOs teach them. For these Baka, their 'plight' is caused by unequal life opportunities, which they believe determination and hard work can overcome. The majority of the Baka in this category tended to reject the concept of indigeneity. They argued that it nurtured stereotypes and encouraged stigma. To them, indigeneity ought to be associated with their other brothers, whom they referred to as 'lazy cowards' (those whom this book calls 'Baka-Baka'). For these Baka who were engaged in guided participation, the tag 'lazy cowards' was appropriate for their other brothers because they did not want to do anything on their own except wait for donations from NGOs.

Contested Belonging and Participation of the Baka in the East Region of Cameroon

The belonging of the Baka is framed within the lines of autochthony and indigeneity. As autochthones, the Baka asserted belonging to the villages/camps where they resided. As indigenous peoples, they asserted their belonging to a global category characterized by being people with a special status, vulnerable, marginalized and discriminated against. However, this belonging of the Baka is highly contested, both by the Bantu and by some Baka. Considering the fact that in the East Region of Cameroon, participation is intricately linked to belonging, it is important to understand how the contested belonging of the Baka influenced their participation in local development.

Participation of the Baka as Regular Eastern Cameroonian Citizens

In the early days of Cameroon's independence, one of the motivations for ejecting the Baka from the forest to resettle them on the roadsides in the East Region of Cameroon was the government's desire to transform them into sedentary agriculturalists. In this way, they could become assimilated and intergrated Cameroonian citizens who worked for national development, a process that was then highly agricultural. At this point we must remind ourselves of the phenomenon that, in Cameroon, in order to progress from colonization to an independent state, the primitive had to become a savage, the savage an indigene, then the indigene must evolve into a citizen who worked for national development; the official policy placed such an emphasis on agriculture that the 'Pygmy' would only be included in the whole process of national development by becoming a farmer, which would permit him/her to emerge as a citizen (Abega and Logo 2005: 121).

This subsection discusses how the participation of the Baka as integrated Cameroonian citizens residing on the roadsides is influenced by the contests surrounding their belonging on these roadsides in contemporary Cameroon. To do this, I will first introduce some contrasting field quotes on the subject of participation from a Baka and a Bantu who both reside on the road-side as regular citizens in East Cameroon.[7] During an in-depth interview in Mballam, the Baka interlocutor said that:

> If they [the Bantu] say that we are forest people and do not belong to this roadside, let them leave our forest to us. They never invite us when they have meetings. Even when the DO [divisional officer, a government administrative official] comes, he only stops there, in their chief's palace, and whatever the Bantu tell him about us, he will listen to; and the next time, we only receive new orders, do this, do not do that, and do not and do not. If they do not consider us as people who also belong to this village, with things that we can also contribute or complain about, let them leave our forest and we will leave their roadsides, since that is how they want things to be. Yes, we are forest people but leave our forest to us and we will leave your village to you (a Baka participant, Mballam, Nov. 2011; my own translation).

Intriguingly, according to Carol J. Pierce Colfer in her book, 'The Equitable Forest: Diversity and Community in Sustainable Resource Management', research for which she also conducted in the East Region of Cameroon, a Bantu said:

> All those Pygmies you see here are only here because they know that the con-servator has brought wine and cigarettes. We have been fighting for compensa-tion ever since the loss of the forest which our ancestors bequeathed us, and for it to be managed as a reserve today. The Pygmies of this village have never shown interest in the course. It seems that they do not consider it to be their problem. We the Bantu are fighting alone (inhabitant of Mintoum village, quoted in Colfer 2004: 120).

These two quotes, extracted from different research conducted in the East Region of Cameroon in different years, suggest that belonging and participa-tion are intricately linked. This intricate link is engraved into the country's constitution, which emphasizes citizenship at two levels: local citizenship and national citizenship. As was mentioned in Chapter 2, Article 55 Part X of the 1996 Cameroon constitution, focusing on regional and local authorities, states that:

> The Regional Council shall be the deliberative organ of the Region. Regional Councillors shall comprise: ... representatives of traditional rulers elected by

their peers ... The Regional Council shall be headed by an indigene of the Region elected from among its members for the life of the Council (Cameroon constitution of 1996).

The clauses *'representatives of traditional rulers'* and *'an indigene'*, extracted from the quote above, emphasize the need for people to belong as autochthones/locals of the localities in a given region before they can participate, even if they are Cameroonians. In other words, they must be 'sons of the soil'. However, as was seen in Chapter 4 and in the quote above from the Baka in Mballam, the Baka are considered as 'strangers' on the roadsides where municipal councils are established. Moreover, most of them live in camps that belong to Bantu villages and are considered the Pygmies of these Bantu villages, as noted by Colfer (2004: 120) above. Nonetheless, I was told by one of the Baka elites who were fighting to have Baka camps recognized as autonomous villages that this process had been halted indefinitely following instructions from the head of state, President Paul Biya.

The government has set up what is called an 'action' for the Baka, referred to in the region as *'promotion de la citoyenneté'* (promotion of citizenship) and as a programme of the national Indigenous Peoples Development Plan (IPDP). It is supervised by the National Programme for Participative Development (known by its French acronym, PNDP) and the subsidiary department of marginalized populations in the Ministry of Social Affairs (hereafter MINAS). The focus of this 'action' is to enable the Baka to engage and participate in civic life within the region and country. This programme has established national identity cards and has distributed these to thousands of Baka people. In the same rubric of promoting the citizenship of the Baka, local councils also distribute national identity cards and marriage certificates to the Baka. However, the question that follows this massive distribution of national identity cards is whether this identity card enforces the Baka's sense of local belonging, and how the Baka engage and participate in community life as citizens.

Although the majority of the Baka now have national identity cards establishing that they are Cameroonian citizens, their belonging as Cameroonians did not immediately confer upon them the status of belonging on the roadsides as local citizens. As already demonstrated in previous chapters, when most Baka claimed to belong to a given municipality in the East Region, where they were born and bred, like all other eastern Cameroonians, some of the neighbouring Bantu people challenged their belonging, arguing that they were strangers on the lands on which they resided. This lack of recognition of their belonging is straining their participation at both municipal and parliamentary levels.

Despite being holders of Cameroonian national identity cards, most Baka can generally only participate by voting for candidates who will represent them at decision-making levels. When they want to present their own candidates (for example, as recounted by Messe Venant during his attempt to run for the position of mayor in 2007), their belonging becomes sharply contested. Based on interviews conducted with some government officials, the Baka can only participate as people from subquarters of Bantu villages or legitimate Baka villages.[8] Pyhälä also noted this in her own report, titled 'What Future for the Baka?' when she said that:

> According to the government (as expressed by the interviewed state representatives), you need to have a legally recognized village chief (referred to as '*chefferie de troisième degré*' in Cameroon) in order to have any political power or representation (2012: 17).

The creation of Baka villages and the appointment of some Baka traditional leaders by the government in early 2000 were lauded as a move towards the recognition of their belonging as local citizens of the East Region. Nonetheless, this programme was suspended,[9] and the belonging and participation of the Baka people as local citizens of the East Region remain greatly contested. Although President Biya mentioned in his 1988 speech during his visit to Bertoua that Pygmies are not second-class citizens (Logo 1998), their belonging as local citizens who can participate in local political processes in the East Region is most often alluded to by Bantus when they want to insult the incompetence of the Baka. This was seen, for example, in the ways that the Bantu expressed discontent about a Bantu-born mayor in Yokadouma who embezzled millions of CFA francs from council funds. The Bantu said that 'it is better to vote for a Pygmy than to vote for that man … giving responsibility to that man is like giving it to a Pygmy' (Robillard 2010: 118).

Two vivid examples of this nuance in participation via the belonging of the Baka as local citizens on the roadsides are elaborated below. The first example is that of Messe Venant, a Baka man born in the late 1960s to a Baka father and a Bantu mother on the roadside of Diang in the Upper Nyong Division of the East Region of Cameroon. Messe explained that in 2007 he wanted to stand as mayor in the Diang municipality. However, the Bantu of the municipality challenged his candidature, arguing that he was from the forest and did not belong as a 'son of the soil' in Diang. Thus, although Messe could vote in Diang as a Cameroonian citizen, the contest surrounding his belonging as a 'son of the soil' in Diang affected his ability to participate in community life by running for high-profile council positions.

In like manner, Helen, a born and bred Baka woman, the national representative of REPALEAC, founder and director of CADDAP, said that her application for the post of senator (by nomination) in 2013 was rejected by the selection committee.[10] According to Helen, her application was rejected on the grounds of what she called a 'lack of grass roots party participation'. In discussing this rejection, she stressed the point that she is a Cameroonian, a woman and a Baka who has been working to protect the rights of Baka people in Baka communities since 2000. The government, she claimed, has collaborated with her in some aspects of her community work. However, she argued that when it comes to what she considered to be 'real' participation, there is always a barrier that is consciously raised to obstruct meaningful participation with the power to change the destiny of the Baka people. Alluding to this rejection of her candidature for the post of a senator, Helen said that it is written in policy documents that the government aims to protect indigenous peoples and to promote women especially. However, when indigenous people want to sit with the government and talk about the issues really affecting them, they are never given a meaningful chance. She stressed that, 'the subject of their belonging is always twisted by local and regional authorities to ensure that the indigenous peoples do not qualify to participate in the appropriate political circles'. Referring to her rejection on the grounds of a 'lack of grass roots party participation', Helen questioned what grass roots actually meant and what the status of Pygmies at the grass roots level is. She identified her rejection with Messe's rejection, which was on the grounds of his forest belonging, and said that in the East Region of Cameroon, the subject of being Pygmies always mingles into everyday living, especially when it comes to participation in influential political spheres. Helen added that it was ironic that even at the national level:

> The Baka people are considered to belong here – in the bush – and not there in Yaoundé [the nation's capital]. If there is an international contract to be signed that demands the signatures of Baka people, we [referring to the government] can go there [to the bush] and meet them [the Baka people] to sign it. In that way, they [the Baka] have participated, after all, their signatures are there in the documents for funders to see (BBP conference, Bertoua, June 2013; my own translation).

Helen's story supports other local-level examples, which have been captured in this section as '*représentation figurative*', associated in the field of political sciences with the metaphor of a figurehead. As was observed in the field, '*représentation figurative*' is a process whereby municipal councils, local Bantu NGOs and some government officials strategically select certain Baka people who, according to them, cannot exercise their civic agency to represent the Baka people during activities. They simply satisfy the funding and reporting obligations of their projects and programmes. This '*représentation figurative*', from my perspective, is an ongoing phenomenon in the region and seeks to fulfil international demands, which require a proof of participation by the local communities (in this case the Baka).

Meyer and Rowan (1977) use the phenomenon of ceremonial coupling to treat organizations as being dependent on societal 'institutions' (legal norms in this context) and try to analyze how organizations behave when these institutions change. This section considers the phenomenon of '*représentation figurative*' as the strategy of political organizations like municipal councils in the East Region of Cameroon to comply with the expectations formulated by international development funding agencies, while at the same time leaving their grass roots operating level unchanged by refusing to recognize the belonging of the Baka as local citizens who can compete for senior positions in municipal councils.

The Baka, '*représentation figurative*' or Participation?

> Despite the intention of the policies and practices of regional balance, the representation of the Pygmies and Mbororo at all levels of the Cameroonian public service is almost zero. Examples of indigenous people being employed are rare in forest revenue management committees, wildlife resource development committees, as well as community forest management associations, which are mostly managed by Bantu residents, who either simply put indigenous populations (Pygmies) aside, or only involve them in very limited numbers, in figurehead positions [*à des positions de figurants*], such that the Pygmies in these positions were quick to realize that they were useless (Nguiffo and Mballa, no date: 6; my own translation).

In the quote above, Nguiffo and Mballa allude to this phenomenon of '*représentation figurative*' and highlight that some Pygmies are already conscious of the phenomenon. During fieldwork, most Baka used the term '*représentation figurative*' when discussing the participation of the Baka at the level of municipal councils. One of them, for example, used a tabularized illustration of the percentage of Baka people living in a particular municipality against the number of Baka municipal councillors participating in local governance in the municipality. Table 5.1 is an extract of this illustration.

Follow-up interviews conducted with some of the few Baka who featured as municipal councillors in the table above revealed dynamics which these Baka characterized as '*représentation figurative*', a term that I will use henceforth because of the lack of a more appropriate word to describe it. In the councils where there were Baka municipal councillors, the ratio of Baka to Bantu councillors (1:25) was always very insignificant, such that the Baka could not significantly participate to alter decisions taken within the council. Moreover, other Baka from the municipality framed the inclusion of

Table 5.1 Representation and participation of the Baka in municipal councils.
Source: Messe Venant, BBP conference presentation, Bertoua, June 2013.

Councils	% of Baka population	Total number of municipal councillors in the council	Number of Baka municipal councillors
Moloundou	60	25	0
Salapoumbé	70–80	25	1
Yokaduma	20	25	0
Lomié	30	25	1
Abong-Mbang	5	25	1
Dimako	7–9	25	0
Messok	45	25	1
Total		**200**	**4**

one Baka member in the council as a blindfolding trick aimed at attracting development money. According to these Baka, the Bantu officials permitted one Baka councillor to feature among their municipal councillors because when development organizations come around with money, the organizations always ask for the Baka, because development money that comes into the region mainly targets the Baka.

During an in-depth interview with one of the Baka chiefs, he mentioned the fact that ensuring the Baka are present does not mean allowing them to participate. To illustrate his point, he referred to one of their brothers who worked as a municipal councillor. The chief argues that the Bantu took their brother on as a municipal councillor because they knew that he could be easily manipulated. The chief insisted that they had more intelligent and learned Baka youths in the camp who wanted to enlist as municipal councillors, but the Bantu rejected them. According to this chief, the Bantu do not want to associate with an intelligent Baka man. Elaborating on the situation, the chief recounted that this Baka municipal councillor is also a traditional healer who treats all the Bantu's ailments for free, because he wants to maintain warm relationships with the Bantu. In conclusion, the chief said of his Baka brother that 'he is there because he is another Bantu. Since he has been there as a councillor, how have we benefited? He spends all his time in the bar drinking with them' (Baka chief, Lomié, Dec. 2011).

During a conference which I organized in Bertoua on the participation of the Baka in local governance and development projects, the Baka participants made mention of the fact that at the level of municipal councils and joint development projects, the Bantu officials responsible for selecting participants often tactically select only 'foolish' Baka people, some of whom could not even read or write well. These Baka participants argued that Bantu officials often use these tactically selected Baka as a pretext for justifying the exclusion of the Baka from decision-making processes within the community. They added that when these Bantu officials tactically select their 'foolish' and alcohol-addicted brothers, they tend to brand and publicize all the Baka as 'illiterates', 'drunkards' and people who cannot do anything for themselves.

Using the example of a lingering 25 million CFA francs (about 40,000 euros) which was deposited at the Dimako rural council for the development of the Baka people in the municipality, these participants said they had only heard that the money had been deposited in the council for their development. They had not been informed about how and when this money would be used. To them, this exclusion was due to the fact that the Bantu had successfully convinced the government and donors that the Baka are incapable of managing resources. They added that the government and donors now believe that if the money is given to a Baka man, he will spend it all on alcohol. While these Baka argued that alcohol abuse has been used by some Bantu to enforce their exclusion from development participation, Oishi has, however, shown that due to 'a strong desire for alcohol and consumer goods, the majority of the Baka spend the[ir] money immediately after acquisition. [Nonetheless, he stresses that] a small number of the Baka try to save money so they can employ the other Baka to expand their cacao plantations' (2012: 115). From this, it may be argued that while some Baka do spend their money on alcohol as Oishi shows, some Bantus seem to use this as an argument against the financial management abilities of the Baka in general, as highlighted by the Baka in the example of the 25 million CFA francs above.

In this example, it was intriguing to find out that while these Baka participants said that they were unaware of the fact that there was a Baka signatory to the 25 million CFA francs, the council's head of service for local development affirmed that indeed, there were two Baka signatories, who also held seats on the steering committee to manage the money. The criteria used to choose these Baka signatories remained arbitrary, especially since there were no Baka municipal councillors in the Dimako council. Moreover, the Baka chief, who is legally recognized as the third-class chief of the autonomous Baka village of Mayos in the Dimako municipality, was among the Baka participants who were not aware of what the money was meant for, who was managing it or when it was to be used.

In a bid to gain a better understanding of this phenomenon of 'représentation figurative', I visited two other municipalities in the Upper Nyong Division where there were Baka councillors. During this field visit, I interviewed a Baka councillor. When I met the councillor, his first words to me were:

> You are with his excellency, a Baka municipal councillor, one of three in the entire East Region of Cameroon.[11] You can also call me chief, because at the same time, I am the chief of a Baka camp, the traditional doctor of the land. I

have a secret that I want to tell you. I cannot talk about my being a councillor without starting with it. It is one of the things that make me feel very proud, and when I see people like you who come here to ask us questions, I like to tell you first, so that you should know that time has changed and Pygmies are now becoming indispensable. You know there is no logging company that can enter here without the Bantu calling me to come and sign. Some white people came to give some money there in the council, but even the mayor could not sign without me. They [the Bantu] cannot get anything now if I do not sign, especially when it is for the Baka people. I am in the committee for Baka people there in the council. So the head of the committee always takes me everywhere he goes. When they make me angry there in the council, I just tell them that I will not sign any documents again, and they start to beg me. They know that if I am not there, things will not move. The white man wants to see a Baka. because at first, Bantu people just used to take all the money. Now things have changed and I must always sign things there in the council (Baka municipal councillor, Lomié, Nov. 2011; my own translation).

According to some Bantu councillors in the same municipality as the municipal councillor quoted above, the election of a Baka councillor onto the council was a 'fill-in-the-gap phenomenon' aimed at easing administrative processes at the level of the council. A councillor who said he had been serving in the council for fourteen years recounted that in the past, when there were no Baka on the council, companies and organizations used to cause them stress by insisting that they include Baka people on their committees. To relieve themselves of this stress, he said they decided to include a Baka in their list during the last municipal elections in 2007.

From the above quote and from discussions, it is clear that the requirement for at least one Baka signatory to appear in documents as an indication of Baka participation in community affairs and development projects is most often abused by some Bantu officials who tactically select certain Baka people whom they consider 'foolish' to represent the Baka. Nonetheless, some of these selected Baka who are considered 'foolish' do actually utilize their agency as solicited signatories. An example of this use of agency may be read in the case of the municipal councillor quoted above, who said that when his Bantu colleagues annoy him in the council or do not meet his demands, he counteracts this by not signing any document that requires his signature. Despite the agency of the Baka municipal councillor above, I would argue that due to the increasing demand from development funders for local beneficiary participation, organizations receiving development funds have devised strategies that will always ensure that the project beneficiaries are represented, without necessarily being able to actively participate.

During the conference I organized on the participation of the Baka in local governance, for example, a Bantu who claimed to be a municipal councillor walked into the conference room and disrupted an ongoing presentation by the head of the council's local development programme. This interrupter, who called himself the council's delegate for community forests, walked into the conference room and asked what the aim of the gathering was and who had authorized the Baka people to sit in the meeting without his knowledge. He went on to add that the Baka people have no right to assist in any meeting at the council, because he represents them at the council. After several attempts to calm him down, he persisted for over thirty minutes. He argued that his colleague, the head of the council's local development programme, who was delivering a presention, had no right to host Baka people in a meeting without his consent. The head of the council's local development programme, for his part, tried to explain the objective of the meeting but this was not to this interrupter's satisfaction. He continued to disturb the event until some of the conference participants, including a police officer and the moderator, told him to stay out of the room. He angrily left, but returned after a while and said:

> You can push me out but you cannot put me out. You cannot do without me. You Baka people who are looking at me, I pity you so much because even though you are attending this meeting, I remain the final signatory for any money that is meant for you people. And let me explain to you how it works, each time I sign and we receive the money, we use it as we desire. After using it, we choose a few Baka and fill their mouths with the leftovers. You the Baka people attending this meeting should know that I have marked all your faces; since you think that you know so much and have started attending meetings without my knowledge, I will not call any of you to sit in the forest committee (conference interrupter, Dimako, June 2013).

This interruption turned out to be very intriguing, because the scene took place during the same meeting in which the Baka mentioned the example of the 25 million CFA francs deposited at the council, which they were unaware had had Baka signatories (at the time of our fieldwork, June 2013).[12] This phenomenon, whereby some Bantu municipal officials exclude the Baka or employ only those Baka who agree to work according to their rules, has also been reported by Robillard (2010). In discussing the phenomemon of influential people and networks ('*hommes forts*' and '*réseaux d'alliance*') in Baka and Bantu relations, Robillard quotes one of her Baka interlocutors, who describes that it is the mayor of the municipality who chooses the presidents of subsections and cells, based on the support that they will give him in return. The following quote stresses the point that the phenomemon of influential people and networks is such that municipal councillors are all the uncles of the mayor:

> All the presidents of the local committees and subsections are put there by the mayor. He chose families who will support him, and in return he supports

them. Many are family members, although some are just his friends. If you look at the municipal councillors, they are all his uncles (Baka interlocutor in Robillard 2010: 105; my own translation).

Taking into consideration the discussions above, as well as the fact that most development funders now demand proof of Baka participation from municipal councils, who are often the implementing partners of these development projects, it may be said that there is a blurring of boundaries between participation and 'représentation figurative'. From this it may be said that the change in development funding requirements, which emphasizes the participation of beneficiaries, is resulting in a change in the nature of social relations between the Baka and their Bantu neighbours. This change in the nature of social relations is shifting from a sharply conflictual continuum towards a manipulative continuum involving 'représentation figurative'. This shift seems to provide one of the underlying explanations for the paradox of collaboration and marginalization respectively raised by Rupp (2011) and Pyhälä (2012). As mentioned in the introductory chapter, Rupp (2011) elaborately challenges stereotypes and illustrates collaborations between the Baka and the Bantu, whereas Pyhälä (2012) extensively demonstrates marginalization, exclusion and violence inflicted on the Baka by their Bantu neighbours. In this light, the 'représentation figurative' of the Baka in community projects may be read as collaboration in the case of Rupp, while the manipulation of the Baka by other parties, like some Bantus, is read as marginalization and discrimination by Pyhälä.

It is also observed that in this nexus of relationships where the Bantu maximize the 'représentation figurative' of Baka, some Baka are also seizing occasional opportunities to get involved and get whatever they can from the opportunities that arise. The Baka chief of Mendjou in Figure 5.3 exemplified this when he recounted that due to his mastery of the way things function, he has benefited from a great deal of training, as well as material assistance from the government and NGOs.

In Figure 5.3, the Baka chief of Mendjou is holding his training certificate on forest management and wearing the uniform of the ruling CPDM party. According to him, if government officials see Baka in the ruling party's uniform, they will assist such Baka. An example of which was his ultra modern house, which he said was built by the Chantal Biya Foundation (owned by the wife of the current president of Cameroon).

Apart from the 'représentation figurative' discussed above, another dimension of Baka participation as local citizens is what the Baka call 'the so-called government inclusion programme', which seeks to integrate young Baka into government positions of responsibility. Through this programme, the government has recruited some Baka youths into the army and others into the

Figure 5.3 The Baka chief of Mendjou with his training certificate.
Source: photograph by the research assistant (Nov. 2011).

national school of forest guards. According to some Baka, these professions were irrelevant for the current development needs of the Baka people. Rather, they argue that by training Baka youths as forest guards, the government is consciously sowing a seed of divide and rule, in which these trained Baka will be employed to police their brothers and prevent them from benefiting from forest resources. In this way, the government action of inclusion was for them a calculated and 'manipulative' action, which in the future may potentially result in more internal conflicts among the Baka. They questioned why young educated Baka students were not rather admitted into the nation's prestigious schools, like the National School of Administration and Magistracy (ENAM), where the nation's high-profile administrators are trained. However, on the part of some government officials interviewed, the decision to train some Baka youths as forest guards and recruit others into the army was, according to them, based on the fact that the Baka have a traditional knowledge of forest conservation and are also good hunters (good in sighting targets). Thus, recruiting Baka youths in these fields is a means of perfecting their know-how.

Conclusion

This chapter accentuates the point that, due to a lack of coordination to ensure that all development interventions have the same long-term vision for the Baka in terms of participation, the resulting differentiation and stratification of the Baka people have led to a vicious circle within Baka society. In this cycle, different development actors come into Baka society with different visions, actions and approaches for the development of the Baka. In return, the Baka engage in these different development interventions. The engagement of different Baka in these different interventions (which have different visions for the Baka) result in internal differentiation among the Baka, which is further reinforced by the constant influx of development resources supporting different development projects with different visions. This phenomenon was captured by some Baka in the following quote:

Each NGO has its Baka that it works with, and in the end, the Baka have very different experiences. This makes the Baka see life in very different ways. But the most important question that we, the Baka, ask ourselves is: Where are all these NGOs taking us to? They have no clear vision for the development of the Baka people, and do not even work in coordination, so that, you will see maybe three or four NGOs working with the Baka in the field of promoting Baka citizenship, but there are many Baka camps where the Baka still do not have national identity cards; whereas, in other Baka camps, you will find a Baka with three or four national identity cards, which is not normal. Even at the national level, there is no one Baka who can always recommend to the government that they should take this or that into consideration when conceiving development plans for the Baka people (Baka participant, BBP conference, Bertoua, June 2013; my own translation).

Pyhälä in her report, 'What Future for the Baka?' stated that:

There are currently no Baka holding office in local, regional or national government, and representation in regional and national institutions is minimal. There are also no forms of consultation, involvement or consent processes with the Baka when it comes to making high-level decisions that bear direct or indirect consequences for them. As a result, the Baka are in no way involved in the decision-making processes around matters that concern them or that affect their rights, and have no political or decision-making power, even in regions where they are the majority of the population (2012: 17).

From the quotes above, it may be said that the Baka do not really participate in community life in the East Region of Cameroon. Nonetheless, there is always a twist when it comes to the subject of the participation of the Baka. This twist is based on the existence of 'figurehead'[13] Baka representation in local government offices, as well as in the management boards of local development aid funds. This 'figurehead' representation is a phenomenon whereby the Baka are theoretically included in local governance by their names being added to the list of participants/beneficiaries of development project proposals/reports, where this inclusion is only allowed as a concession to the demands of development funding organizations, which often stress the need for proof of participation by the project's beneficiaries. This phenomenon has been captured using the term 'représentation figurative'.[14] However, although there is this 'représentation figurative', most Baka occupying the position of figureheads tend to utilize their agency by learning how the organizations in which they are considered to be figureheads are run, so they can start their own local Baka NGOs. This has led to a proliferation of local Baka NGOs in the region.

In the field of development theorizing, the non-participation of people in development projects has often been analysed from the persective that projects were conceived without the effective involvement of their beneficiaries (Hickey and Mohan 2004; Namara 2009). Thus, project goals and activities were incompatible with people's needs, values and cultural systems (Cooke and Kothari 2001). This analysis led development funders to demand that applicant organizations show how their beneficiaries will be involved in all stages of the project's life cycle. This demand has become a panacea in development project funding and evaluation. However, from the discussion of belonging and participation in this chapter, it is clear that there is more to learn about the participation of the so-called 'backward communities' as project beneficiaries. The discussion of 'représentation figurative' by the Baka in local councils and other development projects is one example which shows that the internal dynamics within the category of project beneficiaries can be instrumentalized to facilitate the diversion and misuse of development funds. Also, the contest surrounding the Baka's belonging at the local citizenship level and its influence on their participation in local decentralized development processes suggest that there is more to learn about 'local communities' when emphasizing their participation in development funding and implementation.

Notes

1. 'Rencontre AGGN et les Baka de l'Est Cameroun', by Glory Lueong and Fred Leboh, available online at http://www.youtube.com/watch?v=Gvsqo1Mqf0E&feature=share
2. Non-Baka development actors.
3. The ASBAK members whom I approached claimed to have forgotten the exact name of the international organization that was implementing the project for which they worked prior to founding ASBAK.
4. See the Appendix for an exhaustive list of the programme's activities.
5. According to some of the uninterested Baka, they did not understand why they were being refused access to the forest where these NTFP grew naturally. Nonetheless,

according to one of the community development facilitators, the Baka are impatient people and are not interested in participating in programmes that require time to yield results.

6. For the 'Baka-Bantu', their measure of development was sedentary agriculture, which was packaged with national development during post-independence nationalist policies. So, by reaching development, these Baka meant becoming fully assimilated, 'like the Bantu', as most of them said.

7. One of the field quotes is from my own research while the other is from previous research conducted by another researcher in 2004. These two quotes both come from interlocutors residing within the same division of the East Region.

8. As discussed in Chapter 4, the process of granting villages to Baka people was suspended and most Baka live in 'camps' that are administratively attached to Bantu villages as sub-quarters. In this light, the Baka may belong as assimilated citizens if they integrate into the Bantu villages neighbouring them. This is a subject of contestation, as was discussed in Chapter 4, where the Baka preferred to call their camps 'villages'.

9. The reasons given for this suspension are many and contradictory depending on who is speaking. As seen in Chapter 4, government officials have a different version from Bantu chiefs and elites.

10. In 2013 Cameroon started the implementation of its bi-cameral system of legislation by establishing its first ever senate comprising one hundred senators (three per region). The selection of these senators was both by election and presidential nomination. Seventy per cent of the senators were elected, while thirty per cent were nominated by the president upon application. Helen's application was for one of the nominated seats to represent indigenous peoples.

11. Although he said that he was one of three Baka municipal councillors in the entire East Region of Cameroon, evidence from research as may be read in Table 5.1, notes that there were four Baka municipal councillors as of July 2013 when I was in the field.

12. Since the objective of this research was not to analyse the effective use and accountability of local development funds, I do not have any data on how this money was effectively managed.

13. This metaphor of figureheads is borrowed from political science, where it is used to refer to a nominal leader or head without real power.

14. In the field, the term 'représentation figurative', as used by research participants conveyed an absolutely different meaning from its regular dictionary/academic meaning. Rather, the meaning which participants accorded to the term was associated with the metaphor of a 'figurehead' in political sciences.

Conclusion

ꙮ•ꙮ

This book sought to understand the ways in which the Baka, now living on roadsides in the East Region of Cameroon, assert their belonging in order to participate in and benefit from development interventions. The rationale for focusing on belonging and participation was the fact that, in the East Region of Cameroon, people can only participate in and benefit from development interventions if they belong within the boundaries of the category 'project beneficiaries' as defined by the development interventions.

However, the categorization of 'project beneficiaries' in the region is nuanced by the simultaneous existence of two intertwined social phenomena. The first is the incidence of being 'a local'/autochthon versus being 'forest people'/indigenous, which respectively have specific defining criteria. The second phenomenon is the existence of multiple contrasting development policies and approaches, which include those that 'civilize', assimilate and integrate 'the uncivilized backward savages' to evolve into full citizens, conserve the forest and wildlife resources and finally, protect indigenous cultures at the verge of extinction.

Intriguingly, while the development approach of some development projects seeks to reinforce 'local' autochthony[1] for the Baka, the development approach of other development projects seeks to protect indigenous cultures at the verge of extinction, thereby, aiming to reinforce the indigeneity of the Baka. Amid this intertwining of social phenomena, the Baka have on the one hand been resettled on roadsides to live with 'their Bantus' and become sedentary farmers as 'civilized', assimilated and integrated citizens ('locals').

Yet, on the other hand, they are being presented as indigenous peoples who have a distinct culture to be preserved. Interestingly enough, there are development organizations supporting each of these causes. The state, for its part, constantly switches its support for the two causes. Sometimes it funds activities that promote the sedentarization of the Baka, and sometimes it funds activities that promote their indigeneity. In this regard, it is in the interests of the Baka to assert where they belong to access the available development resources. However, the ways in which they do this remain the question that this book has sought to explore.

Main Arguments

In this book, I argue that amid conflicting development polices and approaches, the Baka assert their belonging in ways that are functionally instrumental. In other words, the Baka assert their belonging not as a group of indigenous peoples. Rather, they assert their belonging in ways that are conflicting. Some Baka assert that they are indigenous peoples, while others see themselves as 'locals'/autochthones. Assertions of the latter often meet with enormous contestations from the Bantu, who by virtue of their relationship to the soil as agriculturalists consider themselves to be the 'locals'. These contests emerge from the ethnoregional political regime, which stresses the need for people to belong as 'sons of the soil' in order to access political power, which in turn enables them to secure development resources for their communities.

These contests also nurse newer forms of conflict between the Baka and the Bantu on the subject of home and 'strangerness'. In these contests, the main concerns are: Who can claim to be a 'local son of the soil' on the roadside, and who is the stranger and why? These concerns are highly contentious, because in the system of ethnoregional political identity, 'locals' who call the roadsides their home have rights to a wide array of resources and benefits. During my research among the Baka, I found that the Baka have begun to call their roadside residences their homes. In this way, they claim to belong there as 'locals'/autochthones and not as 'strangers'. In like manner, these Baka demand to participate and benefit from all municipal offices and resources like their Bantu counterparts. However, the Bantu continually contest and challenge the Baka's belonging to the roadsides as 'locals'.

For most Bantus, the Baka's home is the forest, and they can only belong to the roadsides as 'strangers' or as Bantu subjects. This claim that the home of the Baka is the forest seems to be reinforced by many conservationists, as well as researchers, who decry the destruction of the forest as the destruction of the 'home' of indigenous Baka people (Abega 1998). This is because, while these authors and activists are rational in their fights against deforestation (which I totally support), referring to the forest as the 'home' of the Baka when the Baka have been evicted permanently to settle on roadsides, to my mind shows a lack of understanding about other social processes going on in the region. Framing the forest as 'the home' of the Baka has within it the inbuilt assumption that the Baka can one day return home to the forest, whereas national law forbids this return. This situation seems to suggest that the Baka are stuck at the roadsides. To borrow from Ong, who argues that 'an extraordinary departure in policy ... can be deployed to include as well as to exclude' (2006: 5), one may argue that there is an ongoing process of 'inclusion by exclusion' among the Baka in the East Region of Cameroon, who are stuck at the roadsides as not-quite-local citizens. In this light, I would say that marketing forest conservation primarily as safeguarding the homes of indigenous forest peoples may be valid and useful for other forest people still living in the forest, like those in the Amazon. However, using the same technique for the Baka, who have already been permanently displaced from the forest and are now struggling to make a home on the roadsides in the East Region of Cameroon, is not so helpful. Rather, such marketing helps to amplify new forms of conflicts between the Baka and the Bantu. This is because it gives the Bantu an upper hand to frame the Baka as strangers on the roadsides and as belonging in the forest, which in the context of an ethnoregional political regime has serious implications on their ability to participate in local governance, as well as benefit from local resources.

Another factor enhancing the Baka's contested belonging as 'locals' on the roadsides is the cumulative and conflicting development approaches being implemented in the East Region of Cameroon. On the one hand, there is the sedentarization of the Baka, which translates into relations with the soil on the roadsides; as early as 1961, Baka were already being sedentarized and their younger generations have been born into predominantly agricultural and sedentary roadside camps. On the other hand, however, recent developments in the global category of 'indigenous peoples' have re-invented these Baka as indigenous forest peoples with a 'distinct and marginal culture', because in the past they were hunter-gathers who had no special attachment to the soil. Taking into consideration the fact that the Baka were first being sedentarized and are now being presented as indigenous forest peoples with a 'distinct and marginal culture', the subject of their home and belonging at the local level has come back into question. As a result of their contested belonging as local citizens in the East Region, it is a challenge for them to enjoy the same rights as their Bantu neighbours, especially the sharing of resources derived from forest exploitation.

This recent development in the global approach to development interventions has left the younger agricultural roadside generations of the Baka caught in a dilemma, which divides them between being 'locals' and being indigenous. On the one hand, some of these younger generations tend to attribute forest belonging to their parents and ancestors, arguing that the younger generations belong to the roadsides where they were born. Most of these younger Baka generations challenge the category of indigenous peoples, calling it stigmatizing and a strategy to reinforce the stereotypes held about their incapacity to 'develop' like other Cameroonian 'locals'. For them, the category of indigenous peoples is as derogatory as that of 'Pygmies'. On the other hand, other younger Baka assert that they are indigenous peoples. These Baka have started initiatives aimed at protecting their rights as indigenous peoples. Intriguingly, although the former and latter Baka assert their belonging in different ways, they seem to have one thing in common.

Both are clear about their understanding of the fact that they can never return to the forest – which is now a national domain, and for the most part protected. Thus, both groups try to create a sense of home in their new roadside residences. However, when it comes to this level of making sense of home, again the Baka really differ and are internally stratified. An analysis of how they make use of the concepts of 'roadside camps'/'villages', as well as 'forest' as sites of adherence and homeland permits an insight into the new dynamics surrounding home and belonging for the Baka. The dynamics suggest that as an adaptation mechanism, the Baka are constantly reinterpreting and reinventing the notion of home in their roadside residences. This is different from what current essentialist literature on 'Pygmies' suggests. According to this literature, the Baka have strong connections and attachments to the forest, which is their homeland (Pyhälä 2012).

The above-mentioned adaptive dynamism on the one hand suggests that the Baka who claim to belong to the roadsides as 'locals' tend to authenticate their belonging by using historical narratives, which are compatible with the narrative of 'rootedness in the soil'. These narratives are very similar to those made by the Bantu pertaining to their own belonging to the roadsides. Like their neighbouring Bantus, these Baka stress the fact that they occupied their roadside dwellings in ways that showed their clear control of the land, as required by the government in its 1974 land law. They also refer to their engagement in agriculture prior to the 1974 land law, pointing to palms and other fruit trees that they planted as signifying development of the land and clear control over the land, which the government requires to authenticate citizens' rights to land. In a similar vein, they allude to the graves of their parents and/or grandparents on their roadside dwellings as solid proof that they are rooted on these roadsides, and could thus participate in and benefit from every development intervention aimed at the local inhabitants of the East Region without discrimination of any kind. For those who live in camps that are already upgraded and legalized as villages, they highlight the upgrading of their camps into villages as approval by the government of their authenticity and rights to call the land home. This claim fits well with the mission behind the government's upgrading of Baka camps into villages, which is aimed at minimizing conflicts of belonging and rights to call the land home between the Baka and the Bantu at the local level in the East Region of Cameroon.

On the other hand, the Baka who claim to be 'indigenous peoples' tend to authenticate their being at home on these roadsides by reinterpreting the meaning of their name, 'Baka'. As has been discussed in previous chapters, the word 'Baka' was originally interpreted by previous authors (Dellemmes 1985) and some Baka to mean 'migratory birds' that only land temporarily on a tree branch to eat and rest, and then take off for their next destination. However, with the permanent resettlement of the Baka on the roadsides, the Baka who consider themselves to be indigenous have reinterpreted the appellation to mean 'where man is'. According to this reinterpretation, the Baka were intimately married to their forest environment in such a way that outsiders could hardly notice their presence. Thus, the Baka existed and belonged in the region prior to the arrival of the Bantu, whom they considered to be immigrants.

It is also important to mention that older generations of the Baka who experienced life in the forest tend to be silent when the younger generations say that the older generations belong to the forest because they were born there. Even though these older generations are those who started most of the roadside camps in which they now reside, they often seem less concerned about conceptions of home and belonging when compared to the younger generations born after 1960. On the contrary, these older generations tend to stress their marginalization, poverty, desperation and a disappearance of their culture and values. For them, the majority of their younger generation are fast becoming 'Bantus' and have abandoned the age-long sense of social warmth, solidarity and sharing that existed in their community. On a more specific note, the variation in strategies to authenticate home and roadside belonging among the Baka reflects an internal differentiation and stratification among the Baka.

On the one hand, the Baka who authenticate their rootedness to the roadsides by alluding to their strong agricultural history are considered by other Baka to be Bantus, because they have lost what these Baka consider to be the essence of being Baka. This categorization gives rise to the category of 'Baka-Bantu'. On the other hand, the Baka who take pride in their hunting or fine skills in traditional healing and intimate relationships with the forest tend to refer to themselves as 'Baka-Baka'. For them, they are the 'real Baka' because they still uphold the values and customs of their ancestors. Curiously enough, both categories of Baka call themselves Baka and observe major Baka rites like the *'jengi'* (spirit of the forest). This divide between 'real' Baka and 'Baka-Bantus' seems to be a source of internal conflicts and power struggles among the Baka. In these struggles, most of those categorized as 'Baka-Bantus' consider themselves more 'civilized' than their 'Baka-Baka' counterparts, who they often refer to as 'uncivilized cowards' whose ways are dragging the community backwards. It is interesting to observe that, even among the Baka, the measure of 'civilization' is based on a person's level of assimilation and intergration into mainstream society as conceived in the early 1960s' post-independence national intergration and development policies.

Remarkably, while these conflicts and struggles continue to disunite the Baka, they are quick to blame it on external development organizations and on some Bantus. The Baka argue that the inrush of all sorts of development organizations that claim to be 'helping' the Baka is the major divisive force operating in their community. For them, the 'Baka-land' has become 'a development laboratory' with no clear vision for the development of the Baka people, since each development organization that comes into the region selects and works with the Baka who are compliant with their own development philosophy. In so doing, the Baka argue that this has created internal disorders and conflicts within their community. Nevertheless, since these internal differentiations and struggles are a key discovery of my own research, there is need for further research before it can be ascertained that all internal differentiations among the Baka are caused by external parties. From my research, what is clear about these internal differentiations and struggles is the point that they illuminate new dynamics among the Baka. Also, my research found that a change in development funding requirements, which emphasizes the participation of beneficiaries, is resulting in a change in the nature of social relations between the Baka and their Bantu neighbours. This shift is moving from a sharply conflictual continuum towards a more 'manipulative' and 'representation figurative' continuum. This shift in the nature of social relations between the Bantu and the Baka seems to provide one of the underlying explanations for the paradox of collaboration and marginalization respectively raised by Rupp (2011) and Pyhälä (2012).

Scientific Contribution of the Book

This book makes two key contributions to the existing body of knowledge in sociology and development studies. In sociology, the book contributes to the sociology of social groups and inequality. To underline this contribution, it is important to revisit the original questions that guided my discussions throughout the book. These questions included the following: How do the Baka assert their belonging on the roadsides where they now reside, given the fact that they are presented as indigenous peoples at the same time as being assimilated as integrated citizens? Is there any sense of 'groupness' in the ways in which the Baka assert their belonging on these roadsides? How do the sociopolitical atmosphere clouding the Baka in terms of a structured society, as well as limited resources, influence the dynamics of Baka participation in development interventions?

The answers to these questions show that the Baka are not indifferent to the social processes surrounding them. Far from being merely voiceless and passive consumers of social phenomena in their communities, as they are often projected to be (Pyhälä 2012; Logo 2012), responses from the Baka on the subject of their belonging indicate that they are also social agents with active agency. Indeed, in the East Region of Cameroon, the belonging of the Baka is not a given. Rather, due to the articulations of social needs determined by different conflicting constellations, like the hierarchies between the Bantu and the Baka, as well as among the Baka themselves, the belonging of the Baka is constantly contested and negotiated in different arenas. Moreover, the understanding of the concept of indigenous peoples as invested within Baka communities is not harmonious with the global understanding of the concept. In this regard, there is no sense of *'groupness'* in the ways that the Baka assert their belonging. On the contrary, there is an internal differentiation and stratification among the Baka, which leads to struggles. This observation is compatible with Brubaker and Cooper's suggestion that processes of identification and categorization should be more carefully examined in order to understand the sense of 'groupness' that political and/or social entrepreneurs sometimes seek to achieve (2000).

Based on this, I maintain that although the concept of indigeneity has been employed to empower the so-called powerless and vulnerable indigenous peoples of the world, the same approach may rather crystallize the marginality and exclusion of some Baka (Kuper 2003; Kuper 2005; Geschiere 2009). The Baka categorized as 'Baka-Bantu' hardly consider themselves as belonging to the category of indigenous peoples because, for them, local understandings of the term have reduced it to mean 'Pygmies', or people without any capabilities, thereby limiting their life opportunities. Also, the belonging of these Baka is contested by other Baka ('Baka-Baka'), who consider themselves as 'real' Baka. By highlighting this differentiation, this book illuminates the 'Rupp-Pyhälä' paradox whereby Rupp (2011) portrays the Baka as dynamic, challenging indigeneity as a stereotypic reductive category, while Pyhälä (2012) presents the Baka as dispossessed and marginalized indigenous peoples.

The discovery of an internal differentiation among the Baka illuminates the above-mentioned paradox in that, on the one hand, there are Baka who have been assimilated and integrated into the rest of society (the so-called 'Baka-Bantu'), who sometimes refer to their other Baka counterparts as 'lazy cowards' (*'Les fainéants très paresseux et idiots'*). The dynamism and intergratedness of these 'Baka-Bantu' to the best of my understanding is what Rupp

(2011) bases her argument upon to challenge stereotypes about the Baka. Rupp argues that development organizations should design more balanced development approaches for both the Baka and the Bantu. In her argument for example, she states that 'GTZ's analysis [which distinguishes between the Bantu and the Baka, categorizing the Baka as indigenous forest peoples] reinforces and reinscribes divisive social categories' (2011: 230).

However, on the other hand, the 'Baka-Baka', who consider themselves to be 'real or typical' Baka, portraying themselves as dispossessed, marginalized, discriminated against, exploited, poor and powerless people without any hope for the future, are another differentiated strata among the Baka. It is to these Baka that Pyhälä, in her report titled: 'What Future for the Baka?' (2012), refers when narrating the plight and suffering of the Baka as indigenous peoples in the East Region of Cameroon. I argue that while the blanket categorizations of people as indigenous 'groups' may serve for theorizing social inequality in societies, there is a need to take a leap beyond 'groupness' and explore intra-group internal struggles. This is especially important considering that some Baka who are sedentarized and assimilated (Baka-Bantus), although sometimes discriminated against by their neighbours (because of structural inequalities), consider themselves to be 'civilized' Cameroonian citizens and tend to refer to their 'Baka-Baka' counterparts as 'lazy', 'uncivilized' and 'backward', thus creating a social hierarchy within the Baka communities. To this end, I further argue that the social relevance of 'development' as presented to targeted communities where agriculture equates to 'civilization' and development, as was the case in post-independence Cameroon, tends to initiate structural changes within these communities.

In development theorizing, this book stresses the vulnerability of vulnerable communities. In poverty and inequality analysis (Chambers 1989; Bohle and Watts 1993; Greenberg et al. 1995; Philip and Rayhan 2004), vulnerable communities are considered to be those that suffer most and/or will likely suffer more if some development actions are not taken. However, while the focus has often been on the much-needed development actions, little attention has thus far been paid to coordinating development actors so that their actions contribute to achieving the same long-term development goals for these so-called vulnerable communities. What this book calls 'the vulnerability of vulnerable communities' is the exposure of vulnerable communities to multiple unregulated and uncoordinated development interventions, which end up leaving the communities confused, if not more vulnerable than they were prior to the influx of these development interventions into their communities (Chambers 2006). In some Baka camps for example, the Baka found themselves with three to four national identity cards each, which is not legal in Cameroon, simply because different organizations passed by and thought that the Baka needed ID cards. In other Baka camps there were some Baka with no ID cards. Another illustration is the current Baka cultural centre and museum in Mayos-Dimako, which was originally intended to be a community radio station. Some Baka were trained for six months on community reporting and then were left without a word once the building was converted into a cultural centre. Some of them were later asked by another organization to learn community mapping. According to these Baka, the Baka are tired of the fact that different development organizations simultaneously tell them to do seemingly conflicting things without any clear headway (strategy going forward). One of the Baka elites asked me: '*Où vont-ils avec les Baka?*', meaning, where are these multiple and uncoordinated development interventions going with the Baka people?

Beyond the above-mentioned 'vulnerability of vulnerable communities' is an analysis of the ways in which the Baka now react to development interventions, especially in the context of their participation. Most Baka want their own share of development resources up front. For them, the start of a development project does not neccessarily mean its completion. Thus, since they are unsure of what they might be told in the days or weeks ahead, they say that it is best to demand their share up front. During my own field research for example, most participants asked me what I would give them in return for their answering my questions. At that time, I simply thought that it was because other development and research organizations were in the habit of giving them money to participate in research. However, following the understanding that the Baka demand their own share of development resources up front because they are unsure of future project developments, I argue that development projects need to ensure that the beneficiary communities can trust their activities. Indeed, although some development actors explain this request for upfront benefits by the Baka as an impatient trait, arising from their hunting and gathering background, which does not involve long waiting periods, I argue that clinging to ancestral habits to explain present-day patterns of Baka participation is reductive and closes other windows of social analysis.

Conceptual Outlook

In the course of this book, the concepts of belonging, home, participation and development were explored. The concept of belonging as conceptualized by the Baka had two distinct interpretations, one which fits into the existing discussions of belonging within academia and another which seems to have newly emerged from the field. These two distinct conceptualizations of belonging by the Baka are belonging as an attachment to a place, often expressed as being their home or homeland and authenticated by using the metaphor of 'rootedness in the soil', otherwise understood in the region as local citizenship; and belonging as attachment to a social category of global 'indigenous peoples', which, reinterpreted in the Cameroonian context refers to people who in one way or another are not considered 'rooted in the soil' by virtue of their lifestyle. Indeed, in the conceptualization of belonging expressed in attachment to a place, the Baka tended to deviate from the generally held presumption that people's home is where they originate from, this being the forest in the case of the Baka. Rather, for the Baka, home is where they have established daily emotive experiences of living and thus feel like they belong. This assertion is clear in the way that the Baka use the burial grounds of their loved ones, and their farms and houses to authenticate their belonging as local citizens on the roadsides in the East Region of Cameroon. Nonetheless, when some Baka do not develop these daily emotive experiences and attachments to the roadsides, and where their access and claims to the forest are limited, these Baka tend to conceptualize belonging as attachments to a categorical global community of indigenous peoples.

This dual conceptualization of belonging by the Baka is expressed as two versions of belonging: local citizenship (autochthony) and global citizenship (indigeneity), which gave rights to different claims that tended to conflict with one another, thereby legitimizing exclusion and marginalization. In the context of decentralized local development and governance programmes in the region, being a local at home in the locality and thus belonging as a local citizen, legitimates the rights to participate in local development interventions and governance programmes. The dynamics of Baka belonging to roadside communities as local citizens has heuristic importance for scholars and policy makers on indigenous issues in Cameroon, because it brings to light two dimensions of belonging for the Baka, namely local citizenship and national citizenship. In previous studies on the belonging of the Baka, the focus has often only been on their national citizenship (Pyhälä 2012; Logo 2012), and the government, together with INGOs, has tended to design a citizenship promotion programme specifically for the Baka ('*promotion de la citoyenneté pour les Baka*') aimed at fostering their participation in national life. Nonetheless, as has been discussed in this book, belonging as national citizens in Cameroon does not automatically pave the way for the recognition of citizens' belonging at the local level, since different conditions define belonging at the local and national levels.

Note

1. In the region, autochthony is closely linked to agricultural activity and relations with the soil.

Appendix

❧•❧

The following is a mapping of some local Baka development organizations
Source: Kinkoh Thomas Ngala, Plan Bertoua.

Communities	Existing Institutions	Features
Salapoumbé (Ndongo)	* District Head	Institution that has always existed in this community while not having any legal status in accordance with laws and regulations.
	* Development Committee Salopoumbé	Committee set up in 2009 with the support of Plan Cameroon but not legalized. 10 members (20% of whom at that office are Baka).
Salapoumbé (Ndongo)	* COVAREF	Legalized, created in 2000 to manage funds from the Safari, this committee has a legal personality. 12 members (33.33% Baka).
	* COGE	Committee created in 2004 by a joint MINFI/MINATD order. 9 members (33.33% Baka).
	* CIG Producer of Cocoa	Not legalized, founded in 2009. 10 members (10% Baka). Organization and operational vision unclear.
	* Association Dynamics	Association created in 2005 for tontines and solidarity. 22 members (45.45% Baka). Clear vision for organization and operation.
	* Head of the Community	Institutional break-up of the leadership to the third degree.
	* Village Development Committee (RRC)	Not legalized, committee set up in 2004 with the support of Plan Cameroon. 8 members (all Baka).

Communities	Existing Institutions	Features
	* COGE	Committee created in 2002 by the Lomié City Council to manage forest royalties. 9 members (55.55% Baka).
	* Ndouni Mpeke (Let's Use our Strength)	Not legalized, association founded in 2005. Invests in solidarity and agriculture. 12 members (91.66% Baka). Clear vision for organization and operation.
	* Kounda Tela (The Turtle)	Not legalized, CIG created in 2009. 12 members (91.66% Baka). The main activity is the harvesting of non-wood products. Clear vision for organization and operation.
	* Kana (Name of a Tree whose Fruits Are Used as Condiments)	Legalized, CIG created in 2009. 12 members (all Baka). Main activities are the harvest of non-timber products for sale and the purchase of essential commodities
	* APE (Association of Parents)	Not legalized, association founded in 2003. 7 members (85.71% Baka). Main activity is the education of children.
Diassa	* Head of Camp	Traditional institution not approved.
	* Development Committee	Not legalized, founded in 2008 with support from Plan. 7 members (all Baka).
	* Team SE'EBA	Not legalized, Baka youth group created in 2007 to play football and participate in agricultural activities to improve productivity.
	* Bouma Bo Kpode	Association created in 2004 but no longer exists today.
Abakoum	* Head of Camp	Traditional institution not approved.
	* COGE	Not yet legalized, committee created in 2010. 6 members (33.33% Baka). Main activity is management of forest royalties.
	* CIG (Macabo, Plantain)	Legalized, created in 2009 and chaired by a Baka. Activities: agriculture, crafts, small business.
Bingongol	* Chief	Traditional institution not approved but legitimized by the people.
	* Hot Group	Non-legalized, CIG created in 2003 under the leadership of NGOs. Membership consists exclusively of Baka. Activities: agriculture, village maintenance.
Koungoulou	Head of Camp	Traditional institution not approved but legitimized by the people.
	CVD Motongo (The Beginning)	Not legalized, founded in 2000 without the impetus of NGOs. 15 members (all Baka).
	COGE	Not legalized, founded in 2008 with the support of AAPEC and Plan Committee. 15 members (all Baka).

Communities	Existing Institutions	Features
	We Try	CIG not legalized, CIG created in 2000 after the Plan provided farm equipment. 15 members (all Baka). Main activity: agricultural subsistence.
	APE (Association of Parents)	Association not legalized, founded in 1993. 7 members (71.42% Baka).
Njontal	Deputy Chief	Traditional institution not approved but legitimized by the people.
	CVD Moloulouma	Not legalized, association created in 2000 under the leadership of AAPEC. 41 members (all Baka).
	Ekendji Nadaka (Mixed Friendship)	Not legalized, gathering of Baka and Bantu for a good social environment created in 2006. 18 members (44.44% Baka).
	COGE	Not legalized, committee created in 2000 to manage funds for CVD Moloulouma. 7 members (85.71% Baka).
	AFDAN	Not legalized, association of women created 14 October 1995. 30 members (40% Baka). Activities: agriculture, solidarity.
Bandoum	Head of Camp	Traditional institution not approved.
	CVD Assoconco (Association of Trust of Bandoum Development)	Association not legalized, created in 2004 under the leadership of a community member. 50 members (70% Baka).
	COGE	Not legalized, founded in 1997 with the support of the AAPEC committee. 7 members (42.85% Baka). Activities: management of forest royalties.
	APE	Not legalized, association created in 2002. 9 members (22.22% Baka). Activity: solidarity for school supervision for children.
Bizam	Deputy Chief	Traditional institution not approved.
	CVD Bizam	Not legalized, founded in 1997 by community consensus. 12 members (16.66% Baka).
	COGE	Not legalized, created in 2000 for the management of forest royalties. 8 members (12.5% Baka).
	Nice Friends of Bizam	Not legalized, association created in 1997 to gather and promote solidarity. 19 members.
	Dynamic Youth of Bizam	Not legalized, CIG created in 2000 for agriculture and livestock. 15 members (26.66% Baka).
Grove	Chief	Traditional institution not approved but legitimized by the people.
	CVD Grove (Loukah)	Not legalized, committee created in 2007 under the leadership of Plan. 14 members (all Baka).

Communities	Existing Institutions	Features
	COGE	Not legalized, committee created in 2000 with the support of the NGO SNV for the management of timber royalties. 7 members (all Baka).
	CAF (Club of Friends of the Forest)	Not legalized, CIG created in 2005. 40 members (all Baka). Activities: agricultural aid.
	ASCODEBAK (Community Association of Baka Grove)	Legalized, association created in 2006. 40 members (all Baka). Activities: agriculture, sale of agricultural products.
	APE	Not legalized, association created in 2007. 7 members. Activity: solidarity for school supervision for children.
Ngolle 2	Chief	Traditional institution not approved but legitimized by the people.
	Ndouni Mpeke (Let's Use Our Strength)	Not legalized, CVD created in 2007 under the leadership of NGOs. 150 members (all Baka).
	COGE	Not legalized, committee created in 2010 for the management of forest royalties.
	APE	Not legalized, association created in 2000 to monitor school supervision of children. 6 members (all Baka).
Dympam	Chief	Traditional institution not approved but legitimized by the people.
	CIG Dympam Dynamics	Legalized, CIG created in 2007 consisting of the entire community. Agriculture.
	CVD Dympam	Not legalized, founded in 2003. 6 members (all Baka).
Mass	Deputy Chief	Traditional institution not approved.
	CVD	Legalized, committee created in 1997 under the leadership of members of the community. 20 members (25% Baka).
	COGE	Legalized, committee created in 1997 for healthy management of forest royalties. 8 members (25% Baka).
	Mbaga Me Mbaga	Not legalized, association created in 2004. 12 members (25% Baka). Activities: agriculture, promotion of solidarity.
	ASSORBON (Association of Citizens of Boumba and Ngoko)	Association created in 2007. 25 members (12% Baka). Main activity: agriculture.
	MPA MBO (Bring Your Hands Together)	Not legalized, association created in 2000. 60 members (all Baka). Activities: agriculture, solidarity.
	APE	Association created in 1970. 70 members (25.71% Baka).

Communities	Existing Institutions	Features
Ndjangue	Deputy Chief	Traditional institution not approved.
	CVD Ndjangue	Not legalized, committee created in 2004 under the leadership of Plan. 21 members (all Baka).
	We Try	Not legalized, association created in 2004. 25 members (all Baka). Activities: agriculture, solidarity.
	CIG PRABADE	Not legalized, created in 2009. 19 members (all Baka). Activities: agriculture, solidarity.
Cyrie	Deputy Chief	Traditional institution not approved but legitimized by the people.
	CVD Cyrie	Not legalized, committee created in 2007 under the leadership of NGOs. 9 members (all Baka).
	AOC (Health Committee)	Created in 2002 under the leadership of Nkouak health personnel. 3 members (all Baka).
	COGE	Not legalized, committee created in 2007. 9 members (all Baka).
	Hope	Not legalized, association created in 1999. 30 members (all Baka). Activities: agriculture, tontines.
	DYNAMIC	Not legalized, association created in 2009. 10 members (all Baka). Activities: agriculture, tontines.
	Children's Forum	Not legalized, association created in 2010. 10 members (all Baka). Activities: cleaning the water bridge, protection of the rights and interests of Baka children.
Kendjo	Chief	Traditional institution not approved.
	CVD Kendjo	Not legalized, created in 2006 under the leadership of Plan. 13 members (69.23% Baka).
	COSA	Created in 1996 under the leadership of Nkouak health centre staff. 24 members (25% Baka).
	Let's See, Kendjo	Not legalized, association created in 2003. 8 members (62.5% Baka). Activities: agriculture, sales, solidarity.
Lossou	Chief	Traditional institution not approved.
	CVD Lossou	Not legalized, created in 2002 under the leadership of Plan. 14 members (64.28% Baka).
	OKANI (Let's Go)	Not legalized, association created in 2005 under the leadership of NGOs. 32 members (all Baka).
	Agreement	CIG not legalized, created in 2006. 13 members (92.3% Baka). Activities: agriculture.
	Hope	Not legalized, association created in 2006. 19 members (52.63% Baka). Activities: dance, crafts, agriculture.

Communities	Existing Institutions	Features
Mayos (Dimako)	Chief	Traditional institution not approved, but legitimized by the people.
	CVD (Essayons voir)	Not legalized, founded in 2000. 60 members (22% Baka).
	Solidarity	Not legalized, association created in 2005. 9 members (55.55% Baka). Activities: tontines, solidarity.
	Hand in Hand	Not legalized, association founded in 2004. 6 members (50% Baka). Activities: agriculture, solidarity.
	Deputy Chief	Traditional authority not approved, but legitimized by the people.
Bonando (Petit)	Codebo (Development Committee Bonando)	Not legalized, committee created in 1990 by community consensus. 8 members (37.5% Baka).
	COGE	Not legalized, committee created in 2000. 60 members (13.6% Baka). Activities: management of forest royalties.
	Association of Women of Bonando	Not legalized, association created in 2010. 25 members (all Baka). Activity: agriculture.
	Elephant	Not legalized, ICG farm founded in 2008. 12 members (all Baka).
	Future	Not legalized, ICG farm founded in 2008. 12 members (all Baka).
	Hand in Hand	Not legalized, ICG created in 2008. 12 members. Activity: agriculture, specializing in palm oil.
	Deputy Chief	Traditional institution not approved but legitimized by the people and the administration since 1996.
Kwamb	CVD	Not legalized, committee created in 2005 by community consensus. 15 members (all Baka).
	JEDEM (Youth for the development of Messoume)	Legalized, association founded in 2007. 15 members (66.66% Baka). Activity: community development.
	AFAME (Alliance of Women of Messoume)	Not legalized, ICG created in 2008. 7 members (all Baka). Activities: agriculture, tontines.
	Deputy Chief	Elected and appointed by the District Chief, Mindourou
	COSA	Created in 2006 under the leadership of health center staff. 12 members (all Baka).
Mayos (Mindourou)	Vigilance Committee	Legalized, founded in 1977. 2 members (50% Baka). Activity: controlling all kinds of crime in the community.

Communities	Existing Institutions	Features
	COGE	Not legalized, created in 2008 under the leadership of AAPEC. 7 members (all Baka). Activity: management of timber royalties.
	EPA	Not legalized, created in 1982. 12 members (75% Baka).
	Malouma – Community Fields	CIG not legalized, created in 2001. 200 members (98% Baka). Activities: agriculture, fishing, crafts.
	Children's Forum	Not legalized, association created in 2010. 12 members (41.66% Baka). Activities: promotion and protection of children's rights.
	CIG ASSIMA	Not legalized, created in 2001. 200 members (98% Baka). Activities: agriculture, sale of crops.
	District Head	Not approved, but legitimized by the people.
	CVD Ngolle 120	Not legalized, created in 2009. 8 members (12.5% Baka).
	COVAREF	Legalized, created in 1999 through the initiative of WWF and GTZ. 12 members (25% Baka).
Ngola 120	COGE	Legalized (through a joint MINEF/MINAT order), created in 2004. Activity: management of timber royalties.
	Deputy Chief	Not approved, but legitimized by the people.
	RRC Tengue Yenga.	Not legalized, created in 2010 under the leadership of Plan. 8 members (12.5% Baka).
	COVAREF	Legalized, created in 2000 under the leadership of GTZ. 12 members (8.33% Baka).
Yenga-Tengue	COGE	Legalized and created in 2000 under the initiative of the WWF. 6 members (no Baka).
	SANOFI (Save Our Wildlife)	Not legalized, CIG established in 2006. 42 members (35% Baka). Activities: agriculture, livestock, fish farming.
	ASDEBYM	Not legalized, association created in 2007. 12 members (all Baka). Community and sustainable forestry management.
	AFEBEN	Not legalized, association created in 2000. 100 members (all Baka). Activity: self-promotion for Baka women.
	Head of Camp	
	CODDUMA (Sustainable Development Committee of Mambélé)	Legalized, created in 1985 under leadership of GTZ. 12 members (no Baka).
	COVAREF	Legalized, founded in 2000 through a WWF-GTZ initiative. 12 members (12.67% Baka)

Communities	Existing Institutions	Features
MAMBELE Mambele	COGE	Legalized, founded in 1999 through a WWF-GTZ initiative. 12 members (8.3% Baka). Activity: managing timber royalties.
	Chief	Institution not approved.
	CVD	Not legalized, association created in 2009. 8 members (12% Baka).
	COVAREF	Not legalized, association created in 2000 (WWF/GTZ). 12 members (16% Baka).
Banana	COGE	Not legalized, association created in 2007. 9 members (32.22% Baka). Activity: management of timber royalties.
	Gbiné	Not legalized, association created in 2007. 480 members (all Baka). Main activities: promotion of Baka culture, agriculture. Has a functional orchestra, and sells products in the international music market.
	Chief Baka	Not legalized, created in 2009 (Plan).
	CVD Momboué	8 members (33.3% Baka).
	COVAREF	Legalized, created in 2000 (WWF). 12 members (41.66% Baka).
Momboue	COGE	Legalized, founded in 2004. 9 members (33.33% Baka).
	Chief	Institution not approved
	CVD	Not legalized, created in 2009 (Plan). 10 members (30% Baka).
	COVAREF	Legalized, created in 2000 (WWF/GTZ). 12 members (16.67% Baka).
Nguilili-2	COGE	Legalized, created in 2004 (joint MINEF/MINAT decree). 9 members (22% Baka).
	ASDEFEB (Association for the Development of Baka Women)	Not legalized, association founded in 2000. 40 members (80% Baka). Activities: farming, tontines, solidarity.
	CVD	Not legalized, created in 2007. 12 members (25% Baka).
	COVAREF	Legalized, created in 2000 (WWF/GTZ). 12 members (16.6% Baka).
	COGE	Legalized, created in 1999 (WWF/GTZ). 42 members (8.33% Baka).
Mbateka	DEMOKOGOUE	ICG not legalized, created in 1999. 27 members (all Baka). Activity: cocoa growing.
	Association of Thoughtful Women of Mbateka	Not legalized, association founded in 2000. 15 members (20% Baka). Activities: tontines, savings.
	Deputy Chief	Institution not approved.

Communities	Existing Institutions	Features
	CVD Temba-Track	Not legalized, created in 2009 (Plan). 10 members (10% Baka).
	COVAREF	Legalized, founded in 1999 through a WWF-GTZ initiative. 12 members (25% Baka).
Temba Track	COGE	Legalized, founded in 2004. 9 members (33.33% Baka). Activity: management of timber royalties.
	Chief	Institution not approved.
	CVD	Not legalized, association created in 2009. 8 members (12% Baka).
	COVAREF	Not legalized, association created in 2000 (WWF/GTZ). 12 members (16% Baka).
Menzoh	COGE	Not legalized, association created in 2007. 9 members (32.22% Baka). Activity: management of timber royalties.
	Chief Baka	
	Gbessi Na Sea (Uniting our Hearts)	CVD not legalized, created in 2009. 10 members (32% Baka).
	COVAREF	Legalized, founded in 2000. 12 members (16.67% Baka).
Mbangoye 1	COGE	Legalized, created in 2004 (by MINEF/MINAT). 9 members (22.22% Baka).
	Rural Association for Mbangoye Women's Development	Not legalized, association founded in 2002. 35 members (11.43% Baka).
	AJAM (Association of Young Workers, Mbangoye)	Not legalized, association created in 2009. 120 members (5% Baka). Main activities: health of the city, solidarity.
	Children's Forum	Not legalized, created in 2010. Approximately 270 members, divided into three categories (64.28% Baka).
	Chief	Institution not approved.
	CODEGED (Dioula Committee for Development and Environmental Management)	Legalized, created in 1990 (by the local elite). 10 members (20% Baka).
	COVAREF	Legalized, created in 1999 (by hunting guides/MINFOF leaders). 12 members (16.67% Baka).
Dioula	COGE	Legalized, founded in 2000 with the initiative of WWF-GTZ. 12 members (8.3% Baka).
	WIADEMO	Not legalized, CIG founded in 2008 through the initiative of WWF-GTZ. 12 members (15% Baka). Activity: agriculture.

Communities	Existing Institutions	Features
	Chief Baka	Legalized, created in 1997 by the community
	CVD Ajak	youth. 15 members (6.66% Baka).
	COVAREF	Legalized in 1999 (hunting guides/MINFOF leaders). 12 members (41.66% Baka).
Koumela	COGE	Legalized, created in 1999 through the initiative of MINFI/MINAT. 9 members (33.3% Baka).
	SAYONO	Not legalized, CIG established in 2006. 25 members (all Baka).
	Deputy Chief	Institution not approved.
	COGE 'UNIMBA' (Mballam Union)	Not legalized, created in 2002 (APPEC/MAP). 12 members (all Baka).
	FPC (Forest Peasant Committee)	Legalized, created in 2000 (MINAS/MINFOF/ WWF/Pallisco). 11 members (36.36% Baka).
Mballam	COGE	Not legalized, created in 2009 (Pérade). 7 members (all Baka).
	We Try	Not legalized, created in 2002 (Support Pérade/ MAP). 60 members (all Baka). Activities: agriculture, fisheries.
	EGOUSSOU	Association not legalized, founded in 2008. 44 members (all Baka). Activity: occupational health and safety.
	NGUILOES	Association not legalized, created in 2009. 9 members (all Baka). Activity: protection of the rights and interests of Baka from the village.
	Vigilance Committee	Not legalized, created in 2004. 2 members (both Baka). Activity: security.
	Chief	Institution not legalized.
	CVD 'Minka Mahoua'	Not legalized, created in 1980 by Mr Minka Mahoua, Baka benefactor. 6 members (all Baka).
	CPF	Legalized, created in 2007 (Pallisco). 11 members (36.36% Baka).
Elandjo	Sun	Association not legalized, created in 2001. 11 members (all Baka). Activity: agriculture.
	MAKA (Hand in Hand)	Association not legalized, founded in 2001. 15 members (all Baka). Activity: agriculture.
	EPA	Founded in 1950. 9 members (all Baka).
	Community Field	ICG not legalized, established in 2004. 100 members (all Baka). Activities: agriculture, solidarity.
	Deputy Chief	Institution not approved.
	CVD Mikel	Not legalized, created in 2009 (MAP). 8 members (12.5% Baka).
	COVAREF	Legalized, created in 2000 (WWF). 12 members (25% Baka).
Mikel	COGE	Legalized, created in 1998 (MINEFI/MINAT). 9 members (33.33% Baka).

Communities	Existing Institutions	Features
	Sun Team	Support group, not legalized, created around 2005. 15 members (all Baka). Activity: agriculture.
	Team 2	Support group, not legalized, created around 1990. 16 members (all Baka). Activity: agriculture.
	Boat	Created around 2008. 19 members (all Baka).
	TFSA	Not legalized, aid group created around 2004.
	Chief	Institution not approved.
	GANGA TIMI CVD (Between Us)	Not legalized, created in 2004 (MAP). 25 members (28% Baka).
	Youth Group	Not legalized, association created in 2003. 15 members (all Baka). Activity: agriculture.
Nkoumadjap	Men's Group	Association not legalized, created in 2002. 30 members (33.33% Baka). Activity: agriculture (maize, plantain).
	Chief	Institution not approved.
	CVD and related	Not legalized, established in 2006. 12 members (83% Baka).
	We Try	Association not legalized, created in 2007. 8 members (25% Baka). Activities: agriculture, solidarity.
Nkolbokon	Future	ICG not legalized, created in 2007. 12 members (50% Baka). Activity: agriculture.
	En Avant	Association not legalized, created in 2007. 12 members (41.6% Baka). Activity: agriculture.
	Dance Group	Association not legalized, created in 2007. 12 members (all Baka). Activity: revaluation of Baka culture.
	Chief	Institution not approved.
	CVD	Not legalized, created in 2009 (MAP). 10 members (no Baka).
	COVAREF	Legalized, established in 1999 (WWF/GTZ). 12 members (25% Baka).
Ngolle 125	COGE	Legalized, established in 2004 (MINEFI/MINAT). 9 members (33.33% Baka).
	ICG (Agriculture)	Not legalized, created in 2007. 20 members (20% Baka).
	Baka Chief	Institution not approved.
	CVD	Not legalized, created in 2009 (MAP). 8 members (12% Baka).
	COVAREF	Legalized, created in 2000 (WWF/GTZ). 12 members (16.57% Baka)
Yenga	COGE	Legalized, created in 1999 (WWF/GTZ). 12 members (8.33% Baka).

Communities	Existing Institutions	Features
	Kinoko (Searching with Our Hands)	ICG not legalized, created in 2009. 25 members (16% Baka). Activities: livestock, agriculture, woodland management.
	Chief	Institution not approved.
	CVD 'OBA Weke' (We Try)	Not legalized, created in 2009 (MAP). 7 members (14.3% Baka).
	COVAREF	Legalized, created in 2000 (WWF/GTZ). 12 members (16.6% Baka).
Mbangoye 2	CVD	Not legalized, created in 2009 (MAP). 10 members (no Baka).
	COGE	Legalized, established in 2004 (MINFI/MINATD). 9 members (25% Baka).
	CIG LEAMGBA	Not legalized, created in 2000. Approximately 50 members (33.33% Baka). Activity: cocoa culture.

BIBLIOGRAPHY

AAPPEC. 1969–2001. '32 ans auprès des Pygmées Baka'. pp. 13–15.

Abbot, Dina. 2007. 'Doing "Incorrect" Research: The Importance of the Subjective and the Personal in Researching Poverty', in A. Thomas and G. Mohan (eds), *Research Skills for Policy and Development: How to Find Out Fast*. London: Sage, pp. 208–228.

Abega, Séverin Cécile. 1998. *Pygmées Baka: Le Droit à la Différence*. Yaoundé, Cameroon: INADES Formation.

Abega, Séverin Cécile and Patrice Bigombe Logo. 2005. 'La marginalisation des Pygmées d'Afrique centrale'. Rapport de l'atelier de synthèse sous-régionale consacré à l'étude sur l'autopromotion des Pygmées d'Afrique Centrale qui s'est tenu à Yaoundé, Centre Jean XXIII, Mvolyé du 2 au 4 février 2005. Paris: Afrédit.

ACHPR and IWGIA. 2005. 'Report of the African Commission's Working Groups of Experts on Indigenous Populations/Communities', adopted by the ACHPR at its 28th Session. Copenhagen: IWGIA.

ACHPR and IWGIA. 2006. 'Indigenous Peoples in Africa: The Forgotten Peoples? The African Commission's Work on Indigenous Peoples in Africa'. Copenhagen: IWGIA.

Agrawal, Arun and Kent Redford. 2009. 'Conservation and Displacement: An Overview', *Conservat. Soc* 27: 1–10.

Ahmed, Sara, Claudia Castañeda, Anne-Marie Fortier and Mimi Scheller. 2003. 'Introduction: Uprootings/Regroundings. Questions of Home and Migration', in S. Ahmed, C. Castañeda, A.M. Fortier and M. Scheller (eds), *Uprootings/Regroundings: Questions of Home and Migration*. Oxford: Berg, pp. 1–19.

Ahmed, Sara. 1999. 'Home and Away: Narratives of Migration and Estrangement', *International Journal of Cultural Studies* 2(3): 329–347.

Albiez, Sarah, Nelly Castro, Lara Jüssen and Eva Youkhana (eds). 2011. *Etnicidad, ciudadanía y pertenencia: prácticas, teoría y dimensiones espaciales / Ethnicity, Citizenship and Belonging: Practices, Theory and Spatial Dimensions*. Madrid and Frankfurt: Iberoamericana Vervuert.

Alemagi, Dieudonne. 2011. 'Sustainable Development in Cameroon's Forestry Sector: Progress, Challenges, and Strategies for Improvement', *African Journal of Environmental Science and Technology* 5(2): 65–72 (available online at http://www.academicjournals.org/AJEST).

Amin, Aloysius Ajab. 2008. *Developing a Sustainable Economy in Cameroon*. African Books Collective, Project MUSE (http://muse.jhu.edu/).

Anderson, Benedict. 1991. *Imagined Communities: Reflections on the Origin and Spread of Nationalism*. London: Verso.

Atyi, Richard Eba'a. 1998. 'Cameroon's Logging Industry: Structure, Economic Importance and Effects of Devaluation', Occasional Paper No. 14, CIFOR and TROPENBOS.

Augustat, Karin. 1997. 'Rapport de l'étude socio-économique participative (selon la méthode MARP) à Dioula, sud-est Cameroon'. 20–29 June. Yaoundé, Cameroon: Gesellschaft für Technische Zusammenarbeit.

Babbie, Earl Robert. 2010. *The Basics of Social Research*. Belmont, CA: Wadsworth.

Bahuchet, Serge. 1992. *Dans la Forêt d'Afrique Centrale: Les Pygmées Aka et Baka*. Leuven: Peeters Publishers.

Bahuchet, Serge. 1993. 'L'invention des Pygmées', *Cahiers d'Etudes africaines* 33(1): 153–181.

Bailey, Robert C., Serge Bahuchet and Barry S. Hewlett. 1992. 'Development in the Central African Rainforest: Concern for Forest Peoples', in Kevin Cleaver, Mohan Munasinghe, Mary Dyson, Nicolas Egli, Axel Peuker and Francois Wencelius (eds), *Conservation of West and Central African Rainforests*. Washington, DC: The World Bank.

Bailey, Robert C., G. Head, M. Jenike, B. Owen, R. Rechtman and E. Zechenter. 1989. 'Hunting and Gathering in Tropical Rain Forest: Is It Possible?' *American Anthropologist* 91(1): 59–82.

Baker, Kelly. 2012. 'Identity, Memory and Place', *The Word Hoard* 1(1), article 4.

Balandier, Georges. 1971. *Sens et puissance: les dynamiques sociales*. Paris: PUF.

Ballard, Christopher. 2006. 'Strange Alliance: Pygmies in the Colonial Imaginary', *World Archaeology* 38(1): 133–151.

Barns, Thomas Alexander. 1922. *The Wonderland of the Eastern Congo: The Region of the Snow-Crowned Volcanoes, the Pygmies, the Giant Gorilla and the Okapi*. London: G.P. Putnam's Sons.

Barth, Fredik. 1998. *Ethnic Groups and Boundaries: The Social Organization of Culture Difference*. Long Grove, IL: Waveland Press.

Barume, Albert Kwokwo. 2010. 'Land Rights of Indigenous Peoples in Africa with Special Focus on Central, Eastern and Southern Africa'. IWGIA, Document 115.

Bayart, Jean-François and Peter Geschiere. 2001. '"J'étais là avant": Problématiques politiques de l'autochtonie', *Critique Internationale* 10: 126–128.

Bergman, Jerry. 1997. 'Ota Benga: The Story of the Pygmy on Display in a Zoo'. Retrieved 14.01.2014 from www.rae.org/pdf/otabenga.pdf.

Bhabha, Homi. 1996. 'Culture's in Between', in S. Hall and P. du Gay (eds), *Questions of Cultural Identity*. London: Sage.

Biesbrouck, Karen, Stefan Elders and Gerda Rossel. 1999. *Central African Hunter-gatherers in a Multidisciplinary Perspective: Challenging Elusiveness*. Leiden, Netherlands: CNWS Publications.

Biya, Paul. 1986. *Pour le libéralisme communautaire*. Lausanne: Pierre-Marcel Farme.

Bodley, John H. 1990. *Victims of Progress*. Mountainview, CA: Mayfield Publishing Company.

Boehm, Christopher. 1993. 'Egalitarian Behavior and Reverse Dominance Hierarchy', *Current Anthropology* 34(3): 227–254.

Boehm, Christopher. 1999. *Hierarchy in the Forest: The Evolution of Egalitarian Behavior*. Cambridge, MA: Harvard University Press.

Boisson, F. 1938. 'Le Mandat français au Cameroun', in *Politique étrangère* 3(1):59–67.

Bohle, G. Hans and Michael J. Watts. 1993. 'The Space of Vulnerability: The Causal Structure of Hunger and Famine', *Progress in Human Geography* 17(1): 43–67.

Bradford, Phillips Verner and Harvey Blume. 1992. *OTA: The Pygmy in the Zoo*. New York: St. Martin's Press.

Brand, Laurie A. 2001. 'Displacement for Development? The Impact of Changing State-Society Relations', *World Development* 29(6): 961–976.

Breckenridge, Jenna P., Derek Jones, Ian Elliott and Margaret Nicol. 2012. 'Choosing a Methodological Path: Reflections on the Constructivist Turn', *Grounded Theory Review* 11(1).

Breverton, Terry. 2011. *Breverton's Phantasmagoria: A Compendium of Monsters, Myths and Legends*. Guilford, CT: Lyons Press.

Brisson, Robert. 1999a. *Mythologie des Pygmées Baka I*. Leuven: Peeters (SELAF 376).

Brisson, Robert. 1999b. *Mythologie des Pygmées Baka II (sud Cameroun)*. Leuven: Peeters (SELAF 376).

Broch-Due, Vigdis. 2005. *Violence and Belonging: The Quest for Identity in Post-Colonial Africa*. Abingdon: Routledge.

Brown, Duncan. 2006. *To Speak of this Land: Identity and Belonging in South Africa and Beyond*. Scottsville, South Africa: University of Kwazulu-Natal Press.

Brubaker, Rogers. 2009. 'Ethnicity, Race, and Nationalism'. *Annual Review of Sociology* 35: 21–42.

Brubaker, Roger and Frederick Cooper. 2000. 'Beyond "Identity"', *Theory and Society* 29: 1–47.

Burnell, Peter, Vicky Randall and Lise Rakner. 2008. *Politics in the Developing World*. Oxford: Oxford University Press.

Burnham, Philip. 2000. 'Whose Forest? Whose Myth? Conceptualisations of Community Forests in Cameroon', in A. Abramson and D. Theodossopoulis (eds), *Land, Law and Environment: Mythical Land, Legal Boundaries*. London: Pluto Press.

C169, Indigenous and Tribal Peoples Convention. 1989. Convention Concerning Indigenous and Tribal Peoples in Independent Countries (No. 169). Entry into force: 5 Sep. 1991. Adoption: Geneva, 76th ILC session (27 Jun 1989). Status: up-to-date instrument (Technical Convention).

Campbell, Murray. 1983. *Hunters and Gatherers: African Pygmies and Amazonian Indians, People without a Future?* Auckland, New Zealand: Macmillan.

Canadel. 2010. 'Commune de Dimako, Plan de développement, 2010–2014'. Réalisé avec la Collaboration de Canadel.

Capitaine, René Viard. 1934. *Les Guérés, peuple de la forêt. Étude d'une société primitive*. Paris: Société d'éditions géographiques, maritimes et coloniales.

Catton, William R. 1978. 'Understanding Social Differentiation', *Contemporary Sociology* 7(6): 695–698.

CERD/C/CMR/19. 27 Janvier 2010. 'La situation des droits des peuples autochtones au Cameroun', Rapport supplémentaire soumis suite aux 15e–19e rapports périodiques.

Cernea, Micheal M. 2000. 'Risks, Safeguards, and Reconstruction: A Model for Population Displacement and Resettlement', in M.M. Cernea and C. McDowell (eds), *Risks and Reconstruction: Experiences of Resettlers and Refugees*. Washington, DC: The World Bank.

Cerutti, Paolo Omar, Robert Nasi and Luca Tacconi. 2008. 'Sustainable Forest Management in Cameroon Needs More than Approved Forest Management Plans', *Ecology and Society* 13(2): 36 (available online at http://www.ecologyandsociety.org/vol13/iss2/art36/).

Ceuppens, Bambi and Peter Geschiere. 2005. 'Autochthony: Local or Global? New Modes in the Struggle over Citizenship and Belonging in Africa and Europe', *Annual Review of Anthropology* 34: 385–407.

Chabal, Patrick. 2009. *Africa: The Politics of Suffering and Smiling*. London and New York: Zed Books.

Chambers, Robert. 1989. 'Vulnerability, Coping and Policy', *IDS Bulletin* 20(2): 1–7.

Chambers, Robert. 2006. 'Vulnerability, Coping and Policy' (Editorial Introduction), *IDS Bulletin* 37(4).

Charmaz, Kathy. 2003. 'Grounded Theory: Objectivist and Constructivist Methods', in N.K. Denzin and Y.S. Lincoln (eds), *Strategies of Qualitative Inquiry* (2nd ed.). London: Sage Publications, pp. 249–291.

Charmaz, Kathy. 2006. *Constructing Grounded Theory: A Practical Guide through Qualitative Analysis*. London: Sage Publications.

Charmaz, Kathy and Richard G. Mitchell. 1996. 'The Myth of Silent Authorship: Self, Substance, and Style in Ethnographic Writing', *Symbolic Interaction* 19(4): 285–302.

Che, Victorine Sirri. 2008. 'A Critical Analysis of the Interrelation between Indigenous Livelihoods and Sustainable Forest Management – Integrating Gender Aspects. Case of the Sangha Trinational Conservation Area'. PhD dissertation. Freiburg im Breisgau: University of Freiburg.

Clarke, Adele E. 2005. *Situational Analysis: Grounded Theory after the Postmodern Turn*. Thousand Oaks, CA: Sage.

Coates, Ken S. 2004. *A Global History of Indigenous Peoples: Struggle and Survival*. Houndmills: Palgrave Macmillan.

Cobo, José Martinez R. 1986. 'Study of the Problem of Discrimination against Indigenous Populations'. UN Doc. E/CN.4/Sub.2/1986/7. Geneva: United Nations.

Cohen, David W. and Atieno Odhiambo. 1992. *Burying SM: The Politics of Knowledge and the Social Anthropology of Power in Africa*. Portsmouth, NH: Heinemann; London: James Currey.

Colfer, Carol J. Pierce 2004. *The Equitable Forest: Diversity and Community in Sustainable Resource Management*. Washington, DC: CIFOR.

Cooke, Bill and Uma Kothari. 2001. 'The Case for Participation as Tyranny', in B. Cooke and U. Kothari (eds), *Participation: The New Tyranny*. London: Zed Books, pp. 1–15.

Couillard, Valérie, Jérémie Gilbert, Justin Kenrick and Christopher Kidd. 2009. *Land Rights and the Forest Peoples of Africa: Historical, Legal and Anthropological Perspectives*. Moreton-in-Marsh: Forest Peoples Programme.

Cromer, Sharon. 2011. 'Indigenous Peoples of Africa', written statement by Sharon Cromer, Senior Deputy Assistant Administrator, Bureau for Africa, United States Agency for International Development (USAID), before the Tom Lantos Human Rights Commission, Committee of Foreign Affairs, U.S. House of Representatives. Retrieved 12.05.2011 from http://tlhrc.house.gov/docs/transcripts/2011_05_12_Indigenous_Peoples_Africa/Testimony_Sharon_Cromer.pdf.

Crovetto, Patricia Urteaga. 2005. *Negotiating Identities and Hydrocarbons: Territorial Claims in the Southeastern Peruvian Amazonia*. University of California, Berkeley. Retrieved 22.04.12 from http://gupea.ub.gu.se/bitstream/2077/4499/1/anales_9-10_urteaga.pdf.

Cummings, Vicki, Peter Jordan and Marek Zvelebil. 2014. *The Oxford Handbook of the Archaeology and Anthropology of Hunter-Gatherers*. Oxford: Oxford University Press.

Cutolo, Armando. 2008. 'Populations, citoyennetés et territoires: Autochtonie et gouvernementalité en Afrique', in 'Enjeux de l'autochtonie', *Politique africaine* 112: 5–17.

Dasen, Véronique. 2013. *Dwarfs in Ancient Egypt and Greece*. Oxford: Oxford University Press.

Dawson, Warren Royal. 1938. 'Pygmies and Dwarfs in Ancient Egypt', *Journal of Egyptian Archaeology* 24(2): 185–189.

Dellemmes, R.P. 1985. *Le père des Pygmées*. Paris: Flammarion.

Demuth, Andreas. 2000. 'Some Conceptual Thoughts on Migration Research', in Biko Agozino (ed.), *Theoretical and Methodological Issues in Migration Research: Interdisciplinary, Intergenerational and International Perspectives*. Hampshire: Ashgate, pp. 21–58.

de Quatrefages de Bréau, and Jean Louis Armand. 1887. *Les Pygmées: Avec 31 fig. intercalées dans le texte; Les Pygmées des anciens d'après la science moderne; negritos ou Pygmées asiatiques; Négrilles ou Pygmées africains'; Hottentots et Boschismans*. Paris: J.P. Baillière.

Dkamela, Guy Patrice. 2003. 'Associations, argent et exercice du pouvoir chez les Pygmées Baka de la région de Lomié (Est-Cameroun). Etude en vue d'une recherche des formes appropriées d'action collective', Rapport d'étude. Yaoundé: INADES.

Dkamela, Guy Patrice and Phil René Oyono. 2003. 'Pouvoirs, argent et recomposition sociale chez les Pygmées Baka de l'est-Cameroun', *Africa* 58(3/4), 340–355.

Dorman, Sara, Daniel Hammett and Paul Nugent. 2007. *Making Nations, Creating Strangers: States and Citizenship in Africa.* Leiden: Brill.

Duffy, Kevin.1984. *Children of the Forest: Africa's Mbuti Pygmies.* Long Grove, IL: Waveland Press.

Dunn, Frederick L. 1968. 'Epidemiological Factors: Health and Disease in Hunter-gatherers', in R.B. Lee and I. DeVore (eds), *Man the Hunter.* Chicago: Aldine, pp. 221–228.

Dyson, Mary. 1992. 'Concern for Africa's forest peoples: A touchstone of a sustainable development policy', in Kevi Cleaver, Mohann Munasinghe, Mary Dyson, Nicolas Egli, Axel Peuker and Francois Wencelius (eds), *Conservation of West and Central African Rainforests.* Washington, DC: World Bank Environmental Paper number 1.

Ela, Jean-Marc. 1982. *L'Afrique des villages.* Kartala.

Escárcega, Sylvia. 2010. 'Authenticating Strategic Essentialisms: The Politics of Indigenousness at the United Nations' *Cultural Dynamics*, 22: 3.

Escobar, Arturo. 1996. *Encountering Development: The Making and Unmaking of the Third World.* Princeton, NJ: Princeton University Press.

Eyoh, Dickson. 2004. 'Contesting Local Citizenship: Liberalization and the Politics of Difference in Cameroon', in Bruce Berman, Dickson Eyoh and Will Kymlicka (eds), *Ethnicity and Democracy in Africa.* Oxford: James Currey.

Fanso, Verkijika G. 1989. *Cameroon History for Secondary Schools and Colleges: The Colonial and Post-colonial Periods*, Vol. 2. London: Macmillan.

Feierman, Steven and Janzen, John M. 1992. *The Social Basis of Health and Healing in Africa.* Berkeley: University of California Press.

Fonchingong, Tangie Nsoh and John Bobiun Gemandze. 2009. *Cameroon: The Stakes and Challenges of Governance and Development.* Mankon Bamenda: Langaa Research and Publishing CIG.

Foudouop, Kegne. 1997. 'Elites et intégration nationale au Cameroun sous le régime du renouveau', in Paul Nchoji Nkwi and Francis B. Nyamnjoh (eds), *Equilibre régional et intégration nationale au Cameroun: Leçons du passé et perspective d'avenir.* Leiden and Yaoundé: Cassa T/Monograph.

Garbutt, Rob. 2011. 'The Locals: Identity, Place and Belonging in Australia and Beyond', *Cultural Identity Studies* 22.

Gausset, Quentin, Justin Kenrick and Robert Gibb. 2011. 'Indigeneity and Autochthony: A Couple of False Twins?' *Social Anthropology* 19(2): 135–142.

Gaventa, John. 2004. 'Towards Participatory Governance: Assessing the Transformative Possibilities', in Hickey and Mohen (eds), *Participation: From Tyranny to Transformation? Exploring New Approaches to Participation in Development.* New York: Zed Books, pp. 25–41.

Geertz, Clifford. 1973. 'Thick Description: Toward an Interpretive Theory of Culture', in C. Geertz, *The Interpretation of Cultures.* New York: Basic Books.

Geschiere, Peter. 2005. 'Funerals and Belonging: Different Patterns in Southern Cameroon', *African Studies* 48(2): 45–64.

Geschiere, Peter. 2009. *The Perils of Belonging: Autochthony Citizenship, and Exclusion in Africa and Europe.* Chicago, IL: University of Chicago Press.

Geschiere Peter. 2011a. 'Sons of the Soil: Autochthony and its Ambiguities in Africa and Europe', in J. Abbink and M. de Bruijn, *Land, Law and Politics in Africa: Mediating Conflict and Reshaping the State.* Leiden: Brill.

Geschiere, Peter. 2011b. 'Autochthony, Citizenship and Exclusion: New Patterns in the Politics of Belonging in Africa and Europe', in S. Albiez, N. Castro, L. Jüssen and E. Youkhana (eds), *Ethnicity, Citizenship and Belonging: Practices, Theory and Spatial Dimensions*. Madrid and Frankfurt: Iberoamericana Vervuert, pp. 175–198.

Geschiere, Peter and Stephen Jackson. 2006. 'Autochthony and the Crisis of Citizenship: Democratization, Decentralization, and the Politics of Belonging', *African Studies Review* 49(2).

Geschiere, Peter and Francis Nyamnjoh. 2000. 'Capitalism and Autochthony: The Seesaw of Mobility and Belonging', *Public Culture* 12(2): 423–452.

Giles-Vernick Tamara. 2001. 'A Review of *"Pygmies": Central African Hunter-Gatherers in a Multidisciplinary Perspective: Challenging Elusiveness*, edited by K. Biesbrouck, S. Elders and G. Rossel', *The Journal of African History* 42(1): 117–172.

Gillett, Andrew. 2002. *On Barbarian Identity: Critical Approaches to Ethnicity in the Early Middle Ages*. Turnhout, Belgium: Brespols Publishers.

Glaser, Barney G. 1992. *Basics of Grounded Theory: Emergence Vs Forcing*. Mill Valley, CA: Sociology Press.

Glaser, Barney G. 1998. *Doing Grounded Theory: Issues and Discussions*. Mill Valley, CA: Sociology Press.

Gotz, Graeme and AbdouMaliq Simone. 2003. 'On Belonging and Becoming in African Cities', in R. Tomlinson et al. (eds), *Emerging Johannesburg: Perspectives on the Post Apartheid City*. New York: Routledge, pp. 123–147.

Gramsci, Antonio. 1971. *Selections from the Prison Notebooks of Antonio Gramsci*. New York: International Publishers.

Gray, Peter. 2011. 'How Hunter-Gatherers Maintained their Egalitarian Ways: Three Complementary Theories', in Peter Gray, *Free to Learn: Why Unleashing the Instinct to Play will Make our Children Happier, More Self-reliant and Better Students for Life*. New York: Basic Books.

Greenberg, Jeff, Linda Simon, Sheldon Solomon, Tom Pyszczynski, Eddie Harmon-Jones and Deborah Lyon. 1995. 'Testing Alternative Explanations for Mortality Salience Effects: Terror Management, Value Accessibility, or Worrisome Thoughts?' *European Journal of Social Psychology* 25: 417–433.

Grinker, Roy Richard. 1994. *Houses in the Rainforest: Ethnicity and Inequality among Farmers and Foragers in Central Africa*. Berkeley, California: University of California Press.

Grinker, Roy Richard, Stephen Lubkemann and Christopher B. Steiner. 2010. *Perspectives on Africa: A Reader in Culture, History and Representation*. Oxford: John Wiley & Sons.

Guijt, Irene. 2008. 'Civil Society Participation as the Focus of Northern NGO Support: The Case of Dutch Co-funding Agencies', in A.J. Bebbington et al. (eds), *Can NGOs Make a Difference? The Challenge of Development Alternative*. London: Zed Books, pp. 153–174.

Gupta, Akhil and James Ferguson. 1992. 'Beyond Culture: Space, Identity, and the Politics of Difference', *Cultural Anthropology* 7(1): 6–23.

Hallet, Jean-Pierre. 1973. *Pygmy Kitabu*. London: Random House.

Hallet, Jean-Pierre. 1975. " To Save A People" in Human Potential, a magazine published by The Ambassador International Cultural Foundation, September 1975.

Hastings, Adrian. 1997. *The Construction of Nationhood: Ethnicity, Religion, and Nationalism*. Cambridge: Cambridge University Press.

Headland, Thomas N. 1987. 'The Wild Yam Questions: How Well Could Independent Hunter-gatherers Live in a Tropical Rain Forest Environment?' *Human Ecology* 15(4): 463–491.

Headland, Thomas and Robert Bailey. 1991. 'Introduction: Have Hunter-gatherers Ever Lived in Tropical Rain Forest Independently of Agriculture?' *Human Ecology* 19(2): 115–122.

Hewlett, Barry S. 2000. 'Central African Governments and International NGOs' Perceptions of Baka "Pygmy" Development', in Peter P. Scweitzer, Megan Besele and Robert K. Hitchock (eds), *Conflict, Resistance, and Self-determination*. New York: Berghahn Books.

Hewlett, Barry S. 2014. *Hunter-gatherers of the Congo Basin: Cultures, Histories, and Biology of African Pygmies*. New Jersey: Transaction Publishers.

Hickey, Samuel. 2002. 'Transnational NGDOS and Participatory Forms of Rights-based Development: Converging with the Local Politics of Citizenship in Cameroon', *Journal of International Development* 14(6): 841–857.

Hickey, Samuel and Giles Mohan. 2004. *Participation – From Tyranny to Transformation: Exploring New Approaches to Participation in Development*. London: Zed Books.

Hodgson, Dorothy L. 2002. 'Precarious Alliances: The Cultural Politics and Structural Predicaments of the Indigenous Rights Movement in Tanzania', *American Anthropologist* 104(4): 1086–1097.

Hodgson, Dorothy L. 2009. 'Becoming Indigenous in Africa', *African Studies Review* 52(3): 1–32.

Innes, Mathew. 2009. 'Using the Past, Interpreting the Present, Influencing the Future', in Yitzhak Hen and Matthew Innes, *The Uses of the Past in the Early Middle Ages*. Cambridge: Cambridge University Press, pp. 1–8.

Jacob, Jean-Pierre and Pierre-Yves Le Meur. 2010. *Politique de la terre et de l'appartenance: Droits fonciers et citoyenneté locale dans les sociétés du Sud*. Paris: Karthala.

Jahoda, Gustav. 1999. *Images of Savages: Ancient Roots of Modern Prejudice in Western Culture*. London: Routledge.

Jansen, Stef and Steffan Löfving. 2009. *Struggles for Home. Violence, Hope and the Movement of People*. New York and Oxford: Berghahn Books.

Jenkins, Richard. 1997. *Rethinking Ethnicity: Arguments and Explorations*. Thousand Oaks, CA: Sage Publications.

Jennings, Ray. 2000. 'Participatory Development as New Paradigm: The Transition of Development Professionalism', Community Based Reintegration and Rehabilitation in Post-Conflict Settings Conference, Oct. 2000, USAID, Washington, DC. Retrieved 13.03.2014 from http://pdf.usaid.gov/pdf_docs/Pnacq066.pdf.

Joiris, Daou V. 2003. 'The Framework of Central African Hunter-gatherers and Neighbouring Societies', *African Study Monographs*, Suppl. 28: 57–79.

Kah, Henry Kam. 2010. 'The Culture of Appointments, Arrogance, and Chop Broke Pottism in Cameroon's Contemporary Governance', *Cameroon Journal on Democracy and Human Rights* 4(2): 19–35.

Kent, Sue. 2002. *Ethnicity, Hunter-gatherers, and the 'Other': Association and Assimilation in Africa*. Washington, DC: Smithsonian Institution Press.

Kilian, Christa. 2008. 'Contes des Pygmées Baka du Cameroun', *Schriften zur Afrikanistik/ Research in African Studies* 14.

Klieman, Kairn A. 2003. *The Pygmies Were Our Compass: Bantu and Batwa in the History of West Central Africa, Early Times to c. 1900 ce*. Portsmouth, NH: Heinemann.

Klugman, Jeni. 2002. *A Sourcebook for Poverty Reduction Strategies, Vol. 1: Core Techniques and Cross-cutting Issues*. Washington, DC: World Bank.

Kuper, Adam. 2003. 'The Return of the Native', *Current Anthropology* 44(3): 389–395, 400–401.

Kuper, Adam. 2005. *The Reinvention of Primitive Society: Transformations of a Myth*. London: Routledge.

Law no.5-2011 of Republic of Congo. Retrieved 10.10.2015 from http://www.iwgia.org/iwgia_files_news_files/0115_Loi_n5-2011_du_25_fevrier_2011_portant_promotion_et_protection_des_droits_des_population.s_autochtone.pdf.

Leclerc, Christian. 2012. *L'adoption de l'agriculture chez les Pygmées baka du Cameroun: Dynamique sociale et continuité structurale*. Paris: Editions Quae.

Lee, Danielle Juteau. 2003. *Social Differentiation: Patterns and Processes*. Toronto: University of Toronto Press.

Lee, Richard B. and Robert K. Hitchcock. 2001. 'African Hunter-Gatherers: Survival, History, and the Politics of Identity', *African Study Monographs*, Suppl. 26: 257–280.

Lentz, Carola. 1995. 'Tribalism and Ethnicity in Africa: A Review of Four Decades of Anglophone Research', *Cahiers des Sciences Humaines* 31: 303–328.

Lentz, Carola. 2006. 'Land Rights and the Politics of Belonging in Africa: An Introduction', in R. Kuba and C. Lentz (eds), *Land and the Politics of Belonging in West Africa*. Leiden: Brill.

Lentz, Carola. 2007. 'Land and the Politics of Belonging in Africa', in P. Chabal, U. Engel and L. de Haan (eds), *African Alternatives*. Leiden: Brill.

Léonard, Yves. 2011. *Baka Oral Narratives: A Cultural and Linguistic Analysis and Some Implications for Bible Translation*. Cameroon: SIL.

Leonhardt, Alec. 1998. 'The Culture of Development in Bakaland; the Apparatus of Development in Relation to Baka Hunter Gatherers': Ph.D. dissertation. Princeton, NJ: Princeton University.

Leonhardt, Alec. 2006. 'Baka and the Magic of the State: Between Autochthony and Citizenship', *African Studies Review* 49(2): 69–94.

Lescuyer, Guillaume. 2005. 'Formes d'action collective pour la gestion locale de la forêt camerounaise: organisations "modernes" ou institutions "traditionnelles"?' *VertigO – La revue électronique en sciences de l'environnement* 6(3): 84–90.

Lescuyer, Guillaume. 2007. 'Livelihoods and the Adaptive Application of the Law in the Forests of Cameroon', in L. Tacconi (ed.), *Illegal Logging: Law Enforcement, Livelihoods and the Timber Trade*. London: Earthscan, pp. 167–190.

Lewellen, Ted C. 2003.'Political Anthropology: An Introduction', Third Edition, London, Praeger

Lewis, Paul. 2006. 'We are Frightened by What we See. But is Life Like That? The Baka are a Diminutive Hunter-gatherer Tribe from Cameroon', *The Guardian* (ISSN 0261-3077), 04/25/2006, p. 16.

Logo, Patrice Bigombe. 1998. 'Cameroun: Pygmées, Etat et Developpement. L'incontournable ajustement a la modernité', in *L'Afrique Politique: Femmes D'Afrique*. Paris: Karthala, pp. 255–270.

Logo, Patrice Bigombe. 2002a. 'Le Problème "Pygmée": le besoin d'une citoyenneté multiculturelle', *Les Cahiers de Mutations* 5.

Logo, Patrice Bigombe. 2002b. 'Foresterie Communautaire et Réduction de la Pauvreté rurale au Cameroun: Bilan et tendances de la première décennie', *Bulletin du WRM*.

Logo, Patrice Bigombe. 2006. 'Les élites et la gestion décentralisée des forêts au Cameroun. Essai d'analyse politiste de la gestion néopatrimoniale de la rente forestière en contexte de décentralisation'. Saint Quentin en Yvelines, France: Colloque Gecorev (Gestion Concertée des Ressources Naturelles).

Logo, Patrice Bigombe. 2007. 'Trajectoire de construction progressive de la citoyenneté des "Pygmées" au Cameroun'. Yaoundé, Cameroun: CERAD.

Logo, Patrice Bigombe. 2012. 'Citizens in Quest of Rights? The Citizenship Odyssey of the Pygmies of the Rainforest of Cameroon', paper presented at the biennial conference of the Association of African studies, Cologne, Germany, 30 May – 2 June 2012.

Lund, Christian. 2011. 'Property and Citizenship: Conceptually Connecting Land Rights and Belonging in Africa', *Africa Spectrum* 46(3), 71–75. Retrieved 03.03.2014 from http://journals.sub.unihamburg.de/giga/afsp/article/view/487/485.

Lutz, Ellen. 2007. 'Indigenous Rights and the UN', *Anthropology News* 48(2): 28.

Malkki, Liisa H. 1992. 'National Geographic: The Rooting of People and the Territorialization of National Identity among Scholars and Refugees', in *Cultural Anthropology* 7(1) (Space, Identity, and the Politics of Difference): pp. 24–44.

Malkki, Liisa H. 1995. 'Refugees and Exile: From "Refugee Studies" to the National Order of Things', *Annual Review of Anthropology* 24: 495–523.

Marlowe, Frank W. 2005. 'Hunter-gatherers and Human Evolution', *Evolutionary Anthropology* 14(2): 54–67.

Martiniello, Marco. 1995. *Que sais-Je? L'ethnicité dans les sciences sociales Contemporaines*. Paris: PUF.

Mbaku, John Mukum and Joseph Takougang. 2004. *The Leadership Challenge in Africa: Cameroon under Paul Biya*. Trenton, NJ and Asmara, Eritrea: Africa World Press.

Mballa, Henriette Manga Ndjie Bindzi. 2009. *Les Pygmées face à l'école et à l'Etat. Les Baka de l'Est du Cameroun*. Paris: L'Harmattan.

Mbarga, Hubert Ngoumou. 2013. 'La gestion des forêts communautaires face au défi de la pauvreté et du développement rural', *VertigO – La revue électronique en sciences de l'environnement* 13(3). Retrieved 28.01.2016 from http://vertigo.revues.org/14448.

Meyer, John W. and Brian Rowan. 1977.'Institutionalized Organizations: Formal Structure as Myth and Ceremony', *American Journal of Sociology* 83 (2):340–363.

Mills, Charles W. 1956. *The Power Elite*. Oxford and New York: Oxford University Press.

Mohan, Giles and Samuel Hickey. 2004. 'Relocating Participation within a Radical Politics of Development: Critical Modernisation and Citizenship', in S Hickey and G. Mohan, *Participation – From Tyranny to Transformation: Exploring New Approaches to Participation in Development*. London: Zed Books, pp. 59–74.

Moïse, Robert E. 2014. '"Do Pygmies Have a History?" Revisited: Autochthonous Tradition in the History of Equatorial Africa', in Barry S. Hewlett (ed.), *Hunter-gatherers of the Congo Basin: Cultures, Histories and Biology of African Pygmies*. New Brunswick, NJ: Transaction Publishers.

Molua, Ernest L. and Cornelius M. Lambi. 2013. 'Climate, Hydrology and Water Resources in Cameroon', GEF funded project. Retrieved 27.11.2013 from http://www.ceepa.co.za/docs/CDPNo33.pdf.

Monga, Yvette. 2000. '"*Au village!*" Space, Culture and Politics in Cameroon', *Cahiers d'Etudes Africaines* 160(4): 723–750.

Mulder, Mark Mattijs. 2009. 'A Shared and Contested Heritage: The Dutch and American Expedition to New Guinea of 1926', MA dissertation. Netherlands: University of Amsterdam.

Mwangi, Samuel Muraguri. 2008. *The Pygmy World: The Endangered Bambuti of Congo: The Untold Stories and Sufferings of the Endangered Pygmies in Congo Forests*. Kenya: Olive Marketing and Publishing Co.

Nagel, Joane. 1994. 'Constructing Ethnicity: Creating and Recreating Ethnic Identity and Culture', *Social Problems* 41(1): 152–176.

Namara, Rose Bakenegura. 2009. 'NGOs, Poverty Reduction and Social Exclusion in Uganda', PhD dissertation. The Hague, Netherlands: Institute of Social Studies.

Namara, Rose Bakenegura. 2010. 'Mouthpieces of the Poor or Dancing to the Tunes of Government and Donor? NGOs in Uganda's Poverty Reduction Programmes', in G. Gómez, A. Corradi, P. Goulart and R. Namara (eds), *Participation for What: Social Change or Social Control*. The Hague: ISS and Hivos, pp. 25–43.

Ndobe, Samuel Nnah. 2013. 'Experiences of Indigenous Peoples in Africa with Safeguard Policies: Examples from Cameroon and the Congo Basin, Forest Peoples Program'. Retreived 22.09.2013 from http://www.forestpeoples.org/topics/african-development-bank-afdb/news/2013/04/experiences-indigenous-peoples-africa-safeguard-po.

Ngandjeu, Jean. 2000. 'Elite, "levain du développement local"', in *Cameroun Tribune*, No. 7073/3362.

Ngoh, Julius Victor. 1996. *History of Cameroon since 1800*. Limbe: Presbook.

Nguiffo, Samuel. 2007. 'Social Conflicts Arising from Industrial Logging Practices in Cameroon', in S. Counsell, C. Long and W. Stuart (eds), *Concessions to Poverty: The Environmental, Social and Economic Impacts of Industrial Logging Concessions in Africa's Rainforests*. London: Rainforest Foundation and Forest Monitor, pp. 69–71.

Nguiffo, Samuel and Nadine Mballa. Not dated. *Les Dispositions Constitutionnelles, Legislatives et Administratives Relatives aux Populations Autochtones au Cameroun*. Yaoundé, Cameroon: CED.

Nguiffo, Samuel, Pierre Étienne Kenfack and Nadine Mballa. 2008. *L'influence des lois fonciéres sur les droits des communautés locales et autochtones du Cameroun*. Oxford: Forest Peoples Programme.

Nguiffo, Samuel, Pierre Étienne Kenfack and Nadine Mballa. 2009. 'Historical and Contemporary Land Laws and their Impact on Indigenous Peoples' Land Rights in Cameroon'. Retrieved 02.03.2014 from http://www.forestpeoples.org/sites/fpp/files/publication/2010/05/cameroonlandrightsstudy09eng.pdf.

Niezen, Ronald. 2010. 'The Invention of Indigenous Peoples', in R. Niezen, *Public Justice and the Anthropology of Law*. Cambridge: Cambridge University Press, pp. 105–136.

Nodem, Valery, Jaff Napoleon Bamenjo and Brendan Schwartz. 2012. 'Gestion des recettes tirées des ressources naturelles au niveau des collectivites locales au Cameroun: Redevances Forestières et Minières à Yokadouma, Est du Cameroun'. Yaoundé-Cameroun: RELUFA.

Nyamnjoh, Francis Beng. 1999. 'Cameroon: A Country United by Ethnic Ambition and Difference', *African Affairs* 98(390): 101–118.

Nyamnjoh, Francis Beng. (2010). 'Racism, Ethnicity and the Media in Africa: Reflections Inspired by Studies of Xenophobia in Cameroon and South Africa', in: *Africa Spectrum*, 45, 1, 57–93.

O'Hanlon, Micheal and Robert Louis Welsch. 2000. *Hunting the Gatherers: Ethnographic Collectors, Agents and Agency in Melanesia, 1870s–1930s*. New York and Oxford: Berghahn Books.

Oakley, Peter. 1991. 'Projects with People: The Practice of Participation in Rural Development'. Geneva: ILO, pp. 1–10.

Oishi, Takanori. 2012. 'Cash Crop Cultivation and Interethnic Relations of the Baka Hunter-gatherers in South-eastern Cameroon', *African Study Monographs*, Suppl. 43: 115–136.

Ojong, Vivian Besem and Mpilo Pearl Sithole. 2007. 'The Substance of Identity: Territoriality, Culture, Roots and the Politics of Belonging', *The African Anthropologist* 14(1 & 2): 89–98.

Ojwang, Jackton Boma and Jesse Kanyua Mugambi (eds). 1989. *The S.M. Otieno Case: Death and Burial in Modern Kenya*. Nairobi: Nairobi University Press.

Olwig, Karen Fog. 1998. 'Contested Homes: Home-Making and the Making of Anthropology', in Nigel Rapport and Andrew Dawson (eds), *Migrants of Identity: Perceptions of Home in a World of Movement*. Oxford: Berg.

Ong, Aihwa. 2006. *Neoliberalism as Exception: Mutations in Citizenship and Sovereignty*. Duke University Press.

Owono, Owono. 1997. 'La perception de l'arbre chez les Bakola du Sud Cameroun', MA dissertation. Cameroon: University of Yaoundé.

Oyono, Phil René. 2004. 'One Step Forward, Two Steps Back? Paradoxes of Natural Resources Management Decentralisation in Cameroon', *The Journal of Modern African Studies* 4(1): 91–111.

Oyono, Phil René. 2005a. 'Profiling Local-Level Outcomes of Environmental Decentralizations: The Case of Cameroon's Forests in the Congo Basin', *Journal of Environment & Development* 14(2): 1–21.

Oyono, Phil René. 2005b. 'From Diversity to Exclusion for Forest Minorities in Cameroon', in C.J.P. Colfer (ed.), *The Equitable Forest: Diversity, Community and Resource Management*. Washington, DC: Resources for the Future and CIFOR, pp. 113–130.

Oyono, Phil René. 2007. 'Is Decentralization in Natural Resource Management Leading to Livelihoods Improvement and Sustainability? Evidence from Central Africa', in *Participatory Forest Management (PFM), Biodiversity and Livelihoods in Africa: Proceedings of the International Conference 19–21 March 2007*, Addis Ababa, Ethiopia: Ministry of Agriculture and Rural Development of Ethiopia.

Page, Ben. 2007. 'Slow Going: The Mortuary, Modernity and the Hometown Association in Bali-Nyonga, Cameroon', *Africa* 77(3): 419–441.

Papastergiadis, Nikos. 1998. 'The Limits of the Diaspora: A Conversation with Ashis Nandy', in N. Papastergiadis, *Dialogues in the Diasporas: Essays and Conversations on Cultural Identity*. London and New York: River Oram Press, pp. 101–116.

Paradies, Yin C. 2006. 'Beyond Black and White: Essentialism, Hybridity and Indigeneity', *Journal of Sociology* 42(4): 355–367.

Parker, Lee D. and Bet H. Roffey. 1997. 'Methodological Themes: Back to the Drawing Board: Revisiting Grounded Theory and the Everyday Accountant's and Manager's Reality', *Accounting, Auditing & Accountability Journal* 10(2): 212–247.

Pelican, Michaela. 2006. 'Getting along in the Grassfields: Interethnic Relations and Identity Politics in Northwest Cameroon', PhD dissertation. Halle-Wittenberg, Germany: Philosophy Faculty, Martin Luther University.

Pelican, Michaela. 2009. 'Complexities of Indigeneity and Autochthony: An African Example', *American Ethnologist* 36(1): 52–65.

Pemunta, Vitalis Ngambouk. 2013. 'The Governance of Nature as Development and the Erasure of the Pygmies of Cameroon', *GeoJournal* 78(2): 353–371.

Pénelon, Alain, Luc Mendouga and Alain Karsenty. 1998. *L'identification des finages villageois en zone forestière au Cameroun. Justification, analyse et guide méthodologique*. Série FORAFRI No. 8. Montpellier, France: CIRAD.

Pfaff-Czarnecka, Joanna.2011. From 'identity' to 'belonging' in Social Research. Plurality, Social Boundaries, and the Politics of the Self, In: Ethnicity, Citizenship and Belonging. Practices, Theory and Spatial Dimensions. Albiez S, Castrol N, Jüssen L, Youkhana E (Eds);Madrid: Iberoamericana: 199–219.

Phadnis, Urmila and Ganguly Rajat. 2001. *Ethnicity and Nation Building in South Asia*. Revised edition, London: Sage.

Philip, Damas and Md. Israt Rayhan. 2004. 'Vulnerability and Poverty: What Are the Causes and How Are They Related?' term paper for international doctorate. Bonn: ZEF.

Poole, Peter. 2003. 'Cultural Mapping and Indigenous Peoples', a report for UNESCO, CLT/2003/PI/H/1.

Puddephatt, Antony J. 2006. 'An Interview with Kathy Charmaz: On Constructing Grounded Theory', *Qualitative Sociology Review* 2(3): 1–16 (also available online at www.qualitative-sociologyreview.org).

Pyhälä, Aili. 2012. 'What Future for the Baka? Indigenous Peoples' Rights and Livelihood'. Copenhagen: IWGIA and Plan.

Raffaele, Paul. 2008. 'The Pygmy Plight', *Smithsonian Magazine*.

Rapport, Nigel and Andrew Dawson. 1998. *Migrants of Identity: Perceptions of Home in a World of Movement*. Berg Ethnicity and Identity Series. Oxford: Berg.

RASED. 2006. *Culture and Traditions of the Baka Pygmies.* Plan Cameroon.

Ray Janajit and D.N. Varma. 2008. *Getting to Know the Earth* (revised edition), New Radiant Social Studies. New Delhi: Allied Publishers. Retrieved 24.02.2014 from http://ir.lib.uwo.ca/wordhoard/vol1/iss1/4.

Robillard, Marine. 2010. 'Pygmées Baka et voisins dans la tourmente des politiques environnementales en Afrique centrale', PhD dissertation. Paris: Muséum national d'histoire naturelle (MNHN).

Robinson, Amanda Lea. 2009. 'National Versus Ethnic Identity in Africa: State, Group, and Individual Level, Correlates of National Identification', prepared for Working Group in African Political Economy. University of California, Berkeley.

Rostow, Walt Whitman. 1960. *The Stages of Economic Growth: A Non-Communist Manifesto.* Cambridge: Cambridge University Press.

Roy, Kinmount D. 1890. 'Stanley's Pygmies', *The North American Review* 151(405): 253–254.

Rupp, Stephanie. 2001. 'I, You, They: Forests of Identity in Southeastern Cameroon', PhD Dissertation. Yale University.

Rupp, Stephanie. 2011. *Forests of Belonging: Identities, Ethnicities, and Stereotypes in the Congo River Basin.* Seattle, University of Washington Press.

Rutherford, Jonathan. 1990. 'The Third Space: Interview with Homi Bhabha', in J. Rutherford, *Identity: Community, Culture, Difference.* London: Lawrence and Wishart, pp. 207–221.

Sama, Molem C. 2007. 'Cultural Diversity in Conflict and Peace Making in Africa', *African Journal on Conflict Resolution* 7(2): 193–218.

Samndong, Raymond and Arild Vatn. 2012. 'Forest Related Conflicts in South-East Cameroon: Causes and Policy Options', *International Forestry Review* 14(2): 213–226.

Sarawak, Arau Penan Man. 2007. *Progress Can Kill: How Imposed Development Destroys the Health of Tribal Peoples.* Malaysia: Survival International.

Sarivaara, Erika, Kaarina Maatta, Satu Uusiautti. 2013. 'Who Is Indigenous? Definitions of Indigeneity', *European Scientific Journal*, Special edition, Vol. 1.

Sarup, Madan and Tasneem Raja. 1996. *Identity, Culture and the Postmodern World.* Edinburgh: Edinburgh University Press.

Schebesta, Paul. 1952. *Les Pygmées du Congo Belge.* Brussels: IRSAC.

Schmidt-Soltau, Kai. 2003. Indigenous People ("pygmy") Development Plan for the Participatory Community Development Programme-PNDP, Ministry of Economic Affairs and Regional Development, Cameroon

Schweinfurth, Georg August. 1874. *Im Herzen von Afrika. Reisen und Entdeckungen im Centralen Aequatorial-Afrika während der Jahre 1868 bis 1871. Ein Beitrag Zur Entdeckungsgeschichte von Afrika.* 3 Vols. Leipzig: F.A. Brockhaus.

Scott, James C. 1998. *Seeing Like a State: How Certain Schemes to Improve the Human Condition Have Failed.* New Haven: Yale University Press.

Selin, Helaine. 2003. *Medicine Across Cultures: History and Practice of Medicine in Non-Western Cultures.* Dordrecht, Netherlands: Kluwer Academic Publishers.

Sen, Amartya. 2000. *Development as Freedom.* New York: Alfred A. Knopf. Inc.

Sifakis, Carl. 1984. 'Benga, Ota: The Zoo Man', *American Eccentrics.* New York: Facts on File Inc.

Simo, David. 2006. *Constructions Identitaire en Afrique: Enjeux, Stratégies et conséquences.* Yaoundé: Editions Cle.

Sinang, Joseph Jules. 2005. 'Contribution de l'oralité à l'étude des relations entre les Pygmées Baka et les Bantou au Sud-Est Cameroun, des origines à 1960'. MA dissertation. University of Yaoundé.

Skinner, Elliott P. 1967. 'Group Dynamics in the Politics of Changing Societies: The Problem of "Tribal" Politics in Africa", American Ethnological Society, Proceedings of the 1967 Annual Spring Meeting. Seattle, WA: University of Washington Press.

Starr, Frederick. 1896. 'Pygmy Races of Men', *The North American Review* 162(473): 414–423.

Strauss, Anselm Leonard and Juliet Corbin. 1990. *Basics of Qualitative Research: Grounded Theory Procedures and Techniques*. London: Sage.

Strauss, Anselm Leonard and Juliet Corbin. 1998. *Basics of Qualitative Research: Techniques and Procedures for Developing Grounded Theory*, 2nd ed. London: Sage.

Takougang, Joseph and Milton Krieger. 1998. *African State and Society in the 1990s: Cameroon's Political Crossroads*. Boulder, CO: Westview Press.

Tchoumba, Belmond. 2005. 'Peuples indigènes et tribaux et stratégies de réduction de la pauvreté au Cameroun'. Cameroun: Organisation Internationale du Travail/ Centre pour l'environnement et le développement (CED).

Tchoumba, Belmond and John Nelson. 2006. *Protecting and Encouraging Customary Use of Biological Resources by the Baka in the Dja Biosphere Reserve*. The Forest Peoples Programme/ Centre pour l'environnement et le développement (CED), Cameroun

Topa, Giuseppe, Alain Karsenty, Carole Megevand and Laurent Debroux. 2009. *The Rainforests of Cameroon: Experience and Evidence from a Decade of Reform* (Directions in Development). Washington, DC: The International Bank for Reconstruction and Development/ The World Bank. http://documents.worldbank.org/curated/en/2009/01/11348972/ rainforests-cameroon-experience-evidence-decade-reform

Trilles, Révérend père. 1945. *L'âme du Pygmée d'Afrique*. Paris: CERF.

Tsing, Anna Lowenhaupt. 2005. *Friction: An Ethnography of Global Connection*. Princeton, NJ: Princeton University Press.

Tuan, Yi-Fu. 1977. *Space and Place: The Perspective of Experience*. Minneapolis: University of Minnesota Press.

Turnbull, Colin. 1961. *The Forest People*. New York: Touchstone Books.

Tyson, Edward. 1966 [1699]. *Orang-Outang, Sive Homo Sylvestris: Or, the Anatomy of a Pygmie Compared With That of a Monkey, an Ape, and a Man*. London: Dawsons of Pall Mall.

Udoh, C.T. 1998. 'Ethnicity and National Integration in Nigeria: A Historical Perspective', *Ibom Journal of Social Issues* 5(1).

Unruh, Jon D. 1998. 'Land Tenure and Identity Change in Postwar Mozambique', *GeoJournal* 46(2): 89–99.

Valtonen, Pekka. 2009. 'Baka Rights and Dignity Project, Situation Analysis Complementary Report'. Plan Cameroon.

Van den Berg, Jolanda and Karen Biesbrouck. 2000. 'The Social Dimension of Rainforest Management in Cameroon: Issues for Co-Management'. Kribi, Cameroon: The Tropenbos-Cameroon Programme.

Vansina, Jan. 1986. 'Do Pygmies Have a History?' *Sprache und Geschichte in Afrika* 7(1): 431–445.

Verkuyten, Maykel. 2004. *The Social Psychology of Ethnic Identity*. New York: Taylor and Francis.

Vinding, Diana. 2003. *The Indigenous World 2002–2003*. Copenhagen: IWGIA.

Vinding, Diana. 2006. *Indigenous Peoples and the Millennium Development Goals: Perspectives from Communities in Bolivia, Cambodia, Cameroon, Guatemala and Nepal*. Geneva: ILO.

Vubo, Emmanuel Yenshu. 2003. 'Levels of Historical Awareness: The Development of Identity and Ethnicity in Cameroon', *Cahiers d'Etudes Africaines* 171.

Westin, Charles, José Bastos, Janine Dahinden and Pedro Góis. 2011. *Identity Processes and Dynamics in Multi-Ethnic Europe*. Amsterdam: Amsterdam University Press.

White, Andy and Alejandra Martin. 2002. *Who Owns the World's Forests? Forest Tenure and Public Forests in Transition*. Washington, DC: Forest Trends.

Wily, Liz Alden. 2011. 'Whose Land Is It? The Status of Customary Land Tenure in Cameroon'. A report produced for RFUK, FERN and CED, Yaoundé-Cameroon, Center for Environment and Development.

Woodburn, James. 1982. 'Egalitarian Societies', *Man* 17(3): 431–451.

Woodburn, James. 1997. 'Indigenous Discrimination: The Ideological Basis for Local Discrimination against Hunter-gatherer Minorities in Sub-Saharan Africa', *Ethnic and Racial Studies* 20(2): 345–361.

Yuval-Davis, Nira. 2006. 'Belonging and the Politics of Belonging', *Patterns of Prejudice* 40(3): 197–214.

Websites Consulted

Cheumani, Charlotte. 2012. 'Projet Filets Sociaux au Cameroun: Cadre de Planification en faveur des Populations Pygmées (CPPP)'. Retrieved 06.03.2014 from http:// documents.worldbank.org/curated/en/357521468227701262/text/IPP6410Camer oo00210201300Box377347B.txt.

Chindji-Kouleu, Ferdinand. 'Ethnies, medias et processus démocratique au Cameroun: analyse de contenu de quelques journaux', in *Démocratisation et rivalités ethniques au Cameroun*, UNESCO Management of Social Transformations (MOST) programme. Ethno-net Africa. Retrieved 13.06.2012 from http://www.ethnonet-africa.org/pubs/p95cir3.htm.

Constitution of the Republic of Cameroon, 1996. Retrieved 13.09.2012 from http://www. icrc.org/ihl-nat/0/7e3ee07f489d674dc1256ae9002e3915/$FILE/Constitution%20 Cameroon%20-%20EN.pdf.

FONDAF Cameroun. 'Les groups Pygmées au Cameroun'. Retrieved 20.12.2013 from http:// fondaf-bipindi.solidarites.info/pygmees.php.

International Labour Organization (ILO). 'Origins and History'. Retrieved 02.03.2012 from http://www.ilo.org/global/about-the-ilo/history/lang--en/index.htm.

International Labour Organization (ILO). 'Conventions Nos. 107 and 169: Major differences'. Retrieved 02.03.2012 from http://indigenousfoundations.arts.ubc.ca/home/global-indigenous-issues/ilo-convention-107.html.

International Labour Organisation (ILO). 'Convention No. 107 – Indigenous and Tribal Populations Convention, 1957'. Retrieved 05.10.2015 from http://www.ilo.org/dyn/ normlex/en/f?p=NORMLEXPUB:12100:0::NO:12100:P12100_ILO_CODE:C107.

Intenational Work Group on Indigenous Affairs (IWGIA), Cameroon. 2014. 'Recognition of Indigenous Peoples on Indigenous Peoples' Day'. Retrieved on 20.08.2014 from http:// www.iwgia.org/news/search-news?news_id=1060.

IRIN. 2006. 'AFRICA: Pygmy rights and continued discrimination'. Retrieved 26.06.2010 from http://www.irinnews.org/Report.aspx?ReportId=58647.

IWGIA. 2013. 'THE INDIGENOUS WORLD' Retrieved 14.10.2015 from http://www. iwgia.org/images/stories/sections/regions/africa/documents/2013/Cameroon.pdf

IWGIA. 2014. 'Cameroon: Recognition of indigenous peoples on indigenous peoples' day'. Retrieved 20.08.2014 from http://www.iwgia.org/news/search-news?news_id=1060

Maps of World. 'Cameroon Political Map Showing the International Boundary, Regions' Boundaries with their Capitals and National Capital'. Retrieved 23.11.2013 from http:// www.mapsofworld.com/cameroon/cameroon-political-map.html.

Ministry of Territorial Administration and Decentralisation (MINATD). 'Administrative Divisions of the East Region of Cameroon'. Retrieved 04.09.2012 from http://minatd.cm/gov/site/en/component/%20content/article/81-content/regions/155-region-%20de-l-est.

National Institute of Statistics (NIS) Cameroon. 2012. 'Statistics year book'. Retrieved 28.07.2012 from http://www.statistics-cameroon.org/downloads/annuaire2010/chap2.pdf.

Panapress.com. 2002. 'PANA Belgium: Cameroonian Pygmies Repatriated from Belgium', published online 25.08.2002. Retrieved 16.11.2012 from http://www.panapress.com/Cameroonian-Pygmies-repatriated-from-Belgium--13-461700-17-lang1-index.html.

Plan Cameroon. 2003. 'Pygmies' Journey to Development (Pygmy Rights and Dignity)', Retrieved 30.06.2010 from http://ssl.brookes.ac.uk/ubr/files/8/19-.Pygmy_Rights_Project.pdf.

Sonnè, Wang. UNESCO-MOST Management of Social Transformations Programme: 'De la dynamique de la qualité d'autochtone dans le processus de démocratisation au Cameroun: le cas de la région de Douala', in *Démocratisation et rivalités ethniques au Cameroun*. Ethno-net Africa, undated document. Retrieved 05.05.2012 from http://www.ethnonet-africa.org/pubs/p95cir7.htm.

UNDP. ',About Human Development'.http://hdr.undp.org/en/humandev. Retrieved 02.03.2015

World Bank. 1994. 'Social Assessment Guidelines', 10 May 1994. Retrieved 10.09.2012 from http://web.worldbank.org/archive/website01028/WEB/0__CO-38.HTM.

World Bank. 'IPP86: Indigenous People ("Pygmy") Development Plan for the Forest and Environment Sectoral Programme (PSFE)'. Retrieved 06.03.2014 from http://wwwds.worldbank.org/external/default/WDSContentServer/WDSP/IB/2004/06/01/000012009_20040601150518/Rendered/PDF/IPP86.pdf.

WWF. 2008. 'Protecting Baka Pygmies' Access to Forest Resources in Southeast Cameroon', published 07.07.2008. Retrieved 22.02.2014 from http://wwf.panda.org/who_we_are/wwf_offices/cameroon/news/?139921/Protecting-Baka-Pygmies-access-to-forest-resources-in-Southeast-Cameroon.

WWF. 'Jengi is the Baka Pygmy God of the Forest'. Retrieved 25.09.2012 from http://wwf.panda.org/what_we_do/where_we_work/project/projects_in_depth/jengi_project/people/.

Conference Proceedings

Beyond Being Pygmies (BBP): Generational Gaps and the Future of Baka ('Pygmy') Youths in Participatory Local Governance in Bertoua, Cameroon on 27 and 28 June 2013, organized by Glory M. Lueong in collaboration with Frederick Nchimenyi. A brief documentary summary of the proceedings is available online at http://www.youtube.com/watch?v=Gvsqo1Mqf0E&feature=share.

INDEX

fieldwork, 1, 48, 66, 77, 96, 102, 103, 112, 141, 155, 159
figurehead, 154, 155, 162, 164
firstcomer, 107
FONDAF Cameroun, 33
Forest, 2, 4, 5, 6, 8, 10, 12, 14, 16, 18, 20, 22, 24, 26, 28, 30, 32, 34, 36, 38, 40, 42, 44, 46, 48, 50, 64, 66, 67, 68, 70, 72, 73, 74, 76, 78, 80, 82, 84, 86, 88, 90, 94, 96, 98, 100, 102, 104, 106, 108, 110, 112, 114, 118, 120, 122, 124, 126, 128, 130, 132,134, 136, 138, 140, 142, 144, 146, 148, 150, 151, 152, 154, 156, 158, 160, 162, 164, 166, 168, 170, 172, 174
forest-boundedness, 2

Geschiere, 1, 4, 8, 11, 12, 16, 32, 35, 36, 37, 39, 40, 43, 74, 88, 93, 94, 98, 102, 109, 171

Hallet, 24, 25
headquarters, 46, 101
Helen, 38, 84, 107, 134, 143, 144, 153, 154, 164
hunter-gatherer, 3, 26, 48, 118
hunting, 4, 24, 31, 33, 47, 48, 49, 67, 72, 85, 88, 96, 97, 118, 120, 126, 127, 130, 131, 169, 173

Iliad, 4, 39
ILO, 2, 3, 8, 9, 10, 11, 18, 143, 144
indigene, 30, 33, 51, 70, 71, 77, 91, 150, 152
indigeneity, 4, 8, 11, 17, 30, 37, 41, 45, 49, 50, 58, 61, 63, 69, 70, 80, 81, 87, 88, 91, 93, 108, 150, 165, 166, 171, 174
indigenous, 2, 3, 4, 8, 9, 10, 11, 13, 15, 17, 18, 25, 26, 29, 37, 38, 42, 49, 50, 51, 52, 53, 55, 57, 58, 59, 61, 63, 65, 69, 70, 71, 76, 77, 78, 79, 80, 81, 82, 83, 84, 85, 87, 88, 89, 90, 91, 93, 95, 97, 102, 108, 113, 126, 139, 142, 147, 150, 154, 155, 164, 165,166, 167, 168, 169, 170, 171, 172, 174
INGOs, 1, 11, 29, 51, 55, 69, 70, 80, 126, 128, 132, 136, 139, 146, 149, 174
Ituri forest, 2, 24, 25

Kadey, 26
Koumadjab, 44, 67, 80, 116

latecomer, 107
law 90/053, 34
law no. 5-2011, 4, 18
les Dualas, 123, 124, 125, 136, 139
les Obamas, 123, 124, 125, 136
local citizens, 66, 152, 153, 155, 160, 167, 174
Logo, 2, 19, 23, 24, 25, 26, 30, 32, 33, 44, 72, 94, 96, 102, 107, 121, 126, 128, 138, 151, 153, 171, 174
Lom and Djérem, 26
Lomié, 49, 86, 100, 139, 145, 156, 158

Mayos-Dimako, 68, 81, 85, 104, 173
Mballam, 18, 51, 76, 77, 78, 100, 115, 134, 137, 146, 151, 152
Mbororos, 11, 37, 63
Mbuti Pygmies, 2, 118
Mendjou, 51, 110, 130, 160, 161
Messe Venant, 38, 71, 134, 141, 143, 153, 156
Moloundou, 29, 47, 51, 66, 67, 69, 70, 79, 88, 101, 117, 122, 123, 125, 129, 130, 132, 136, 137, 138, 156
mongolou, 80
multi-ethnic, 31, 116
multiparty, 8, 30, 35, 43, 90

nation state, 30, 109
national citizenship, 16, 79, 93, 151, 174
Natives, 31
native-stranger divide, 36, 37
NGOs, 11, 15, 23, 39, 48, 49, 51, 53, 69, 70, 73, 75, 77, 78, 81, 84, 130, 134, 137, 138, 142, 143, 144, 145, 146, 147, 149, 150, 154, 160, 162, 163
Nomedjo, 44, 51, 119, 127
non-timber forest products, 147

on the ground understandings, 42, 63
Oubangui, 95

Participation, 2, 14, 29, 35, 142, 143, 145, 147, 149, 150, 151, 153, 155, 157, 159, 161, 163